D £20·00
A)

TRANSFORMATIONS IN MODERN EUROPEAN DRAMA

The essays in this volume derive from an international conference on modern European drama held at the Humanities Research Centre, Canberra. The principal focus of attention is upon questions of dramatic transmission and translation. Most of the essays are concerned with what happens when plays from the modern European repertoire are performed in countries or times other than those for which they were originally intended.

Ian Britain looks at Ibsen's reception in England, and David E. R. George at Ibsen in Germany. Maria Shevtsova examines recent productions of Chekhov in France; Kyle Wilson, recent theatrical experimentation in the Soviet Union. Martin Esslin and L. A. C. Dobrez write about Samuel Beckett's recent work for theatre and radio; and Michael Butler discusses Max Frisch's new work, *Triptychon*. John Willett discusses a number of practical problems relating to dramatic translation and, in a second essay, examines the literary relationship of W. H. Auden and Bertolt Brecht.

Ian Donaldson is Professor of English and Director of the Humanities Research Centre at the Australian National University, Canberra. He is the author of *The World Upside-Down: Comedy from Jonson to Fielding* and *The Rapes of Lucretia: A Myth and its Transformations* and the editor of *Jonson and Shakespeare* and *Ben Jonson: Poems*.

The Humanities Research Centre/Macmillan Series

General editor: Professor Ian Donaldson, Director of the HRC

This series is designed for publications deriving from the Humanities Research Centre of the Australian National University, Canberra. The series, which is an occasional one, will include monographs by the academic staff and Visiting Fellows of the Humanities Research Centre, and collections of essays from the Centre's conferences and seminars.

Ian Donaldson (*editor*): JONSON AND SHAKESPEARE

Ian Donaldson (*editor*): TRANSFORMATIONS IN MODERN EUROPEAN DRAMA

J. E. Flower: LITERATURE AND THE LEFT IN FRANCE

Oliver MacDonagh, W. F. Mandle and Pauric Travers (*editors*): IRISH CULTURE AND NATIONALISM, 1750-1950

TRANSFORMATIONS IN MODERN EUROPEAN DRAMA

Edited by

Ian Donaldson

in association with
Humanities Research Centre
Australian National University, Canberra

First published 1983 by
THE MACMILLAN PRESS LTD
London and Basingstoke
Companies and representatives
throughout the world

Distributed in Australia by
Australian National University Press
PO Box 4, Canberra ACT 2600

ISBN 0 333 33421 3

Printed in Hong Kong

Contents

Preface

The essays in this volume derive from a conference on modern European drama held in the Humanities Research Centre of the Australian National University, Canberra, in July 1979. As the title of the volume suggests, the conference was principally concerned with problems of dramatic change: with what happens when plays from the modern European repertoire are performed in countries or times or media other than those for which they were originally intended. Superficially, drama may seem, especially in the modern world, to be one of the most international of all art-forms, freely travelling across national and cultural boundaries. Yet plays also obviously undergo a variety of changes, linguistic and otherwise, as they pass from one social context to another, and as time brings about its own changes in social and political perception and expectation. A production of a play by Brecht in Australia in the 1980s may be quite a different thing from a production of the same play in Germany in the 1930s. An adaptation for radio or screen may (likewise) be quite a different thing from a stage performance. These questions of translation, transportation, transmission, transformation (the words varied, but *getting it across* was a constant theme) were uppermost in the minds of most of the speakers at the conference.

Several of the papers, such as those by Martin Esslin, L. A. C. Dobrez and Michael Butler reproduced in this volume, were concerned with dramatic transformations of another kind: with the ways in which dramatists such as Samuel Beckett and Max Frisch return in recent works to themes and ideas that have occupied them for many years.

Unhappily, not all the papers given at the conference can be reproduced here, and the remaining papers deserve to be briefly mentioned. Andrzej Drawicz (Warsaw University) discussed the present-day reputation and interpretation of Chekhov in the Soviet Union; Victor Emeljanow (University of New South Wales) looked at the reputation of Chekhov in England between 1909 and 1945; while Jeremy Ridgman (University of Queensland) examined the recent adaptation of *The Cherry Orchard* by Trevor Griffiths at the Nottingham Playhouse. Bernard Dukore, of the University of Hawaii, discussed the film versions of Shaw's *Pygmalion* and *Major Barbara*, which were screened during the conference. Martin Esslin, former Head of BBC Radio Drama, spoke with authority on the subject of radio drama. Michael Addison (San Diego) spoke about productions of Beckett in America; while Vicki Ooi, of the University of Hong Kong, spoke about the problems of presenting Brecht's plays in Cantonese to Chinese audiences who are familiar with many of the Chinese theatrical devices which Brecht introduced into his plays for exotic or distancing effect. Martin Esslin, John Willett and Wal Cherry (Flinders University, South Australia) led a lively symposium on the work of Bertolt Brecht.

The conference was much concerned with practical questions of theatrical (and musical) interpretation. And perhaps the most pleasurable of the week's many activities were the transformations wrought, and translations illustrated, by Sydney actors Ralph Cottrill and Robyn Neven and singer Robyn Archer in a context set by John Willett and explained in the paper that opens this volume.

                                                        I.D.

Notes on the Contributors

Ian Britain is a Lecturer in the Department of History at Melbourne University. He is the author of *Fabianism and Culture* and is now working on a social history of Edwardian theatre in England and Australia.

Michael Butler, Senior Lecturer in German at the University of Birmingham, is the author of *The Novels of Max Frisch* (1976), and is currently working on a book on Frisch's drama. During 1979 he held a Visiting Fellowship at the Australian National University's Humanities Research Centre, Canberra.

L. A. C. Dobrez is a Senior Lecturer in English at the Australian National University, Canberra. He has published articles on Samuel Beckett and on Australian literature.

Ian Donaldson, Professor of English and Director of the Humanities Research Centre at the Australian National University, Canberra, convened the HRC's 1979 conference on modern European drama. His latest book is *The Rapes of Lucretia* (Oxford University Press).

Martin Esslin, Professor of Drama at Stanford University, was Head of BBC Radio Drama until 1977. Amongst his many books on aspects of the modern theatre are *Brecht: A Choice of Evils* (1959), *The Theatre of the Absurd* (1962), *The Peopled Wound: The Plays of Harold Pinter* (1970), *Artaud* (1976) and *An Anatomy of Drama* (1976).

David E. R. George is the author of *Ibsen in Deutschland* (1968) and *Deutsche Tragödientheorien vom Mittelalter bis zu Lessing* (1972). He is Senior Lecturer in Comparative Literature at Murdoch University, Western Australia.

Maria Shevtsova, Lecturer in French Studies at Sydney University, has worked with Bernard Dort and Jacques Scherer at the Institut d'Études Théâtrales, Paris University, and with Jacques Leenhardt at the School of Social Sciences, Paris (EHESS); and has taught at the University of Paris V.

John Willett is joint editor of the US and UK editions of the collected writings of Bertolt Brecht, much of whose work he has translated. His books include *The Theatre of Bertolt Brecht* (1959), *Expressionism* (1970), *The Theatre of Erwin Piscator* (1978) and *The New Sobriety* (1978). While a Visiting Fellow at the Humanities Research Centre, Australian National University, Canberra, in 1979, he worked on a study of theatre in Germany between 1918 and 1933.

Kyle Wilson is a postgraduate student in the Department of Slavonic Languages at the Australian National University. During 1978 and 1979 he was an exchange scholar at Moscow State University engaged on research on Soviet theatre. He is at present working in the Australian Embassy in Warsaw.

1 Translation, Transmission, Transportation

JOHN WILLETT

I

Most people agree that theatres in the English-speaking world need to import foreign-language plays: the argument is self-evident. But how in fact do they do so? There are from the start a number of different approaches, which tend to lead to rather different results. Case (a): a management wants to do a play which has been a great box-office success on the European continent. Case (b): a subsidised theatre wants to do a play because it has heard interesting reports of it; here commercial motives are secondary. Case (c): the author's London or New York agent gets a translation done in order to interest theatres in it. Case (d): a radio organisation — mostly the BBC — decides to broadcast a play and commissions a translation, which may later find its way into the theatre. Case (e): a publisher commissions a translation which has above all got to be readable. Case (f): somebody — a playwright, an academic, a retired colonel or a clergyman's wife, falls for a foreign play and translates it on spec. off his or her own bat.

There's no telling which of these methods is going to work best: all six can and do produce disastrous flops, but sometimes they don't. And there are further vital differences. Is the translation made with a theatre in mind or for the benefit of students of the drama? Or both? If intended for the theatre, has it already been worked on by actors — for better or worse? Is this going to be the sole authorised translation? Is it done from the original language or from a translation into something less exotic? And is it a fair representation of what the author himself wrote, or has it been what they call 'adapted for the English or American stage'?

1

I don't want to overrate the role of the translator, because I think there's an unfortunate tendency nowadays to treat translation as if it were very nearly as important as original writing. This is consoling for those of us who translate, but of course it's nonsense. All the same there is a very wide range of possibilities here, and some of them in my view are unlikely to work. Very briefly, I think that if a translation is going to be used for more than a single production it has got to give us what the author wrote, without improvements and without cuts. The director has to make these for himself, not accept somebody else's view of the play. I'm against translation monopolies (as happened with Shaw in Germany, for instance); I agree with the Brechts, who will let anybody with a reasonable idea of what he is doing make his own version. I think that the text that plays best is likely to be the most publishable, but not necessarily *vice versa*. I'm very mistrustful of translations from an intermediate language. And I'm doubtful about the London National Theatre's policy of only allowing recognised (or recognised by them) playwrights to translate, because they don't always achieve the first essential, which is to understand and appreciate the original play.

Here's a good modern European play, possibly a great one. What's the translator's responsibility? *Not* to change its structure; that's a dramaturg's or director's job, though of course it may be the translator who goes on to fulfil that role for a given production. Not to accommodate the dialogue to the actors; this may be quite against the author's intentions, and anyway the actors may be only too inclined to do that for themselves. No, his real responsibility, in my view, is to communicate the story and the characters as the author conceived them and to reproduce as far as possible his *use* of language. That's to say, first of all his communication of character through modes of speech; secondly his variation in levels of language – high-flown and colloquial, prose and verse, and so on; and thirdly his use of songs. These are the fundamental problems of any translation, and to my mind an awareness of different speech-rhythms is essential if the translator is to solve them; a play can be killed if its translator has a tin ear. Mere howlers and mistranslations are much less significant, because they are so easily put right. But of course they are what any critic of a given translation is likeliest to pick on. If someone translates 'goddess' as 'cabbage' he looks a fool. Yet this is much less serious than rendering a solemn, measured, formal speech by short, jaunty colloquial sentences; because when this happens it cannot be put right without doing all the work over again.

The trouble is that our convention of criticising translations is wrong-headed. And this applies to books almost as
much as to plays. If something sounds or reads like whatever
kind of English we are used to, with all its colloquialisms
and clichés, then it is assumed to be good - for the simple
reason that most critics can't or don't judge by the original. The translation 'flows'; the actors find it easy to
speak. But not all plays are *meant* to flow, and some of the
most interesting dialogue - that of the German Expressionists for instance, or Auden's in *Paid on Both Sides* (to take
an English example) - is *not* easy to speak, at least until
the actor gets used to it. Read Brecht on Peter Lorre's
performance in *Man Equals Man*; Brecht made him speak in a
deliberately broken, jerky way, as the text in fact
demanded, and the Berlin critics thought he was being either
incompetent or affected. Here's another small example from
Georg Kaiser's *From Morn to Midnight*.[1] In Ashley Dukes's
translation - which he made around 1922 out of love for the
play (I think) and which was historically important because
it really introduced Expressionism to the English and
American theatre - there's a scene at a six-day cycle race
where the Cashier tells one of the officials that he'll put
up money for a sprint prize. In Dukes's version their
exchange goes,

A prize of a thousand marks! For how many laps?
As many as you please.
How much shall we allot to the winner?
That's your affair.

Dukes has ironed out the flat oddity of this dialogue, which
really goes,

A prize of a thousand marks! For how many laps?
Whatever you want.
How much to the winner?
Whatever you want.

Once you start normalising such language you can easily
alter a character and ruin a whole play.

The problem, then, is to assimilate without over-assim-
ilating; to embrace but not to smother; to make the play
intelligible and interesting to our own audience without
making it an Australian, American or English play. And that
further raises the tricky questions of accent, slang and
context. Now, in the English theatre there are certain modes
of speech which actors are happy to slip into: one is the
regional accent, West Country rustic or North of England;

another is army talk, I suppose because so many older and
middle generation actors did some kind of military service.
But of course these can be wildly inappropriate, both
culturally and chronologically; if I'm supposed to be
listening to the Greeks outside Troy, for instance, I do *not*
want to be taken back to an Aldershot NAAFI. It may be all
right in certain cases, where it's the actor's natural mode
of speech. But so often the assumed accent is phoney. And,
as for slang expressions, when intelligently employed (which
they often aren't) they may make dialogue sound contemporary
at the moment of writing, but they date as quickly as
yesterday's pop tunes and only too easily strike a false
note in a translation unless deliberately used for period
effect.

Of course it's impossible to lay down a firm rule about
this. Some plays have to be situated in their period, and
the audience must be encouraged to look at them with a
historian's eye. (I'm not talking about costumes and set,
but about the text and its interpretation.) Others can speak
directly to the present day. Others again can be *made* to
speak directly, but will not then be saying what the author
meant. It's my feeling, for instance, that English audiences
– who are anyway quite neurotically anxious to laugh at the
least provocation in the first ten minutes of a play – have
a tendency to interpret any play about unfamiliar kinds of
European as being a family comedy about funny foreigners.
Mrozek's *Tango* came out like that at the Aldwych, I thought,
and so indeed did Stoppard's *Travesties* (which is essentially a European rather than an English play).

Shifting the context is a tricky business, even when the
author is long dead. I don't for instance find that updated
Shakespeare really works, though it was different with
Brook's *Midsummer Night's Dream*, whose framework was timeless, and I should love to have seen the Czech *Romeo and
Juliet* staged by Burian in the first winter after the 1939-
45 war, when the Renaissance setting emerged from the wartime dreams of a group of prisoners in a concentration camp
(presumably Buchenwald, where Burian himself was). But I've
come across this kind of transplantation most often with
Brecht – an author whose claim to make politically significant statements rather conflicts with his wish to establish
'model' productions for others to absorb. In *The Caucasian
Chalk Circle* he himself uses a framework for an ancient
story to make it intelligible; so it's clearly legitimate
for a dramaturg or director to change this framework if it
no longer does so for our audiences. But introducing new
political allusions and pointers, to my mind, is likely to
be a mistake – for instance, to make *Arturo Ui* a satire on

some dictator other than Hitler, or to try to turn *Drums in the Night* into a serious political play, or to garnish the opera *Mahagonny* with projections of later political events. The only answer is to think anew in each given case, which is certainly what the author would have done himself. When Strehler, for instance, shifted *The Threepenny Opera* to America in the 1920s, with Keystone Cops in lieu of Victorian peelers, Brecht loved it; in fact he encouraged him to go farther in situating it among the New York Italian-American community. Not that this made it less of a period piece; it just brought the period of its setting closer to that of its writing.

I was asked to talk about my own experience in this connection, and all I can say is that it has been limited, *ad hoc* and quite inconsistent. Confronted with Brecht's adaptation of *The Tutor*, I found that his added scenes with the Leipzig students were really only relevant for a German audience, while a lot of what he'd cut from Lenz's highly confused original was marvellous stuff. So I went back to Lenz and made my own version: doubtless a very disloyal act. Then in Adelaide in 1975 Wal Cherry got me to help with *The Threepenny Opera*, which we tried to make accessible by presenting it as a work brought back from Europe – along with various other infections – by the returning troops after World War I; in other words we shifted it back ten years instead of trying to bring it up to date – the latter being something I doubt that its slightly dated satire would stand. I did a new translation of *Mother Courage* into a kind of artificial North Country English, which I don't really think anglicises it but does correspond to Mother Courage's character and mode of speech, and does try to capture the kind of verbal dynamics necessary to keep this long, often rather flat, play moving. (Brecht's language does this, but his translators don't.) Then Robyn Archer, Wal Cherry and I schemed out an Australian version of *Puntila* which we hope to see put on under the title *Jack Punt Esquire and His Mate Matt*.

This is a real transportation of Brecht's drunken Finnish landowner and his doings, though it entails very little tampering with the text. The reasons: (a) as a Finn Puntila never made the grade with English audiences, though they ought by rights to find this a most congenial play; (b) he's a very credible Australian grazier, who will be intelligible in London as well as here; (c) his relationships with his employees and his daughter are recognisable Australian ones; (d) Punt's part-proprietorial, part-physical sense of his country and its landscape play the same role as in the original; (e) I think the Aussie accent suits Brecht as long as it's natural and not laid on – it's sharp and it's tough and it has the right sardonic flavour. Our only two real problems in shifting the story lock, stock and barrel to the South Australian semi-desert were, first, that poverty is hardly an issue in Australia, and, secondly, that the so-called Finnish stories about ruling-class harshness and self-interest have to be rewritten in Australian terms. Here is a sample:

Post-
Mistress: They know what they are up to all right. Must be some reason why they get so rich. There was this squatter down our way hired an Aboriginal to guide him across a fifty-mile stretch of Jackson's Desert in the drought of 1908. The Abbo knew there was a waterhole somewhere half-way across but he wasn't sure if it had dried up, so the squatter took charge of all their water till the black found it. There was a sandstorm, so the boss got frightened and promised him a horse if they got across all right. When they'd found the hole and filled up and had a wash he spoke up again and said, 'If you find the right track and we don't run into trouble I'll see you get a sheep.' Then they came on a track and he said, 'Keep it up and you'll have earned that watch, mate.' A couple of miles outside Waggaroona he was talking about a sack of corn, then when they got in he handed the Abbo five bob and said, 'You took your time, didn't you?' We're too stupid for their jokes and tricks and we fall for them every time. Know why? Because they look just the same as our sort, and that's what fools us. If they looked like dingos or redback spiders people might be more on their guard.

When we read the play in 1978, Cherry's directing student (who wasn't a fool by any means) asked me how come Brecht knew these stories about Australia. So I think this play really does transplant.

Finally, a tricky problem, those scenes of Brecht's about life in Nazi Germany called *Fear and Misery of the Third Reich*, or in their wartime version *The Private Life of the Master Race*. Wal Cherry wanted a translation to direct in San Diego, so I made one. I never liked the wartime framework, with its German soldiers in an armoured half-track, which seemed like a half-hearted attempt to shift

the work forward from the 1930s, when it was written.
So I went back to Brecht's original text, which ties the
scenes together with a long poem faintly reminiscent of
Gottfried Keller and introduces it all as a *Heerschau*, a
march-past — Hitler's review of his forces before the
impending war. But I historicised this for the benefit of
young audiences who had got punchdrunk with anti-Nazi horror
stories — true ones and fiction so mixed up that they no
longer know where they are. And instead of 'march-past' I
called it 'Private Viewing'.

What do we know about the wretched Hitler?
Villain of endless comics, harrowing television dramas
The man we love to hate — or should do if we're dutiful
Good students and worthy offspring of that noble
generation
Which liberated Europe, knocked down Dresden, teamed up
with Stalin.
Well, are those dotards right with their forty-year old
obsessions about the Nazis
Or is it all a hoax? For we've also heard of a visionary
Hitler
Selfless and charismatic, who brought his country out of
chaos
Built roads and factories, created order and purpose
Spread confidence in clean-limbed, clear-eyed German
Youth.
Nor were his Nazis cowards. Their predestined road to
power
Demanded bloodshed, the unflinching acceptance of
necessary violence
Without which nothing changes
How different from our world of aimless mediocrity and
tame contentment
Whose packaged visions boast commercial sponsors,
advertising soap or sex aids
To an invalid society gently jogging to the grave!
We need alternatives, an underground, flamboyant
anarchists
Who'll spit on all the system stands for. As for what it
so flatly stood against
Might that not need reviving, or at least bear closer
inspection?

So we chose to look at those Nazis: set aside *Holocaust*
with its piled-up horrors
And dug out images of their daily life, their homes and
kitchens

A few old clips, scenes from those better, fairer times
Before the war, before the mass extermination of unwanted
   persons
Had blackened the Führer's name. For instinct had made us
   curious
To see what sort of movement, formed from what sort of
   people
In what condition, what sort of thoughts thinking
He led against our fathers. We staged a private viewing.

Like Brecht's own prologue, whose style and rhythms it
imitates, this then leads into the first three stanzas of
the long linking poem:

And now the lights start fading
So they can come parading
Before your critical eyes.
Watching the little antics
Of these misplaced romantics
You might get a surprise.

The murky newsreels flicker
Past jackboot and swastika
To show you the rank and file.
It's not their gross excesses
But their endless pettinesses
That make them seem so vile.

All timid and obedient
They'll do what's most expedient
They'll sneak and brag and lie.
And you who never knew them
Now get a chance to view them
As they go marching by.

They in turn are followed by the first of Brecht's realistic, laconically written scenes.

II

The further illustrations which followed took the form of an
exercise-*cum*-parlour game for two highly skilled performers:
actors Robyn Neven and Ralph Cottrill. Shortly beforehand
they had been given two episodes from modern plays, each in
three different English language translations, which they
were asked to play as they would be inclined to play them on

encountering them for the first time. The object was to
provide the audience (and indeed the introducer) with some
idea of the different interpretations, associations, tempi
and feelings of comfort or discomfort imposed by variations
in translation. So the two performers were given absolutely
minimal previous instructions; moreover, they were neither
of them familiar with the plays.

We began with the dialogue between Anya and Trofimov at
the end of Act II of *The Cherry Orchard* in the translations
by Ronald Hingley (for the Oxford Chekhov edition), Michael
Frayn (for the National Theatre in London) and Trevor
Griffiths.[2] In this case the audience were told beforehand
what was being performed and asked to watch out for the
varying implications. My own impressions – without any knowledge of the original text – were that the Griffiths text
dictated a much more aggressive approach by Trofimov, due
perhaps in part to Ralph Cottrill's prior assumptions about
the translator's viewpoint. At the same time it lapsed once
or twice into false bathos, like the deliberate pauses in
Anya's 'Isn't it ... wonderful here ... today ...?', answered by Trofimov's 'Yes. Perfect weather.' It raised the
question (in the ensuing discussion) whether Trofimov's
political speeches were addressed to a Russian or a modern
British public.

Both Hingley and Frayn seemed to leave the play in its
proper historical context. But Hingley's version slightly
slowed the actors down, because the words lacked momentum
and discouraged quick exchanges. It had not, unfortunately,
occurred to me to time the different performances, but over
the whole length of the play there could well be a substantial time-difference. Without any use of false colloquialisms, the Frayn version had the greater sparkle and pace.

For the second example – three translations of Scene i of
Schnitzler's *Reigen*, or *La Ronde* – the audience were asked
to guess the author of the play and the names or approximate
dates of the translators. They were in fact Frank Marcus,
Eric Bentley and Keene Wallis, whom the actors chose to play
in, respectively, their natural voices, English cockney, and
American. Despite the absurdity of suddenly hearing Austrian
place-names dropping like exotic stones into an apparently
UK or US episode between a tart and a soldier, the least
dislocated version (Marcus's) seemed the least effective.
However, none of the three came near to capturing the
flavour of the original, which handles an authentic Viennese
low-life idiom with terseness and elegance. Martin Esslin
having been ruled out on the grounds of special knowledge –
borne out by his subsequent graphic description of the
locale – it took a little time for the audience to identify

the author. It was agreed that for social as well as
stylistic reasons the best Austrian playwrights are particularly hard for our theatres to assimilate - the nineteenth-
century comedian Nestroy being the outstanding case, to our
great loss.

The choice of examples was conditioned by the translations
available to hand, so, regrettably, no truly modern play
could be included. Instead the actors performed two more
extracts involving modern translators who were likely to be
well known, though not their translations. The first was the
episode from Goethe's *Faust I* where Faust, having seen
Margarete, wants Mephistopheles to get her for him. This was
played first in the almost unspeakable mid-nineteenth-
century translation by Bayard Taylor, with its lines like

> Yet, pray, don't take it as annoyance!
> Why, all at once, exhaust the joyance?

then, more ambiguously, in that by Anna Swanwick:

> But do not fret, I pray; why seek
> To hurry to enjoyment straight?

Walter Kaufmann's modern version followed, then finally
Louis MacNeice's with its sometimes Byronic (rather than
Goethean) touches of neat wit. It was an amusing exercise
for actors and audience, few of whom guessed the play and
none the identity of the last translator (Esslin, an old
colleague of his, tactfully *tacente*). But each version had
its ridiculous aspects. Again, perhaps, Goethe into English
doesn't go.

I had told the audience that we were going to cheat, and
we did so with three versions of Coriolanus's 'There is a
world elsewhere' monologue. These were translations made by
myself (who had not got the original indelibly in my ear)
from the standard German Shakespeare - Schlegel; the
standard French Shakespeare - Jean-François-Victor Hugo;
and Brecht's *Coriolanus* adaptation of the 1950s. As
delivered by Ralph Cottrill (himself a former RSC actor)
these came out respectively as pseudo-Shakespearean verse, a
rather pompous prose speech and an aggressive jerky tirade.
The speech itself was easily identified, the translations
less so, nobody guessing the French.

From comments made after these four assorted demonstrat-
ions it seemed that the main point had got across. Even
specialists were surprised at the enormous differences - of
interpretation, of rhythm and of overall tone - which the
choice of translation is liable to make. Of course, many of

the actors' immediate interpretations would have been ironed
out in rehearsal, whether by themselves or by the director.
But the issue to be illustrated was that of the initial
start (or twist) given by the actors' natural reactions to
the text before them. Not forgetting that directors on the
whole are not primarily dramatic scholars: many, indeed,
have been actors themselves.

III

To conclude the morning we had an informal, yet forceful,
performance of (mainly) Brecht songs by Robyn Archer. They
included theatre songs from various plays, an early song to
a tune of Brecht's own devising, a Communist marching-song
(vintage 1931-2), a wartime anti-Nazi song broadcast by the
US Office of War Information, and some of the Hollywood
Elegies, which expressed his feelings about California in
the 1940s. They were by all three of his principal composer
associates: Kurt Weill, Hanns Eisler and Paul Dessau. Just
to show that Brecht wasn't the only pebble on the Weimar
beach, they were offset by two non-Brecht songs, while there
was also one of the songs which Weill wrote after his emi-
gration to America, for a musical play by Maxwell Anderson.
In some cases alternative translations were used or indepen-
dently read: thus I read W. H. Auden's translation (for the
National Theatre) of Eilif's song from *Mother Courage*, after
which we had my own version, based on the Kipling original,
sung to Dessau's fiendishly difficult setting. Similarly the
Barbara Song from *The Threepenny Opera* was sung with verses
translated by Bentley, Marc Blitzstein and Willett/Manheim.
The Benares Song from *The Little Mahagonny* was sung in the
home-made English ('Is here no telephone?') attributed to
Brecht but actually due to his collaboratrix Elizabeth
Hauptmann.
'Lust' from *The Seven Deadly Sins* in Auden's translation
showed Brecht and Weill collaborating (in 1933) on a sung
ballet; it was their last completed work together and the
first either man wrote in exile. The 'Song of the Flow of
Things' from *Man Equals Man* showed how the playwright
cannibalised one of his city-poems of the mid 1920s and
interpolated it, together with a sung refrain, in a play
about Kipling's India; the music (c. 1950) was by Dessau.
The wartime 'Song of a German Mother' is one of Brecht's and
Eisler's most moving anti-Nazi songs; the Hollywood Elegies
are a more private song-cycle reflecting (musically)
Eisler's partial return to his Schoenbergian roots - its

last section, 'The Swamp', is now known to relate to the
drug-addiction of the actor Peter Lorre. 'Seashells from
Margate' (1928) is a virulent satire on Shell Oil from one
of Piscator's productions; the music is by Weill but the
words by Felix Gasbarra, no particular friend of Brecht's.
Finally, 'The ballad of the Sailor Kutteldaddeldu', with its
picture of a drunk German sailor losing all the presents he
had bought in Sydney, is a quasi-theatrical piece by the
sailor poet Joachim Ringelnatz, who appeared (or was, anyway, announced to appear) in the cabaret programme following
the 1922 première of Brecht's play *Drums in the Night*. Its
music is by Wilhelm Grosz, later famous on a slightly different plane as a composer of ''Twas on the Isle of Capree
that I Met Her', with which he earned the bread of exile.

The intention of this coherently eclectic mixture was to
illuminate Brecht's varying dramatic use of song and the
kind of problems which it poses for non-German audiences and
performers. Much of the most interesting part of the ensuing
discussion, however, was Robyn Archer's account of how she
got to know these songs, and what they have meant to her.
'Would you describe yourself as an entertainer?' somebody
had asked. She had indeed started as one, singing Country
and Western and the like in South Australian clubs and pubs
in the intervals of reading English at Adelaide University.
Then in 1974, when the Festival Centre was opened, Justin
McDonnell, then administrator of the South Australian Opera,
proposed that she should sing one of the two sisters in *The
Seven Deadly Sins* under the direction of Wal Cherry. The
success of this led to her casting as Jenny in Cherry's 1975
production of *The Threepenny Opera* with the same company,
also to a public recital involving many Brecht songs. *Never
the Twain* a Brecht-Kipling collage, followed, again under
Cherry's direction. Thereafter she was in the National
Theatre's Brecht song and poetry programme *To Those Born
Later* (1977), when she met Dominic Muldowney and Georg
Eisler, the composer's painter son. Then in 1978 she
included further Brecht items in her *Kold Komfort Kaffee*
programme at Nimrod with John Gaden, and also gave (with
Michael Morley) a song-recital at Sydney Opera House entitled *Brecht and Co*. And the point of all this to her? 'I
had found something where I could sing *and* think.'

A happy end-note. After leaving the conference she went to
Sydney to hear the Brecht song and poetry programme of
Ekkehard Schall, Brecht's son-in-law and the (virtuoso)
leading actor of the Berliner Ensemble. Within hours of

meeting for the first time they were improvisedly singing the Tango from *The Threepenny Opera* together for ABC Television, Schall singing in German, Archer in English.

This, to my mind, is the kind of unforced marriage of cultures over which the theatre and its students can only rejoice.

NOTES

1. We had read this to an audience at the Nimrod Theatre, Sydney, a fortnight earlier, with Ralph Cottrill as the absconding Cashier.
2. Trevor Griffiths's version of *The Cherry Orchard* had been discussed in another paper earlier in the conference by Jeremy Ridgman of the Department of English at Queensland University.

2 A Transplanted Doll's House: Ibsenism, Feminism and Socialism in Late-Victorian and Edwardian England

IAN BRITAIN

How does a dramatist begin to make an impact in a foreign country? While the processes involved doubtless vary from dramatist to dramatist, and from country to country, any explanation of these will need always to demonstrate the relationship between the nature of the dramatist (or reputed nature) and the predilections of his early supporters and critics (their tastes, sensibilities, world-view). The social history of drama — especially modern drama — is still in a relatively primitive state, partly because of the very limited, often perfunctory, attention which social historians have chosen to give to the arts in general and their audiences. Many inadequacies will remain, owing to basic inadequacies in the evidence itself. It is difficult enough, for instance, trying to work out how a dramatist makes an impact in his own country. The level and distribution of applause at performances, even if there were any regular or reliable records of these, would tell little about the particulars of an audience's response, and the casual snatches of foyer chat may tell us more about the social pressures of theatregoing (interesting in themselves, admittedly) than about genuine feelings regarding a play and the ways in which it evoked those feelings in individuals. But there are more tangible kinds of evidence — press reports, private letters, and other documents traditionally used by any kind of historian — which have been insufficiently exploited, and, where exploited at all, often misinterpreted. Such deficiencies can be discerned in the accounts of Ibsen's initial reception in England, which have been content on the whole to catalogue some of the better-known transplants of

his dramatic work and record some of the major critical
responses, without really explaining how and why certain
people were prompted to make or sponsor those transplants in
the first place. It is the purpose of this paper to point up
these deficiencies and gaps, and to suggest ways in which
they can (at least partially) be repaired. Ultimately there
can be no accounting for taste – or distaste – in drama or
any of the other arts; but this should not stop the historian of these phenomena from hazarding some speculations
based on the evidence which survives.

I

The first professional production of *A Doll's House* in
London, in June 1889, was not the first attempt to transplant Ibsen's play to English soil, but the roots laid in
the decade before were rather flimsy. In 1882, Henrietta
Frances Lord published a translation which disposed of
Ibsen's title and called the play after its central character, Nora. For Mrs Lord, the more obvious themes and tensions conveyed by the original title were not the only ones,
or even the most important ones, to be enacted in Ibsen's
play. In the preface to her edition (and to her later translation of *Ghosts*) she depicted Ibsen's works as a text not
simply for the feminist cause but also for Christian
Science, the Karma philosophy and the doctrine of 'Twin
Souls'.[1] Fortunately, these bizarre appropriations did not
lead her to tamper with his plot or with the spirit of his
dialogue – which is more than can be said for some subsequent treatments. Two years after her translation was
brought out, an 'adaptation' of *A Doll's House* was staged in
London, which in addition to discarding Ibsen's title, so
altered plot, dialogue and characterisation as to out-
bowdlerise the most ruthless expurgations of Shakespeare.
The title chosen for this adaptation – *Breaking a Butterfly*
– reflected the way in which it contrived to trivialise,
sentimentalise and melodramatise the issues in Ibsen's
original.
     The spectacle he had presented of a middle-class wife and
mother, well provided-for by a respectable husband, and
showered with affection, suddenly deciding after eight years
of marriage to leave home and family because the very se-
curities of her existence had threatened her proper functioning as an individual, was obviously considered too
unseemly or too absurd or too un-English for the average
Victorian audience to swallow. Whatever the reasons, the two

playwrights responsible for *Breaking a Butterfly* - Herman and Jones - invented a new and much more soothing ending and a string of new or scarcely recognisable characters along the way. Nora's husband was turned into a model of saintly forbearance, willing to take on himself the blame for her past indiscretions; and she herself was shown as sweetly repentent for her indiscretions, and properly grateful for his generous protection against their consequences.[2]

This emasculated version of Ibsen's play was presented as one of the opening attractions of the new Prince's Theatre in London. Over the next few years, small groups of aspiring actors, who were freer from commercial, West End pressures, attempted to stage Ibsen's play as it had been originally conceived. Their efforts, however, would appear to have done it little more justice, and to have made little impact even in the negative sense of bringing Ibsen notoriety. In 1885 William Archer, who was to emerge as the major translator of Ibsen in the following decade, noted pessimistically that Henrietta Lord's 'clumsy but conscientious' version of *A Doll's House* had been used as the basis for a performance in 'one or two narrow circles', but that these productions - one by students of the School of Dramatic Art, and another by an amateur theatrical club at a hall in Argyle Street - had been 'little noticed by the press' and had 'certainly not reached the general public'.[3]

Another amateur performance took place early in 1886; and, judging from its venue - a private drawing-room in Bloomsbury - and from the nature of its audience and participants, it would seem to have been the work of a quite self-consciously 'narrow circle'. Its chief organiser made a point of inviting 'only people who we know do love and understand Ibsen already, or those who will love and understand him, and who in turn will go on preaching him to others . . . just a few people worth reading *Nora* to'.[4] A sense of public mission, on behalf of Ibsen, is none the less detectable here, and made clearer in an earlier letter by the same writer which spoke of 'a real duty to spread such great teaching' as Ibsen offered: 'my little effort', the letter went on to say, with reference to the forthcoming reading, 'is just a poor beginning'.[5]

In fact, it turned out to be a more portentous beginning than any of the other performances by enthusiastic amateurs at the time. The organiser of the performance was Marx's daughter, Eleanor, who also played the part of Nora. Eleanor's common-law husband, Edward Aveling, played the part of Nora's husband, Torvald Helmer; William Morris's daughter, May, was cast as Mrs Linde; and the role of the blackmailer, Krogstad, was taken by Bernard Shaw: each of these had already achieved, or was about to achieve, considerable prominence in the British socialist movement, as well as being associated in various ways with the cause of women's emancipation.

If we can trust his account of the evening, penned some thirty years afterwards, Shaw took a rather less earnest interest in the proceedings than Eleanor Marx. He recalled how he 'chattered and ate caramels in the back drawing-room (our green room) whilst . . . Nora brought Helmer to book at the other side of the folding doors'.[6] This irreverence may well have been a conscious check on his part of the truly 'deadly' seriousness with which, as he later observed, controversial authors were apt to be treated when their work was first known.[7] He may also have been reacting against the slightly cliquish atmosphere. In his own play *The Philanderer*, written in 1893, he was to highlight some of the dangers involved in turning Ibsen into a cult. That play, however, showed no disrespect for Ibsen himself; by then Shaw had become an even more dedicated purveyor of Ibsenist teachings than Eleanor Marx, having completed his famous exegesis, *The Quintessence of Ibsenism*, two years before.

For all his subsequent scoffing at the proceedings, some of the seeds of his enthusiasm may well have been sown on the occasion of Eleanor's *Doll's House* reading. Certainly, it was his first exposure to Ibsen in performance, and was remarkable in foreshadowing, if not facilitating, the special interest which the Norwegian's work aroused among socialist groups in England. The nature and extent of that interest have never been properly appreciated or documented, and the reasons for it never explored.

The socialists' interest in Ibsen was not reflected merely by enthusiastic support: some of his work (and, on occasion the whole Ibsen corpus) provoked vigorous criticism or outright attack from within their circles. Their role in the early Ibsen movement was complex and manifold, defying easy categorisation; but, in order to clarify it in the first instance, it is perhaps best considered under certain broad headings, relating to the various capacities in which the socialists were engaged: performers and producers of Ibsen's work on the stage — both professional and amateur; translators, editors and publishers of Ibsen texts in English; debaters in the controversy which raged over his themes; and more passive or unobtrusive roles, such as the audiences at these debates, the audiences for his plays in the theatre, and his reading public. The evidence relating to these various capacities is uneven and far from complete, but there is enough to suggest that the socialists' role in each of them was, when not dominant, always substantial.

II

At the time that *A Doll's House* was given its public première in London, its producer, Charles Charrington, and its
leading actress, Janet Achurch – Charrington's wife – were
being irresistibly drawn into socialist circles through
their personal and professional connections with the participants in Eleanor Marx's private production of 1886. In
1888, for example, Charrington had produced Edward Aveling's
dramatisation of *The Scarlet Letter*; and it may have been
through this early contact that his active interest both in
socialism and in Ibsen were first roused. Besides producing
the 1889 première of *A Doll's House*, he took the role of
Dr Rank, and later of Nora's husband; and, in the years of
the 'Ibsen boom' which followed, he played Dr Relling in *The
Wild Duck* (1894) and Aslaksen in a turn-of-the-century production of *The League of Youth*, which he also directed. The
sponsor of this production was the Stage Society, set up in
1899 by Frederick Whelen, a clerk of the Bank of England who
became a prominent member of the Fabian Executive Committee
in the following decade. The Stage Society was, in effect,
an affiliated organisation of the Fabians, drawing much of
its audience from their number.[8]
     Charrington himself had joined the Fabians in 1895,
perhaps under the influence of Shaw (who had become
infatuated with his wife after seeing her in *A Doll's House*
in 1889,[9] and had managed to remain a close friend for
years afterwards). While eschewing the militant socialism of
the Avelings, Charrington's political involvements were far
from dilettantish, and he managed to combine them very
effectively with his theatrical activities. He was elected,
like Whelen, to the Fabian Executive Committee, serving on
it between 1899 and 1904; he delivered lectures to the
Fabians and affiliated groups on the theatre and various
other subjects; and he contributed to Fabian literature with
a tract on municipal pawnshops.[10]
     As late as 1907, he and Janet Achurch made a notable
appearance at the first Fabian summer school, held in North
Wales. She had long since become famous for her interpretation of Nora, not only in England but also on tour in
Australia, New Zealand, India and Egypt; and in addition she
had created the leading role of Rita Allmers for English
audiences in the London première of *Little Eyolf* in 1896,
and had played Ellida Wangel in a 1902 production of *The*

Lady from the Sea. The Charringtons' appearance at the summer school resulted in a number of sessions being devoted to
the theme of 'Modern Dramatists'. Charrington gave several
lectures on the subject – three specifically on Ibsen, and
one of them incorporating a reading from *An Enemy of the
People*, which, according to the log-book of the school, was
'much appreciated by the audience.'[11]

In the decade before, there had been an amateur performance of the same play by the Liverpool branch of the Fabian
Society; and, if we can credit the recollections of one of
the participants,[12] Ibsen himself had been so struck with
the group's interest that he was prepared to write another
play specially for its members. Evidently nothing came of
the enterprise. In 1900, the Fabians' keenness for getting
up actual performances of Ibsen was shown again by the
involvement of several of the London group in a production
of *A Doll's House*, mounted in aid of the Indian Famine Fund
of that year.[13] And, in 1905, the Society's most prominent
theatrical personality after Shaw and Charrington, Harley
Granville Barker, included *The Wild Duck* in his momentous
season of plays staged at the Royal Court in association
with the theatrical manager, J. F. Vedrenne. He also took
the leading part of Hjalmar Ekdal in that production. The
Royal Court venture had grown out of Whelen's Stage Society,
in which Barker had been involved as an actor from early on,
playing the role of Erik Bratsberg in Charrington's production of *The League of Youth* in 1900.[14] Barker was to
follow Whelen and Charrington onto the Fabian Executive
Committee, serving between 1907 and 1912.

Mrs Theodore Wright, one of the foremost professional
Ibsen actresses after Charrington's wife, was another member
of the Fabian Society, and had been well known in advanced
political circles since the days of the First International.
She created the role of Mrs Alving in the controversial
London première of *Ghosts* in March 1891. Shaw, in recollect-
ing that production, noted how Mrs Wright had even held Karl
Marx in conversation, and had played and recited before him
as well as before William Morris. She was also an acquaintance of Eleanor Marx.[15]

III

Eleanor Marx herself never fulfilled her youthful ambition
of becoming a professional actress; but, for long after her
private production of *A Doll's House*, she and her husband
continued and extended their passionate mission on behalf of

Ibsen. It was not an indiscriminate passion, however; and it had some rather unusual aspects. These were reflected in her attitudes to the translating and publishing of Ibsen's work, in which activities she - and several others with direct or indirect links with the socialist movement - became closely involved.

There is no evidence to show that Mrs Lord, whose translation of *A Doll's House* Eleanor had used in her private production, was a member of any socialist organisation; though in 1885, on completing the first English translation of *Ghosts*, she had it published in serial form in the socialist periodical *To-day*,[16] edited at the time by H. H. Champion, a prominent official of the Social Democratic Federation (SDF). Eleanor herself specially learned Norwegian in order to produce other Ibsen translations, and her version of *En Folkefiende* (entitled *An Enemy of Society*) was included in a seminal edition of Ibsen in English, published in 1888.[17] This edition also contained translations by William Archer of *Pillars of Society* and *Ghosts*. Archer was certainly no socialist, official or otherwise; though he came into close and friendly contact with a number of socialists (notably Shaw) through his prominence in various rationalist, secularist and other heterodox or anti-establishment circles. The editor of the 1888 volume, Havelock Ellis, had no formal connections either with any of the major socialist organisations, such as the Socialist League (to which Eleanor Marx belonged), the SDF, from which the League had split off, or the Fabian Society, of which Shaw was an early member. Ellis, however, did not deliberately eschew socialism as Archer was wont to do. He remained an active member of those proto-Fabian groups formed in the 1880s, the Progressive Association and the Fellowship of the New Life; and, at the same time as sharing their undogmatic ethical-humanist concerns, he tried to give these greater solidity by setting them in a more definite socialist framework than many other members of the group were prepared to do.[18]

Eleanor Marx, for no specified reason, considered Ellis's edition of Ibsen 'a very unwise selection for a *first* volume in English'; and her own contribution does not seem to have brought her much reward or personal satisfaction: writing to her sister, Laura, about her translation of *An Enemy of the People*, she confided rather wearily, 'I'm hacking chiefly . . . for the munificent sum of £5 . . . .'[19]

Her lack of enthusiasm for *An Enemy of the People*, or at least for the project associated with it, contrasts with the special interest the play aroused among other socialists, such as the Fabians in Liverpool and the participants in the

Society's first summer school. When Herbert Beerbohm Tree's
production of *An Enemy of the People* visited Manchester in
January 1894, Alexander Thompson, a popular columnist in
Robert Blatchford's socialist newspaper, the *Clarion*, wrote
a glowing notice[20] which in no way reflected or anticipated the antagonism towards Ibsen adopted by the editor of
that paper a few years later. Blatchford's attitude is one
of the few examples of outright hostility to Ibsen in the
socialist ranks; and in any case seems to have developed
only after he became acquainted with Shaw's interpretation
of the Norwegian's work.[21] In 1897, while discussing
Blatchford's attacks on Ibsen, a columnist in Keir Hardie's
newspaper, the *Labour Leader*, averred, 'many a socialist
might be proud of writing' *An Enemy of the People*.[22]

Eleanor Marx's relative lack of enthusiasm for this play
also contrasts with her own championship of *The Lady from
the Sea* - a work of Ibsen's in which none of her fellow
socialists (apart from Aveling and Shaw) expressed much
interest. In the discussion following a lecture on Ibsen
given by her husband to the Playgoers' Club in May 1891,
Eleanor contributed a 'fervent defence' of this work.[23]
She had produced a translation of it the year before which
was published with an introduction by Edmund Gosse, the
critic who is usually accredited with first introducing
Ibsen's name to the English public, through some articles he
wrote in the early 1870s.[24] Perhaps because Eleanor's
heart was in this project rather more, and because she
regarded it less as mere hack work, her translation of *Fruen
fra Havet* appeared 'far superior' to her version of *An Enemy
of the People* - in Shaw's eyes at least.

The occasion of Shaw's remarks on the translation - a
letter to the actress Alma Murray[25] - suggests that he was
judging it on the basis of its potential effectiveness on
stage rather than as a linguistic exercise; he himself was
unacquainted with Norwegian, though he was aware of some of
the technical difficulties involved in translation work,
having made an abortive attempt in 1888 to render *Peer Gynt*
into English verse with the help of a Norwegian scholar.[26]
Eleanor's version of *The Lady from the Sea* was in fact used
for the first staging of that play in England - a production
mounted by her husband at Terry's Theatre, London, in 1891.
Shaw (along with other critics)[27] noted grave inadequacies
in the production; though he found fault not with the translation but with the actress's interpretation of the central
role of Ellida Wangel.

IV

Shaw was respectful of Eleanor's services to Ibsen, not just in her capacity as a translator but also as an active polemicist on the dramatist's behalf. In fact, apart from his own performance in the debates on Ibsen held at the Playgoers' Club in the early nineties, Shaw seems to have remembered only Eleanor's contributions as having any pertinence or bite. Dismissing the Club on the whole as 'an assemblage of barloafing front-row-of-the-pit-on-a-first-night dilettanti', he claimed that he and Eleanor had been 'much in the position of a pair of terriers dropped into a pit of rats'.[28]

This description rather distorts the proceedings at the Club, and fails to take account of the pronouncements of several other Ibsen enthusiasts in the debates. These included Aveling himself, who gave papers on Ibsen to the Club as well as defending him in the discussions following other people's papers.[29] He was a gifted linguist, who included a mastery of Norwegian among his accomplishments and may well have been responsible for first introducing Eleanor to Ibsen's work. He was sufficiently conversant with it by the early 1880s to expose the Herman and Jones adaptation of *A Doll's House* as a complete travesty compared with the Frances Lord version; and in collaboration with Eleanor he published a number of other articles referring to Ibsen in relation to topics of mere general cultural and social interest, including the woman question.[30] If we are to credit contemporary accounts – including those of Eleanor's father's collaborator, Frederick Engels – Aveling was one of the first to incorporate elements of the typical Ibsen drama into his own works for the stage.[31] He is also on record as enthralling audiences of the Playgoers' Club with his readings from *Ghosts*. The Club's journal reported that he 'was at his best . . . in bringing out the hypocrisy of Parson Manders; and the cynicism of Engstrand'.[32]

This is rather ironical, in that hypocrisy and cynicism – albeit of a bohemian rather than of a bourgeois variety – were just the kind of vices for which he himself had become infamous among his socialist colleagues. According to Eduard Bernstein, the German Marxist (and later revisionist) who had come to live in London in 1888, Aveling provided the model for the character of Louis Dubedat, the unscrupulous artist, in Shaw's play *The Doctor's Dilemma*.[33] In view of Aveling's record as an embezzler and seducer, it was difficult for Eleanor's friends to explain her long and fatal attraction to him – truly fatal, in that a moment of deep despair over his peculations and infidelities finally

prompted her to take her own life.[34] That was in 1898,
when the battle for Ibsen had already substantially been
won. The general odium attaching to Aveling's name should
not allow one to forget his bold campaigning at the height
of that battle. To hold an audience's attention to *Ghosts*,
without provoking the 'abusiveness' and 'convulsive
fury'[35] which characterised reactions to the first professional production of the play a few weeks after the meetings at the Playgoers' Club, was a considerable feat in
itself. Ibsen's depiction in *Ghosts* of the ravages of
venereal disease had lent the play a special notoriety all
over Europe, and such subject-matter proved particularly
sensitive in the England of the early 1890s, which was still
experiencing the shock-waves from the debates of the previous decade over the Contagious Diseases Acts.[36]

Among the other Ibsen champions mentioned in the report of
the Playgoers' Club but unacknowledged by Shaw were a
'Mr Bernstein' (evidently a reference to the same socialist
luminary who later spotted the resemblance between Aveling
and Shaw's Dubedat);[37] J. T. Grein, the Dutch-born
theatre-critic and experimentalist who was to stage the
notorious London première of *Ghosts*; and Israel Zangwill,
the Jewish novelist with whom Eleanor Marx had just collab-
orated in writing a sequel to *A Doll's House*, published in
the pages of the socialist periodical *Time*.[38]

Shaw recalled years later how several 'literary people'
in the 1890s used to write 'futile sequels' to *A Doll's
House*.[39] At the time, however, he seems to have regarded
such exercises as having a certain sociological significance
and polemical value. He himself had published one the year
before Zangwill's and Eleanor Marx's appeared, and in the
same periodical.[40] It came as a rejoinder to a yet earlier
sequel - by the novelist Walter Besant[41] - which had
struck Shaw as 'a representative middle class evangelical
verdict on the play', and important to counter for that very
reason.[42] Besant does not seem to have been as conservative as the general run of anti-Ibsenites: he had risked
his popular reputation as a writer by raising some delicate
social issues in his works, and he had even been described
to Shaw, about a year earlier, as a potential convert to
socialism.[43] Even so, his grimly moralistic speculations
about the fate which overtook Nora Helmer's family when she
abandoned it at the end of Ibsen's play provided Shaw with
an excellent opportunity for entering into the fray again on
Ibsen's behalf, and presenting a completely different
verdict on the play from a completely different viewpoint.
The sequel written by Zangwill and Eleanor Marx was a rather
less aggressive exercise - indeed, to any eye untrained in

detecting parody, positively accommodating in its avowed aim
to produce an ending to Ibsen's story which would accord
with the demands of 'sound English common sense'.[44]
Entitled '*A Doll's House* Repaired', it effected transformations in the action and characterisation which surpassed
even those of Herman and Jones. The doll's house is repaired
in this version by Nora returning to Helmer in a mood of
great contrition and despair, and submitting to his plans to
keep their marriage going on a platonic basis - just for
appearance's sake. The story ends not with Nora slamming the
front door on Helmer, but with Helmer slamming the bedroom
door on Nora.

The more recent chroniclers of Ibsen's reception in
England have referred to the contributions of individual
socialists such as Shaw and the Avelings. None of them, however, has noted - as contemporaries and near-contemporaries
were quick to note - the peculiar concentration of interest
in Ibsen and the 'New Drama' among those who belonged to
'the literary fringe of the Fabian Society and other reform
and revolutionary organisations'. These last words are
Holbrook Jackson's, and are to be found in his book on the
1890s, written only a decade or so after the events they
recount.[45] Jackson himself was leader of the Fabian Arts
Group, set up in 1907, and one could quibble with his
account only on the grounds that it tends to exaggerate the
confinement of Ibsen's appeal to some special or marginal
sections of the socialist movement; and that it fails to
suggest the variations which can be found in socialist
responses to the Norwegian dramatist and his beliefs.

There were, in fact, a number of individual littérateurs
and artists in England outside the socialist movement who
took a vigorous interest in Ibsen and his cause - including
Gosse and Archer (mentioned above), and George Moore, Henry
James, Max Beerbohm, Thomas Hardy, W. B. Yeats and James
Joyce. Among any definable political or artistic groups,
however, the strongest and most conspicuous signs of
interest in Ibsen's work were undoubtedly to be found in
socialist circles. The extent of interest within these
circles, it needs to be stressed, was wide and pervasive -
by no means limited to those engaged in literary and
theatrical life; or merely to the London-based members of
socialist organisations. At the same time, it also needs to
be stressed that socialist interest in Ibsen was not consistently adulatory nor uniformly sympathetic. During the
1890s, his work and his ideas became the focus of heated
debates inside as well as outside the socialist movement. In
Robert Blatchford's attacks on Ibsen and Shaw in the later
part of the decade, there were even echoes of the hysterical

denunciations which had appeared in the non-socialist press after the première of *Ghosts* in 1891.[46] The moral implications of Ibsen's ideas – at least as spelt out by Shaw in Shaw in *The Quintessence of Ibsenism* and the Fabian Society lecture on which that book was based – gravely disturbed a number of other socialists. The most notable of these were Annie Besant and William Clarke, both of whom had contributed to the famous *Fabian Essays in Socialism*, published in 1889, but who had then quitted the Society in disenchantment, not long afterwards. Their apostasy was not necessarily or solely due to their disagreements with Shaw over Ibsenism, but they must have felt alienated by the sympathetic reception accorded his thesis by most of their colleagues. There were certainly vehement protests – including a very articulate one from Mrs Besant herself – against Shaw's celebration of Ibsen as a poetic dramatist whose special significance lay in the challenge he presented to traditional ethical values and social ideas; but Shaw's rejoinders to these protests were received with as much rapturous enthusiasm by most of the audience as his original exposition had been.[47]

V

In some recollections published in 1912, the leader of the SDF, H. M. Hyndman, dismissed Ibsen as 'a portentous purveyor of commonplace . . . logrolled into being considered a genius'.[48] This display of bored indifference to Ibsen was a very uncharacteristic response among English socialists; and Hyndman implied, in another section of his memoirs, that Ibsenist ideas, as expounded and celebrated by Shaw, were not (and could not be) so lightly dismissed in the 1890s. Referring to the 'merciless castigation' of these ideas by Herbert Burrows in the SDF's newspaper, *Justice*, he commended the fact that his colleague had 'seriously' addressed himself to confronting the issues which Shaw had raised. According to Hyndman, Shaw himself had made his lecture simply an excuse for travestying Ibsen as 'a pleasing little side-issue of a joke'.[49] If we turn to Burrows's original article on Shaw's lecture, we find no sign at all of Hyndman's boredom with Ibsen, and an even greater readiness to protect the latter from any misrepresentation by Shaw. Outlining Shaw's thesis about Ibsen's persistent repugnance for traditional ideals, Burrows concluded, 'Those who really know Ibsen's works know that his message is nothing of the kind'.[50]

There were other members of the SDF who were actively
sympathetic towards Shaw as well as Ibsen. For example,
J. L. Joynes (a former pupil and master at Eton who had been
sacked from the school for his advanced political opinions)
wrote to Shaw to say how riveting he had found his explanation of Ibsenism.[51]

H. H. Champion — another upper-middle-class, public-school
rebel who found himself among the Fabians in the early 1880s
and then gravitated to the more militant Federation — has
been attributed by a contemporary with publishing first
editions of both Shaw and Ibsen.[52] There is no trace of
such editions in book-form; and the attribution probably
refers to the serialisation of two novels by Shaw and of the
Henrietta Lord translation of *Ghosts*, in the periodical *To-
day*, the publication of which had been taken over by
Champion at the end of 1883.[53] In 1894, ill-health forced
him to leave England for Australia, where he was on the committee of a group in Melbourne which called itself the
Playgoers' Club — perhaps in imitation of the London body in
which Shaw and the Avelings had been prominent. One of the
aims of the Club, he explained, would be to arrange for the
performance of controversial works such as *The Wild Duck* and
Ghosts, which had no likelihood of being staged publicly in
Australia, and to organise a series of discussions on such
plays.[54] What happened to this venture is not clear; it
probably dried up for want of support.

VI

This was not so great a problem in England, where the
socialists, again, would seem to have been a big enough and
an impressive enough force in the community to give Ibsen's
plays the initial boost they needed in order to become,
within a few years, a regular part of the repertoire. On the
composition of audiences at early Ibsen productions, it is
difficult to obtain much precise or reliable information;
but most observers — of varying political complexions — are
in accord about the fairly special or cliquish nature of
these audiences, and several comment expressly on the high
proportion of socialists among this clique.[55]

In a review of the première of *A Doll's House* in June
1889, J. M. Barrie noted that 'the Ibsen pit . . . differed
from its predecessors' as much as the play performed differed from the average burlesque. 'Discussions about which
was the best of Ibsen's plays, what was their thesis and
what their value went on all over the pit. . . . Possibly

the fact that none of the characters are "sympathetic" would
have spoiled any ordinary pit's interest in the play. . . .'
This section of the audience, at least, seemed to be 'enthusiastic about Ibsen before it came to the theatre'. There
were only a few who had not 'already worshipped Ibsen in
book covers, either because he is one of the great minds of
our age or because it is the fashion with the clique'.[56]
If Barrie's observations are correct, this would suggest
some sort of correlation between the purchasers or readers
of that seminal edition of Ibsen's plays, produced the year
before by Havelock Ellis, and the kind of theatregoer who
patronised the early Ibsen performances.

According to Clement Scott, one of the most vehement anti-
Ibsenites among London's theatre-critics at the time,
Ibsen's plays would barely have survived on the English
stage were it not for his following among 'socialistic' and
like-minded cranks.[57] Evidence from such a hostile source
should be treated with caution, though the nature of Scott's
occupation allowed him a close and continuous insight into
the composition of Ibsen's audiences; and his observations
tend to be borne out by the (admittedly more random) impressions of other commentators, close to the socialist
movement. For instance, William Morris – though himself no
great enthusiast for contemporary theatre in any form[58] –
noted of *A Doll's House*, a few weeks after its professional
première, that 'Socialists obviously look on the play as
making for Socialism, and are enthusiastic about it'.[59] On
the same day the SDF's newspaper, *Justice*, urged all its
subscribers to see the play: it was, the newspaper noted,
'one which no socialist should miss'.[60]

After attending a revival of *A Doll's House* in London in
1892, the trade-union leader John Burns noted in his diary
that the theatre had been 'half-filled with socialists',
including Graham Wallas (a co-contributor with Shaw, William
Clarke and Annie Besant to the *Fabian Essays*[61]) and
W. S. Sanders, a current member of the SDF who later became
a Fabian.[62] Both Burns and Wallas, as well as H. S. Salt,
the food reformer and collector of socialist verse, were
spotted by Shaw at the *Hedda Gabler* première a year earlier
– Burns in the gallery; Wallas and Salt in the pit, 'in
company', Shaw noted, 'with a large and intelligent contingent of Fabians'.[63]

VII

The writings of many other prominent socialists – particu-

larly those attached to the Fabian Society — contain references and allusions to Ibsen which reflect a considerable
acquaintance with his works, either as they appeared on the
English stage or in book-form. In stating what interested
them about the Norwegian's work, few of these socialists
were as explicit as Shaw had been in *The Quintessence of
Ibsenism* and in the Fabian Society lecture on which he based
that book. Moreover, none of them had his opportunities as
the regular theatre-critic for a popular periodical (the
Saturday Review) to enter into such great detail on the
matter. In many cases, they may have been unconscious of, or
unconcerned about, the underlying reasons for Ibsen's
interest, simply feeling some kind of instinctive affinity
with the dramatist and his outlook on society and human
nature. For the historian attempting to ascertain these
underlying reasons it may be a useful starting-point to
work out the possible bases of the affinity by considering
what kinds of relationship existed between Ibsen's social
background, the situations he presented in his plays, and
the backgrounds and situations of his socialist supporters.
    Not only because of the lack of detailed evidence
available, but also because of the ambiguities in the
evidence, generalisations relating to this subject are
hazardous, though the ambiguities in themselves provide good
grounds for some reasonably wide-ranging hypotheses. The
most obvious explanation for the particular interest in
Ibsen shown by the socialists is that many of them, as
William Morris noted, hailed Ibsen as 'another fighter in
the ranks of the socialist cause',[64] and appropriated his
work and ideas for the advancement of that cause. The
problem with this automatic association of Ibsenism and
socialism is twofold. First, there is the simple question of
its legitimacy: to what extent was it truer to Ibsen's
actual beliefs than, say, Mrs Lord's appropriation of Ibsen
to tenets of Eastern philosophy and religion? Second, it
neglects to take account of those socialists who clearly
dissociated socialism, as currently practised, from Ibsenism
— or at least from the Shavian brand of Ibsenism. Such
exceptions, if they can be called that, were to be found not
only among those socialists, such as Mrs Besant, William
Clarke and Robert Blatchford, who suffered a more or less
vehement reaction against Ibsenism. William Morris himself
tried to correct the impression that the two creeds were
associated by asserting that Ibsen was 'a clever playwright
but no socialist'.[65] And the same point was hammered home
to a socialist audience by none other than Shaw. Though he
is usually depicted as popularising the idea of an association between socialism and Ibsenism and thereby distorting

Ibsen's ideas, he in fact insisted in his Fabian Society
lecture on the dramatist that the latter was 'not a
socialist'. Further, Shaw claimed that, if Ibsen's plays had
any application (real or potential) to the current socialist
movement in England, it was not as a confirmatory text of
that movement's basic beliefs, but rather as an implied
critique of the tendency of socialism to eschew practical
considerations in pursuit of abstract ideals.[66] In his
refined version of this lecture, published as *The Quintessence of Ibsenism*, Shaw avoided all reference to Ibsen or
Ibsenism in connection with socialism; and in the second
edition of the book he ranked him with Strindberg as a
'Arch Individualist'.[67]

If he was in danger of distorting Ibsen's views at all, it
was in playing down, not exaggerating, the connections between the dramatist's ideas and socialism; though it would
be unfair to call this a distortion in view of Shaw's
repeated insistence that 'Socialism means practically the
nationalization of land and capital and nothing else'.[68]
Ibsen was never a socialist in this sense and he never
attached himself to any kind of socialist organisation. It
needs to be remembered, however, that he resolutely refused
to become committed to any political group, and that he
declared on at least one occasion a favourable interest in
socialism as 'one of the forces of the future'.[69] Born
into the family of a small merchant and businessman, with
far from radical inclinations, Ibsen revealed his rebellious
temperament from a early age. In his teens he proclaimed
himself a freethinker, thereby defying the pietist teachings
of his childhood, and at the outbreak of the revolution in
France, in February 1848, he thrilled to the republican
cause in a manner which alarmed the conservative populace of
the small provincial town where he was staying at the
time.[70] In the face of his middle-class background, he
came to support wholeheartedly the cause of the working-
class, berating those of the left who did not make this
cause their own;[71] and he displayed throughout his
writings - though most conspicuously in his naturalistic
'social' dramas - a deeply critical or sceptical attitude
towards several of the most sacred bourgeois institutions
and conventions (including the prevailing concepts of marriage, the family, the role and status of women, the Church
and the commercial system). On the surface, then, even
though Ibsen was not a socialist as such, it is not difficult to account for the interest he held for so many socialists in England - especially those of middle-class origins
themselves. The Fabians, an almost exclusively middle-class
body,[72] were particularly prominent among Ibsen's

admirers, and it is significant how most of the other
socialists referred to above as evincing some interest in
Ibsen also came from a middle-class background (John Burns
and W. S. Sanders, coming as they did from an artisan or
working-class background, were exceptions).

Whatever the true nature of Ibsen's position on socialism
- and it remained an elusive and ambiguous one - the sense
of sharing a similar social background to him, and of
experiencing a comparable form of rebellion against that
background, may have been sufficient to attract the initial
attention of the bulk of the socialists under discussion
here. Shaw's case is particularly pertinent in this respect.
Both he and Ibsen were the sons of businessmen and, moreover, businessmen who had failed under the pressures of the
competitive commercial system and had turned increasingly to
drink.[73] Though he may not have known how close were the
parallels between his own background and Ibsen's, Shaw
instinctively associated himself with the Norwegian dramatist and a long line of other 'middle-class revolutionists' -
by no means all of them socialist in their beliefs or
affiliations. In a 'lay sermon' he published in 1912, he
observed that

it is in the middle-class itself that the revolt against
middle-class ideals breaks out. . . . Neither peer nor
laborer has ever hated the bourgoisie as Marx hated it,
nor despised its ideals as Swift, Ibsen and Strindberg
despised them. . . . I defy any navvy, or any duke, to
maul the middle-class as Dickens mauled it, or as it is
mauled to-day by Wells, Chesterton, Belloc, Pinero, the
young lions of the provincial repertory theatres, or
G. Bernard Shaw.[74]

VIII

With particular reference to Shaw's work and times, feminism
has been seen as 'an important element in political socialism',[75] and there were clearly some connections between an
adherence to these two overlapping causes and an enthusiasm
for Ibsen. In reviewing the writings of the German socialist
August Bebel on women's social and economic status in the
past, present and future, Eleanor Marx and Edward Aveling
stated,

the truth, not fully recognised even by those anxious to
do good to woman is that she, like the labour-classes, is

in an oppressed condition. . . . Women are the creatures
of an organized tyranny of men, as the workers are the
creatures of an organized tyranny of idlers. . . .[76]

This statement was made as far back as 1886, the year of
their *Doll's House* production; and it was not a completely
fortuitous irony, perhaps, that in the concluding passages
of their review the Avelings should have used as a text the
words of Ibsen's do-gooding tyrant in that play, Torvald
Helmer. They looked forward to the time when a 'Socialistic
state', having cleared away the 'mists and miasmata of the
capitalist system', would facilitate, in the sexual relationships of man and woman, the 'complete, harmonious, last-
ing blending of two human lives'. The realization of such an
ideal, they claimed, needed four things: 'love, respect,
intellectual likeness and command of the necessaries of
life'. Under socialism, the last of these things was

absolutely ensured to all. As Ibsen makes Helmer say
to Nora, 'Home life ceases to be free and beautiful
directly its foundations are borrowings and debts.' But
borrowings and debts when one is a member of a community
and not an isolated man fighting for his own hand, can
never come. . . .[77]

Ibsen himself, in a speech he delivered a year earlier to
the artisans at Trondheim, connected the degraded condition
of women in contemporary society with the degraded condition
of the working classes; and, while making no reference to
socialism, he contended that

the transformation of social conditions which is now being
undertaken in the rest of Europe is very largely concerned
with the future status of the workers and of women. That
is what I am hoping and waiting for, that is what I shall
work for, all I can.[78]

That Ibsen's work - especially *A Doll's House* - should have
struck certain socialists who were in the vanguard of the
women's movement as a valuable feminist text is perfectly
understandable. Their use of his plays in this way
represents one of the more justifiable appropriations of his
work by contemporaries for extra-theatrical purposes. But
as an explanation of Ibsen's appeal to socialists, it is
inadequate.

To begin with, there was no *automatic* alliance between
socialists and feminists, just as there was none between
socialists and Ibsenists: the pattern of allegiance to these

various groups and their beliefs was complex and uneven. On one hand, by no means all advocates of women's rights (political or otherwise) were socialists or even socialist sympathisers. And among the general run of feminists, it is difficult to find instances of that passionate advocacy of Ibsen which can be found among the socialists in particular, or, indeed, of any passionate hostility towards him such as can be found in a few other socialists. Ibsen's work, rather than becoming an object or focus of intense involvement and active campaigning on the part of the women's movement as a whole, would seem to have provided little more then some convenient symbols for that movement's propaganda and an occasional, though not a fundamental nor even particularly vital, source of inspiration. Havelock Ellis's wife, Edith Lees, while as passionate about Ibsen's work as her husband, could only say of *A Doll's House* that it 'drove thinking women *further together* towards their emancipation'.[79] The same could be said of several other works of literature, as she intimated by linking Ibsen's play in this context with Olive Schreiner's novel *The Story of an African Farm* (1883). The figure of Nora Helmer in *A Doll's House* was an apotheosis of the 'New Woman' in literature, but she had a long line of predecessors, as well as rivals and successors;[80] and it is remarkable – considering the heat which the Ibsen controversy in general produced – how infrequently the debates over women's suffrage and over broader feminist issues managed to reflect in any explicit way the impact of *A Doll's House*.[81]

On the other hand, not all socialists were feminists, and some of them were quite prominent in the ranks of the antisuffragists, viewing the cause of women's rights – in the political sense at least – as a dangerous distraction from the cause of the working class as a whole.[82] These included the SDF's leader, H. M. Hyndman (for whom, as we have seen, Ibsen's plays exercised no appeal) and Ernest Belfort Bax – a colleague of Eleanor Marx's in the Socialist League yet one of the 'idealist' brand of socialists whom Shaw had attacked in his Fabian Society lecture on Ibsen.[83] There were other socialists who, while they were avowed admirers of certain aspects of Ibsen's work, expressed a positive distaste for his exploration of feminist themes. Beatrice Webb, for instance, found great stimulation and solace in Ibsen's two great poetic dramas, *Brand* and *Peer Gynt*, which her husband, Sidney, read out to her in 1897;[84] but on accompanying Shaw to a revival of *Pillars of Society* some four and a half years later, she walked out before it was over, displaying a marked impatience with its 'old fashioned stuff' about 'Truth and Freedom and Emancipation of Women'.[85] Having enjoyed a quite remarkable independence for a girl brought up in Victorian England, she was never as concerned about women's rights questions as she was about so many other social issues. In the 1880s she had even ranked herself among the anti-suffragists; though she was to moderate this position under the influence of her husband and was eventually to recant it.[86]

A favourite of the Webbs among the Edwardian generation of Fabians, Rupert Brooke,[87] showed almost as much enthusiasm for Ibsen in his Cambridge days as he did for running the university branch of the Fabian Society.[88] In addition to seeing and reviewing Ibsen's plays, which had come to enjoy popularity among Cambridge undergraduates,[89] Brooke expressed his keenness to mount productions of them, writing in 1911 that, 'If the Cambridge Stage Society wants a stage-manager for Ibsen, they'll know where to come.'[90] By 1913, however, he was showing signs of disenchantment with Ibsen's works - partly because of their feminist implications. In an address he gave in that year, he judged Ibsen 'rather unhealthy' compared with Strindberg. The latter, he claimed, 'had been born into a community suffering from a "woman's movement"' which tried to preach 'that denial of sex called feminism, with its resultant shallowness of women and degradation of man. Feminism disgusted Strindberg.' For all his weakness and excesses, Strindberg had at least had the courage, as Brooke saw it, 'to declare that men are men and women women'.[91]

Ibsen would probably have been more surprised than distressed to have himself identified with the brand of feminism which Brooke stigmatised, though he had been the victim of similar kinds of identification made in his lifetime by hostile critics - including other members of the Fabian Society, such as Robert Blatchford.[92] The feminist label, even as applied in a much simpler and milder manner to describe an advocate of women's social or political claims, was one which Ibsen had been careful to eschew. In 1898, addressing the Norwegian Women's Rights League at a banquet which it had organised in his honour, he denied having worked consciously, or exclusively, for women's rights: 'I am not even quite clear', he claimed, 'as to just what this women's rights movement is. To me it has seemed a problem of humanity in general. And if you read my books carefully you will understand this.'[93]

Shaw's views were at least as equivocal as Ibsen's. This is a point which needs stressing, in view of the way he has usually been labelled, so unambiguously, as a feminist.[94] In his account, published in 1913,[95] of the Norwegian's third-last play, *Little Eyolf*, Shaw clearly understood - and

applauded – the fact that Ibsen was as sensitive to the
oppression of men by contemporary marital practices as to
that of women. In later years, he actually criticised Ibsen
for not giving sufficient emphasis to the man's side of the
story. Shaw claimed that as far back as 1894, in writing
Candida, he had turned the tables on Ibsen by 'showing that
in the real typical doll's house, it is the man who is the
doll'.[96] The balance of relationships in *Candida* is in
fact much more complex and sophisticated than this account
suggests; and Shaw came as close to misreading his own early
views on the roles and status of the two sexes in contemporary society as he did Ibsen's. As he never abandoned his
basic respect for Ibsen, however, his later misreadings only
confirm that Ibsen's reputation as a feminist was not a crucial factor – and certainly not the only one – in winning
the general support he received in English socialist
circles.

IX

In view of the myth of Shaw's 'socialist' interpretation of
Ibsenism, and in view of the obvious programmatic interest
which such a play as *A Doll's House* had for those in the
vanguard of the women's movement,[97] it is easy to over-
estimate the importance of Ibsen's political, social or
moral 'message' in arousing interest in his work. Shaw's
interest in particular has nearly always been accounted for
in these terms – to the extent that he has been charged
with remaining indifferent or insensitive to the artistic
and dramatic qualities of Ibsen's work.[98] If we examine in
detail Shaw's and the other socialists' responses to Ibsen,
we shall find that most of them were just as interested in
Ibsen's capacities as a poetic dramatist and in the ways in
which his plays worked as theatre, or failed to work.

A few examples will have to suffice. When Rupert Brooke
became disenchanted with Ibsen's plays, it was not only because of his increasing irritation at their allegedly feminist themes; Brooke had also begun to perceive weaknesses in
the construction of the plays he saw and to bristle at the
limitations of their severely realistic dialogue and plot-
ting.[99] Conversely, we find Havelock Ellis, an early and
enthusiastic preacher of Ibsen's social gospel, and the
Reverend Percy Dearmer, a leading Christian socialist and
also an active Fabian, celebrating the Norwegian dramatist's
artistic capacities in the same breath as expounding his
social message or argument. Indeed, if anything, both these

writers tended to play down the didactic elements in *A Doll's House*.[100]

On looking back at how Ibsen had made his initial impact on him, Shaw asserted that it was 'the magic of the great poet' which had opened his eyes 'in a flash' to the 'importance of the social philosopher'. There is reason to doubt the suddenness of this process; Shaw spent a good part of the 1880s[101] forming those ideas which found final shape in *The Quintessence of Ibsenism*; but it is not unlikely that his views on Ibsen's social philosophy should have evolved with, and partly through, his appreciation of Ibsen's art. It is significant in this respect how often, in explaining the Ibsenist philosophy, Shaw referred to the Norwegian as a great poet or playwright or artist, rather than as a philosopher, and alluded to his works (including the non-verse plays) as dramatic poetry.[102] While deliberately concentrating in *The Quintessence* on expounding what he saw as Ibsen's overall message – the tyranny of idealism – he was also intent on revealing the Norwegian dramatist as a genuine 'pioneer in stage progress', using but at the same time subverting and transcending the forms and conventions of the nineteenth-century French comedy of intrigue.[103] In a long Appendix to the first edition of *The Quintessence*, he addressed himself specifically to the technical and emotional problems of doing Ibsen justice in performance – problems which arose precisely because, in Shaw's words, 'the whole point of an Ibsen play' lay in exposing 'the very conventions', melodramatic and idealistic, 'upon which are based those by which the actor is ridden'.[104] In his original Fabian Society lecture on Ibsen, Shaw had announced his conviction that it was on the stage 'alone' that the true extent of Ibsen's power could be conveyed and appreciated;[105] and his individual notices of Ibsen productions throughout the 1890s, while by no means inattentive to Ibsen's social and moral themes, placed the weight of emphasis on the dramatic potency of those themes and their theatrical realisation – or lack of realisation – in the particular performance under review.[106]

X

Shaw's appreciation, however, of Ibsen's dramatic art, and the similar appreciation shown by various other socialists, does no more to explain the germination of their particular interest in the Norwegian dramatist than their responsiveness to his ideas. That explanation is to be sought in the

way in which, and the extent to which, both his art and his
ideas served to crystallise the socialists' own personal and
political dilemmas. Sidney Webb once intimated that no novel
- and he might well have been speaking of any form of
literature - was of deep interest to him unless he found
himself coming into it and therefore learned something of
personal significance.[107] It would be too easy to dismiss
this as characteristic of Webb's co-called philistinism;
self-identification of this kind is probably something we
all pursue and experience in reading literature, even if we
avoid making it so crucial to our assessment and enjoyment.
It was certainly characteristic of other socialists in their
response to Ibsen, and there was much in his plays, beyond
his beliefs, for them to identify with, at least indirectly
and intuitively.

Webb himself, as he hinted in the same passage, was
sceptical of the individualist elements in Ibsen's beliefs
which the Shavian interpretation had stressed; though he
would 'not condemn' these, conceding that the 'Ibsenite'
theme of the necessity of 'self-realisation' may be of particular importance to women 'just now'.[108] Furthermore,
the situations and words of some of Ibsen's characters
became a part of Webb's frame of reference in summing up
some of his colleagues' dilemmas, if not his own.[109]

There was a particular aspect of Ibsen's individualistic
beliefs which may well have served to dampen the enthusiasm
of one of his most fervent champions among the socialists,
Eleanor Marx. We have seen how, in *The Woman Question*, written in conjunction with her husband, she had stressed the
importance of enjoying the full resources of the 'community'
in establishing the best material basis for sound relationships in the home, and had alluded to the futility of the
'isolated man fighting for his own hand'. This had come as a
rider to a quotation, made half-approvingly, from one of
Ibsen's most conservative and unprepossessing characters; it
could also be seen as an implicit criticism of one of
Ibsen's heroes, Dr Stockmann in *An Enemy of the People*. For
Stockmann showed a particular relish for the role of the
'isolated man' fighting the will of the majority; he not
only practised the role, but also preached it as a principle; and it is not surprising that that principle should
have been taken as representing Ibsen's own central theme in
the play. Eleanor's scepticism about the worth of such a
principle might well account for her feelings of dissatisfaction in being commissioned to translate *An Enemy of the
People*, and her reservations about an edition which should
include that play but not *A Doll's House*.

However distasteful they might have been to her, the par-

ticular beliefs   of Ibsen revealed in *An Enemy of the People*
were not sufficient to turn Eleanor against him in any way;
and there   are   grounds   for suggesting   that the beliefs he
revealed in   *The Lady from the Sea*, though much more congenial to her, were far from being the only factor accounting for her much more positive enthusiasm for that play.

The Lady from the Sea broadly resembles *A Doll's House* in
taking   as one of its central themes the question of women's
rights   in sexual and family relationships;   though it represents a more elusive and more ambiguous treatment of this
theme.   The lady in question, Ellida Wangel, does not find
the liberation she is seeking by leaving her husband, as
Nora does, but by making a quite conscious and considered
decision to stay with him after he has given her complete
freedom of choice in the matter. Her option was to go away
with an alluring sailor, and suspected criminal, with whom
she had contracted a mystical alliance before her marriage.
The alliance was rooted in a passion for the sea which
Ellida shared with the sailor; there was nothing rationally
explicable about it. Before her husband gave up his posses-
sive claims on her, the prospect of consolidating her
alliance with the sailor presented itself as less an option
than a compulsion. It both reflected and portended a relationship that was at least as oppressive as her marital
bonds, and which was also a source of real dread, for all
its promises of fulfilling her deepest romantic yearnings.
There is certainly a double edge to her final decision: what
looks like a victory for rationality could also be interpreted as a victory for safe conventionality. But it is more
than anything a victory for freedom of will, which she could
not have won or, rather, not have sustained, if she had gone
off with the sailor.

The spectacle of a husband allowing his wife complete
freedom to choose between himself and another would have
had an obvious appeal to anyone in the radical vanguard
of the late-Victorian women's movement; and one can only
conclude that it was the ambiguities in Ibsen's exposition
which made the play a less popular feminist text than *A
Doll's House*.[110] It was also not nearly as widely publi-
cised in England, for all of Eleanor's efforts to give it
currency.

Her earlier interest in *A Doll's House* has been partly
explained in terms of the play's relevance not only to her
views on women's rights but also to her own situation *vis-
à-vis* her notorious common-law husband. Her first biographer
has noted that 'she must often have felt as if she were a
Nora — a stranger to her husband', quoting in support a
letter written to Havelock Ellis at the time of her private

production of *A Doll's House* in which Eleanor confessed,
'There are some people one gets to know at once . . . and
others that one is a stranger to after a lifetime passed
together.'[111]
  The parallel is plausible; but there was a still closer
one between Eleanor's situation and Ellida's in *The Lady
from the Sea*, which helps account for her special commitment
to that play, despite its ambiguities on the theme of
women's rights. The sailor whom Ellida finds so alluring is
actually called 'the Stranger'; and in both his irrational
attraction for Ellida and in his reputation as a criminal,
Eleanor may well have seen reflections and extensions of the
personality of Edward Aveling, for whom she herself felt an
awful fascination in spite (or perhaps partly because) of
his notoriety as an embezzler and his powerful attraction
for and to other women. It is not impossible that even
Aveling's interest in the play may have stemmed in part from
an intuitive identification with the Stranger; but there are
some clear hints from Eleanor of her tendency to see broad
parallels between the situations and people in Ibsen's plays
and the situations and people in the life she lived. These
parallels were what she singled out in a very early attempt
to explain the Norwegian dramatist's appeal to her. Writing
to Shaw in 1885 about her plans to organise a reading of *A
Doll's House*, she said of Ibsen,

> the more I study the greater I think him. How odd it is
> that people complain that his plays 'have no end' but just
> leave you where you were, that he gives no *solution* to the
> problem he has set you! As if in life things 'ended' off
> either comfortably or uncomfortably. We play through our
> little drama, & comedies, & tragedies, & farces & then
> begin it all over again. If we *could* find solutions to the
> problems of our lives things wd. be easy in this weary
> world.[112]

Eleanor's eventual 'solution' to her problems with Aveling
was suicide: it was her particular tragedy perhaps that she
did not even have Ellida's option, in finally giving up 'the
Stranger' to whom she was so powerfully drawn, of holding on
to the anchor of a conventional marriage.
  This explanation of Eleanor's interest in Ibsen remains a
hypothetical one in the last analysis; and, even if the
evidence for it were more than just suggestive, it would
still remain something of a special case, inapplicable in
its details to the experience of other socialist enthusiasts
for Ibsen. At the same time, it does provide a clue to the
possible processes by which Ibsen's works and ideas came to

acquire so great a significance in socialist circles - and
not only for his enthusiasts in those circles. To be aware
of that significance, most socialists did not need to identify with Ibsen's situations and characters in such a highly
personal manner as Eleanor seems to have done; but those
personal dilemmas which she found crystallised in his plays
had broader social, political and moral ramifications which
could not but have affected all of her fellow socialists to
some degree. Over various issues - including such questions
as the respective rights and wrongs of marriage and 'free
love' - they had to decide how far to take their rebellion
against bourgeois conventions and ideals; and Ibsen's plays
came to present an important testing-point in this respect,
particularly for socialists of middle-class origins themselves. The more extreme forms of rebellion embodied in some
of his plays - for example, the apparent advocacy of freedom
from any binding marriages or from any overriding duty to
one's spouse and children - provided the focus for a general
dilemma among the socialists and therefore a subject of considerable controversy within their ranks. Any explanation of
his impact on the socialists has to take into account not
only those in their number who liked and championed him but
also those who felt prompted to attack him or at least to
attack his more extremist representatives among their colleagues. His importance to them is underlined by the fact
that they could be found fighting about him as well as for
him.

XI

One must be wary of oversimplifying the battle-lines, for
that would be to oversimplify the tests Ibsen presented and
the dilemmas he crystallised in his works. If some socialists, like the Webbs, remained equivocal about Ibsen, there
were others, like Edward Carpenter, whose response was never
hostile but not passionately enthusiastic either. In a book
of essays on 'Art and Its Relation to Life', Carpenter wel-
comed Ibsen, together with Zola and Whitman, as pioneers in
'the healthy and natural treatment' of sexual themes in
literature. He claimed, however, that 'the world still waits
for anything like a large and artistic treatment of this
grand subject' and that 'the outlines sketched by Whitman'
had been developed 'less healthily' by Zola and Ibsen.[113]
He gave no explanation of this judgment. In view, however,
of his well-publicised interests in the role of the homosexual in society and his own sexual inclinations,[114] it

is possible to argue that his reservations about Ibsen and
Zola sprang partly from the fact that they neglected to
deal, explicitly or implicitly, with homosexual themes and
tensions in their work. Some of Whitman's writings certainly
lent themselves more easily to homoerotic interpretation,
even if they did not openly celebrate homosexual love, and
for Carpenter they may thereby have represented a more profound, or at least more complex, crystallisation of human
dilemmas and delights. On the level of his personal
emotions, as well as of his particular social concerns,
there was more for him to identify with in Whitman's poems
than in either Zola's novels or Ibsen's plays.

Even a more passionate enthusiast for Ibsen like Eleanor
Marx may have had a passing sympathy at times with critics
like William Clarke, who attacked the Norwegian dramatist
for the 'pronounced Anarchism' in his writings.[115] The
kind of individualism represented by Stockmann in *An Enemy
of the People*, which may have been at the root of Eleanor's
dissatisfaction with that play, had some clear anarchistic
implications. Shaw for one brought these out in the course
of writing about Ibsen in an anarchist newspaper. 'The function' of the 'philosophic anarchist', he claimed in the
pages of *Liberty* in 1895 , was to 'combat the attempts that
are constantly being made to arrest development by using the
force of the state to suppress all departures from those
habits of the majority which it pretentiously calls its
morals'.[116] This statement has definite echoes of
Dr Stockmann's thunderings against the tyranny of the majority in the last act of *An Enemy of the People*.

'The strongest man is he who stands alone', was Stockmann's motto; and his creator's own determination to 'stand
alone', reflected in his refusal to commit himself to any
group or party ideology, exposed a side of his nature which
was not just apolitical but actually anti-political. He
expressly preached a form of anarchism on occasion. 'The
state must go' he told the Danish critic, Georg Brandes, in
1871:

That is the revolution I shall join in. Undermine the concept of the state, set up free choice and spiritual kinship as the one decisive factor for union, and that is the
beginning of a liberty that is worth something. Changing
the form of government is nothing more than tinkering with
degrees, a little more or a little less - rotten, all of
it.[117]

'Special reforms' were ultimately futile in Ibsen's eyes;
and 'revolutions in externals' were 'mere trifling. What is

all important is the revolution in the spirit of man.'[118]

It is at first sight puzzling that other socialists not only failed on the whole to emulate William Clarke in his vigorous criticisms of Ibsen's anarchist and individualist tendencies, but should also - with exceptions like Eleanor Marx - have shown such an unreserved enthusiasm for a play which endorsed those tendencies more overtly than any other. The attraction of *An Enemy of the People* for the Fabians, for instance, is particularly surprising, considering that one of the basic characteristics of Fabianism was a faith in the worth of 'special reforms' in gradually bringing about socialism.

There are two possible explanations of why Ibsen's individualist and anarchist sentiments did not break the bonds of affinity with him that so many English socialists of similar social origins appear to have felt. First, those sentiments were neither consistent nor completely unqualified. The individualism of Stockmann in *An Enemy of the People* was never so vehemently anarchistic in tone as the sort of beliefs Ibsen articulated in his private correspondence. Despite the associations Shaw made in 1895 between a crusade against majority opinion and philosophic anarchism, he had insisted a few years earlier, in his section on *An Enemy of the People* in *The Quintessence of Ibsenism*, that Ibsen's views there 'must not be confounded with Anarchism' in the sense of 'idealization of the repudiation of Government'.[119] And, indeed, in the famous speech Ibsen made in 1895 before the artisans of Trondheim, he himself made some accommodating references to 'our government' and 'our representatives', expressing the hope not that they would be abolished but that they would be ennobled by the infusion of those two great forces of the future, women and workers.[120] Ibsen's outright advocacy of anarchism was confined to his letters and, perhaps, his conversation - sources that were inaccessible at the time to anyone who was not on intimate terms with him.

A second explanation of Ibsen's attractiveness to British socialists in the face of his individualist and anarchist tendencies is that there were several members of socialist groups in England who themselves shared these tendencies, at least to a small degree, and who did not see them as necessarily incompatible with socialism. Shaw and Morris both flirted with anarchism of one kind or another in the eighties, while ultimately rejecting it.[121] The latter joined with Eleanor Marx herself, as well as Aveling, Belfort Bax and others, in severing formal links with Hyndman's SDF, partly because of the 'political opportunism' displayed by the organisation in its preoccupation with 'electioneering' and getting socialists into 'our sham parliament'. The alternative body set up by the breakaway group, the Socialist League, aimed to work for the revolution through propaganda and educational programmes directed at the working classes. 'Mere politics' was to be eschewed.[122] In its initial stages, the League was not opposed to parliamentary action *in toto*; but its anti-political leanings attracted many outright anarchists to its ranks, and by the late eighties these had come to dominate most of its activities. Even the Fabian Society, as Shaw pointed out, did not escape the 'influenza of anarchism' in its early years.[123]

Considering that the socialist movement in England was capable of harbouring, and on occasions even assimilating, these seemingly unorthodox elements, it is not so surprising that Ibsen should have maintained a wide appeal for many prominent supporters of the movement, especially as his more extreme anarchist pronouncements were seldom made public.

His open questioning, in *An Enemy of the People*, of some of the basic assumptions underlying current concepts of democracy, including the rights of majorities, might also have appealed to the more authoritarian or elitist side of certain socialists. Shaw's support of the 'strongest man' principle became notorious in the 1930s, as it led him into sympathies with Fascism. A continual tension between elitist and egalitarian tendencies is particularly discernible in the Fabians' political, social and cultural attitudes;[124] and there was also a strong anti-liberal streak in the thought of several of their most prominent leaders.[125] The sort of democratic system which Dr Stockmann singled out for attack in *An Enemy of the People* was precisely the liberal-bourgeois kind which socialists in general felt to have serious limitations, even if they did not all denounce it with the same vociferousness and felt – as the Fabians did – that it was worth exploiting and 'permeating' for their own ends.

Many socialists – again, particularly those from a middle-class background – may have identified themselves with the doctor in his revolt against the social selfishness of the 'solid liberal majority', ignoring the fact that he really relished the role of the lone rebel and was not a member of any anti-establishment political organisation. Even those in socialist groups who recognised Stockmann's resolute individualism would not in all cases and in all respects have been alienated by it. In the preface to the edition in which Eleanor Marx's translation of *An Enemy of the People* appeared, Havelock Ellis pointed out that, though Stockmann declares that 'the strongest man upon earth is he who stands alone', his very actions in the play have been 'genuinely

social, prompted by genuinely social motives'.[126] Shaw was
to claim in his Fabian Society lecture on Ibsen that in a
sense the way to socialism was through individualism, and in
his discussion of *An Enemy of the People* in *The Quintessence
of Ibsenism* he spoke of the vital role in social progress of
'pioneers', or isolated proponents of 'new developments' –
precisely of the Stockmann stamp.[127] Sydney Olivier, one
of Shaw's colleagues on the Fabian Society Executive, and
the contributor of the chapter 'The Moral Basis of Socialism' to *Fabian Essays*, showed in that chapter how it was
possible for socialists to see individualism not as the
antithesis of their doctrine but as intimately (even organi-
cally) connected with it:

Socialism appears as the offspring of Individualism,
as the outcome of individualist struggle, and as the
necessary condition for the approach to the individualist
ideal. The opposition commonly assumed in contrasting the
two is an accident of the new habitual confusion between
personality and personalty, between a man's life and the
abundance of things that he has. Socialism is merely
Individualism rationalised, organised, clothed, and in its
right mind.[128]

XII

If the individualist and anti-political elements in Ibsen's
writings and make-up did little to detract from his general
appeal among socialists in England – and to a certain extent
even enhanced that appeal – the same may perhaps be said
for his more conservative tendencies. These were strong
enough at times to cut right across the dominant radical
currents of his thought. A staunch republican, he yet
hankered after medals and honours awarded by European
monarchs and earned the contempt of his colleague and rival
Bjornstjerne Bjornson by continually sporting these
decorations. This practice merely heightened the extraordinary formality of his mode of dress, which, according to
one observer, was 'more suited to a rich merchant or banker
than a philosopher or poet'.[129] A sworn enemy of any kind
of political oppression, especially of one state by another,
he was yet incapable of responding with any degree of
enthusiasm to Garibaldi's attempts to liberate Rome from
papal domination in the late 1860s, regarding these in fact
as a threat to the serenity of a place which had afforded
him such ideal conditions for working in the past few

years.[130] A would-be anarchist and flouter of bourgeois
conventions, he could yet castigate, in terms that were
worthy of the most respectable, law-abiding of citizens, an
actor who had attempted to make illicit profits out of his
work.[131]

These random examples of the conflicting impulses in
Ibsen's personality suggest a powerlessness on the dramatist's part to escape completely the fetters of his middle-
class heritage in the pursuit of his 'advanced' political,
social and moral convictions. There is reason to believe
that Ibsen, as a renegade from institutional religion, was
also powerless to rid himself of all the effects of his
childhood exposure to pietist doctrines. This spiritual
dilemma of his becomes clearly evident to any attentive
reader of *Emperor and Galilean* or *Ghosts* or *Rosmersholm*, in
which the problems of reconciling Christian ethics with
worldly joy reveals itself as a marked preoccupation of the
author and his characters. On the other hand, the influence
of Ibsen's middle-class background in nurturing a conservative strain in his personality is less readily apparent in
his plays, covered up as it is there by the vehemence of his
onslaughts on bourgeois values and institutions.

At the same time, it is important to note that, even if
some of his supporters have perceived the conservative element in Ibsen – either intuitively or through a particularly
close analysis of his work and the extensive criticism on
it – they would not necessarily have been alienated. A
look at a small sample of the diaries, letters, memoirs and
published writings of socialists (particularly middle-class
socialists) based in England in the late-Victorian period,
and the comments they made there concerning either their own
predilections or those of their colleagues, suggests that
many of these figures were scarcely immune from the prejudices, or resistant to all the habits, associated with
their class, and were often aware of the conflicting
impulses in their own make-up.[132] Conceivably, therefore,
the conservative undertone in Ibsen may in itself have
touched off a responsive chord in British socialists from a
social background similar to the playwright's, and served to
build up, rather than diminish, the affinity which many of
them apparently felt with him. One can do little more than
speculate on this as a possible general factor, in view of
the lack of specific reasons given by most English socialists for any interest in Ibsen which they expressed. That
this is not an entirely fanciful proposition, however, is
perhaps suggested by the following comment by one of the
younger generation of Ibsen enthusiasts (Holbrook Jackson)
on Bernard Shaw. In his book on the 1890s, published in

1913, Jackson observes that Shaw is really

> an apostle to the Middle Class, as, indeed, he is a prod-
> uct of that class. He displays all its characteristics in
> his personality and his art, what are called his eccentri-
> cities of thought and expression being little more than
> advertisements of his own respectability. Puritanical,
> economical, methodical, deeply conscious of responsibility
> and a sound man of affairs, he sums up in his own person-
> ality all the virtues of the class satirised by Ibsen
> in *The Pillars of Society*. An examination of his most
> 'advanced' ideas urges the point, for even his dialectic
> is bourgeois from its nicest subtleties to its most out-
> rageous explosions. . . . As a Socialist he invariably
> appeals to the bourgeois instinct of self-interest, and
> much of his philosophy is a modern variation of the
> bourgeois ideals of self-help and self-reliance – namely
> self-assertion.[133]

If this contemporary summing-up of Shaw's attitudes and
inclinations is in any way a valid one, it would seem to
bear out the notion that the affinity which a middle-class
socialist such as himself felt with Ibsen was based not
simply on a shared hostility to the values of their class,
but also, paradoxically, on an instinctive adherence to some
of those values.

It was an affinity which certain socialists, whose adherence to the ethical values of their class and age proved
unremitting, could not share; they could contemplate an
overturning of the current socio-political order but not
of the moral order. Ibsen's ideas, as bodied forth in his
art, and his very art-forms, together served as a challenge
to all aspects of the old order, and were – as interpreted
by Shaw at least in his deliberately provocative manner –
especially subversive of conventional morality. The extent
of the challenge, the degree of effective subversion, were
not as far-reaching as Shaw made out; but their very limitations and equivocations probably made Ibsen's plays a more,
rather than a less, accurate reflection of the socio-political, moral and aesthetic objectives of most of his socialist
supporters in England. The complex of political attitudes
and conflicting personal impulses evident in his plays and
elsewhere brought to the surface the dilemmas and self-
conflicts of his bitterest critics in the socialist movement
as well as those of his sympathisers; and that, fundament-
ally, is what made his work so significant for all these
so-called 'middle-class revolutionists'.

NOTES

Place of publication is London, unless otherwise stated.

1. *Nora* (1882) pp. x–xii; *Ghosts* (1890) pp. v–viii.
2. See the review by Edward Aveling, *Nora* and *Breaking a Butterfly*, *To-day*, I (June 1884) pp. 473–80.
3. 'Ibsen in England', *Dramatic Review*, 4 Apr. 1885, p. 147. Cf. H. Granville Barker, 'The Coming of Ibsen', in Walter de la Mare (ed.), *The Eighteen Eighties* (1930) p. 193.
4. Eleanor Marx to Havelock Ellis, Jan. 1886, printed in Ellis, 'Eleanor Marx – II', *Adelphi*, XI (Oct. 1935) p. 35.
5. Ibid., Dec. 1885, p. 35.
6. Preface to *The Irrational Knot* (1931) p. xix.
7. *The Quintessence of Ibsenism*, 2nd edn (1913) p. 182.
8. For details, see Norman and Jeanne MacKenzie, *The First Fabians* (1977) pp. 305–6; C. B. Purdom, *Harley Granville Barker* (1955) pp. 8–9, 12–13; and Purdom's edition of *Bernard Shaw's Letters to Granville Barker* (1956; New York, 1957) pp. 2–4.
9. See Shaw's Diary, 16, 21, 22 June 1889, in British Library of Political and Social Science. Cf. Shaw, *London Music in 1888–89* (1937) pp. 148–51.
10. *Fabian Tract no. 91* (1899). Cf. *Fabian News*, Feb. 1897, pp. 47–8; Apr.–May 1889, pp. 5, 10.
11. See Mabel Palmer (*nee* Atkinson) – organiser of the summer schools – to Mrs G. D. H. Cole, 1 July 1955, enclosures and photographs, p. 2, Box 9 of Fabian Society Collection, Nuffield College, Oxford (hereafter 'FSC'). Cf. the appreciation of the Charringtons by Ashley Dukes (himself connected with the Fabians and a participant in their summer schools) in '*A Doll's House* and the Open Door', *Theatre Arts Monthly*, XII (Jan. 1928) pp. 21–38.
12. 'Gray Quill' (pseud.), 'The Liverpool Fabian Society: Some Memories of Strenuous Days and Personalities that are Gone', press clipping (*c.* 1920s) in FSC, Box 8.
13. *Fabian News*, Apr. 1900, p. 8.
14. *Shaw's Letters to Granville Barker*, p. 4.
15. Shaw, *Our Theatres in the Nineties*, III (1932) pp. 180, 182; Shaw to Charrington, 30 Mar. 1891, in *Bernard Shaw: Collected Letters*, vol. I: *1874–1897* (1965) p. 289; Shaw, *The Quintessence of Ibsenism*, 1st edn (1891) p. 139.
16. *To-day*, III (1885) pp. 29f., 65f., 106f.

17. Havelock Ellis (ed.), *The Pillars of Society and Other Plays* (1888).
18. See Isaac Goldberg, *Havelock Ellis* (1926) p. 34; Sheila Rowbotham and Jeffrey Weeks, *Socialism and the New Life: The Personal and Sexual Politics of Edward Carpenter and Havelock Ellis* (1977) p. 147; Vincent Brome, *Havelock Ellis, Philosopher of Sex* (1979) p. 54. Though cf. Phyllis Grosskurth, *Havelock Ellis* (1980) p. 61.
19. Eleanor Marx to Laura Lafargue, 30 Oct. 1888, in International Institute of Social History, Amsterdam (IISH), Marx/Engels Archives, section G, fol. 307. Cf. her letter to Havelock Ellis, *c.* Aug. 1888, cited by Ellis in *Adelphi*, XI, p. 37.
20. *Clarion* (Manchester), 3 Feb. 1894, p. 3 ('Stageland' column by 'Dangle' - pseudonym for Thompson).
21. See my article, 'Bernard Shaw, Ibsen and the Ethics of English Socialism', *Victorian Studies*, XXI (1978) pp. 395-8.
22. Charles Tierney, 'Our Parisian Newsletter', *Labour Leader*, 6 Mar. 1897, p. 78.
23. Report in *Playgoers' Review*, 15 May 1891, p. 178.
24. See, for example, 'Ibsen's New Poems', *Spectator*, 16 Mar. 1872, pp. 344-5; 'A Norwegian Drama [*Peer Gynt*]', ibid., 20 July 1872, pp. 922-3; 'Ibsen, the Norwegian Satirist', *Fortnightly Review*, XIX (Jan. 1873) pp. 74-88.
25. Shaw, *Collected Letters*, vol. I, p. 272.
26. 'How William Archer impressed Bernard Shaw', in Shaw, *Pen Portraits and Reviews* (1932) pp. 19-23.
27. See, for instance, the reviews in *The Times*, *Daily Telegraph*, *Gentlewoman*, *Referee* and the *Hawk*, repr. in Michael Egan (ed.), *Ibsen: The Critical Heritage* (1972) pp. 245-51; *Dramatic Notes*, 11 May 1891, pp. 101-3; William Archer, Introduction to *Collected Works of Henrik Ibsen (1906-21)*, vol. IX, p. xxvi.
28. Shaw to Charles Charrington, 30 Mar. 1891, ibid., p. 288.
29. See *Playgoers' Review*, 16 Mar. 1891, pp. 106-8; *Dramatic Opinions*, 9 Dec. 1891, p. 2, and 11 May 1892, p. 3. Cf. John Stokes, *Resistable Theatres: Enterprise and Experiment in the Late Nineteenth Century* (1972) pp. 12-14.
30. See Edward's review of the two early versions of *A Doll's House* entitled *Nora* and *Breaking a Butterfly*, in *To-day*, I, pp. 473-80, and in *Our Corner*, III (May 1884) p. 306; his notices of other plays in *Dramatic Review*, 4 Apr. 1885, p. 151, and *Dramatic Opinions*, 18

May 1892, pp. 1-2; Edward and Eleanor's *The Woman Question* (1886) pp. 15-16, and their joint reviews in *Dramatic Notes*, 1890, pp. 1335-7, and 1891, pp. 85-9.

31. Engels to Paul Lafargue, 17 May 1889, in Frederick Engels/Paul and Laura Lafargue Correspondence, vol. II (Moscow, 1960) p. 254. Cf. review of Aveling's *The Jackal* in *Dramatic Notes*, 28 Nov. 1889, p. 148.

32. *Playgoers' Review*, 16 Mar. 1891, p. 106.

33. Bernstein, *My Years of Exile* (1921) pp. 162-3.

34. For details, see Chushichi Tsuzuki, *The Life of Eleanor Marx 1855-1898* (Oxford, 1967) chs 12-13; Yvonne Kapp, *Eleanor Marx*, vol. II (1976) pp. 677-721.

35. William Archer, Introduction to *The Prose Dramas of Henrik Ibsen*, vol. IV (1901) p. xxii; 'Ghosts and Gibberings', *Pall Mall Gazette*, 8 Apr. 1891, p. 3.

36. See F. B. Smith, 'Ethics and Disease in the Later Nineteenth Century: The Contagious Diseases Acts', *Historical Studies*, XV (1971), pp. 134-5. For examples (not cited by Smith) of the connections made by contemporaries between *Ghosts* and the Acts, see unsigned article in *Truth*, 5 Mar. 1891, pp. 485-9.

37. Cf. Bernstein, *My Years of Exile*, p. 160, where he recounts a story of Eleanor Marx speaking at the Playgoers' Club and making a potent impression there.

38. Israel Zangwill and Eleanor Marx, *'A Doll's House Repaired'*, *Time*, 16 Mar. 1891, pp. 239-53.

39. In Shaw, *Pen Portraits and Reviews*, pp. 19-23.

40. 'Still after the Doll's House: A Sequel to Mr Besant's Sequel to Henrik Ibsen's Play', *Time*, Feb. 1890, pp. 197-207.

41. 'The Doll's House - and After', *English Illustrated Magazine*, Jan. 1890, pp. 315-23.

42. Shaw to Charles Charrington, 28 Jan. 1890, in Shaw, *Collected Letters*, vol. I, p. 239.

43. Grace Black to Shaw, 8 Mar. 1889, in Shaw Papers, British Library (BL) Add. MS. 50511, fol. 293.

44. In *Time*, 16 Mar. 1891, p. 239.

45. Holbrook Jackson, *The Eighteen Nineties* (1913) p. 254.

46. *Clarion*, 30 Jan. 1897, p. 37; 13 Feb. 1897, p. 50; 27 Feb. 1897, pp. 65-6.

47. See my analysis of the reactions to Shaw's lecture, in *Victorian Studies*, XXI, pp. 393-4.

48. H. M. Hyndman, *Further Reminiscences* (1921) p. 220.

49. Ibid., pp. 204-5.

50. 'Socialism of the Sty', *Justice*, 26 July 1890, p. 2.

51. Joynes to Shaw, 21 Nov. 1891, in Shaw Papers, BL Add MS. 50511, fol. 253.

52. Frank Harris, *My Life and Loves* (1964) p. 382.

53. See Henry Pelling, *Origins of the Labour Party*, 2nd edn (Oxford, 1965) p. 24.

54. Champion to Bernard O'Dowd (undated), O'Dowd Collection in H. A. Pearce Papers, National Library of Australia, MS. 2765, ser. 1, folder 5.

55. I have come across only one notice − reviewing the 1889 production of *The Pillars of Society* − which suggests that early audiences for Ibsen were in any way 'representative' of the average theatre-going public: see *Dramatic Notes*, 17 June 1889, p. 92.

56. J. M. Barrie, 'What the Pit Says − Ibsen at the Novelty', *Time*, XXI (July 1889) pp. 79−80.

57. See his unsigned article in *Truth*, 5 Mar. 1891, pp. 488−9.

58. See Shaw on the reasons for Morris's lack of interest in the modern theatre − 'William Morris as Actor and Dramatist' (1896), repr. in *Pen Portraits and Reviews*, pp. 210−17. Cf. Philip Henderson, *William Morris: His Life, Work and Friends* (Harmondsworth, Middx, 1973) p. 405.

59. 'Notes on News', *Commonweal*, 22 June 1889, p. 193.

60. 'A Play with a Purpose', *Justice*, 22 June 1889, p. 1.

61. Wallas's contribution to this volume contains a favourable reference to Ibsen: *Fabian Essays in Socialism*, 1st edn (1889) p. 147.

62. Entry for 19 Apr. 1892, in Burns Papers, BL Add MS. 46312, fol. 17.

63. Shaw to Elizabeth Robins, 20 Apr. 1891, in Shaw, *Collected Letters*, vol. I, p. 291.

64. Morris to Charles Tierney (undated), cited in Tierney's article in the *Labour Leader*, 6 Mar. 1897, p. 78.

65. Ibid.

66. For a full discussion of Shaw's arguments on this point, see my article in *Victorian Studies*, XXI, pp. 382−5. Cf. 'Discards from the Fabian Lectures on Ibsen and Darwin when publishing them as *The Quintessence of Ibsenism* & the *Methuselah* Preface', Shaw Papers, BL Add. MS. 50661, *passim*.

67. *The Quintessence of Ibsenism*, 2nd edn (1913) p. xv.

68. Shaw Papers, BL Add. MS. 50661, fol. 33. Cf. my article in *Victorian Studies*, XXI, pp. 389−92.

69. See William Archer's report of a conversation he had with Ibsen in 1890 − letter to Shaw, *c*. Aug. 1890, Shaw Papers, BL Add. MS. 50660, fol. ii.

70. See Michael Meyer, *Henrik Ibsen*, Vol. I: *The Making of a Dramatist 1828-1864* (1967) pp. 55−7.

71. Ibsen to Laura Kieler, cited in Meyer, *Henrik Ibsen*, vol. III: *The Top of a Cold Mountain* (1971) p. 152.

72. For a succinct analysis of the social composition of the Fabian Society, see E. J. Hobsbawm, 'The Fabians Reconsidered', in his *Labouring Men* (1968) pp. 255-9, 268-9.
73. See Meyer, *Henrik Ibsen*, vol. I, pp. 28-9; Shaw, *Sixteen Self Sketches* (1949) pp. 11-12, 45.
74. 'What About the Middle Class . . .?', pt. II, *Daily Citizen* (Manchester) 19 Oct. 1912, p. 4.
75. Robert Skidelsky, 'The Fabian Ethic', in Michael Holroyd (ed.), *The Genius of Shaw* (1979) p. 117.
76. *The Woman Question*, p. 6.
77. Ibid., pp. 15-16. Cf. Havelock Ellis's review of Bebel's writings, and his similar use of *A Doll's House* as a text for elucidating 'the question of the independence of women' : 'Women and Socialism', *To-day*, I (1884), esp. pp. 362-3.
78. Printed in James W. McFarlane (ed.), *Ibsen: A Critical Anthology* (Harmondsworth, Middx, 1970) p. 104.
79. *Essays by Mrs Havelock Ellis* (Berkeley, NJ, 1924) p. 41, cited in Vineta Colby, *The Singular Anomaly* (1970) p. 242 (emphasis added). Cf. Swanhilde Bulan, '*A Doll's House* Revisited', *Votes for Women*, 17 Feb. 1911, p. 8.
80. See Gail Cunningham, *The New Woman and the Victorian Novel* (1978); Patricia Stubbs, *Women and Fiction: Feminism and the Novel 1880-1920* (Brighton, 1979).
81. For one example of this impact, recollected many years later, see Frances Stevenson, *Lloyd George: A Diary*, ed. A. J. P. Taylor (1971) p. 43.
    I am grateful to Dr Brian Harrison, who has made a detailed study of the debates over feminist issues in his book *Separate Spheres* (1978), for confirmation on this point of Ibsen's general influence in the period 1880-1914.
82. Harrison, *Separate Spheres*, p. 41. Cf. Lily Bell, 'A Socialist View of the Woman's Movement', *Labour Leader*, 6 Feb. 1897, p. 43.
83. Shaw Papers, BL Add. MS. 50661, fols 10-11, 27-8.
84. See Beatrice Webb's Diary, 18 Jan. 1897, typescript version, in Passfield Papers, London School of Economic and Political Sciences.
85. Shaw to Sidney Webb, 26 July 1901, in Shaw, *Collected Letters*, vol. II, pp. 366-7.
86. Beatrice Webb, *My Apprenticeship* (Harmondsworth, Middx, 1971) pp. 353-4; cf. Harrison, *Separate Spheres*, pp. 83, 92.
87. See Sidney Webb to Lujo Brentano, 29 Jan. 1911, in Norman MacKenzie (ed.), *The Letters of Sidney and Beatrice Webb* (Cambridge, 1978) vol. II, pp. 366-7.

88. For Brooke's connection with the Cambridge Fabian Society as a committee member and president, see the branch's reports and lists of meetings (1909-13) in his papers at King's College Library, Cambridge. Cf. Geoffrey Keynes (ed.), *The Letters of Rupert Brooke* (1968) pp. 70, 79-80, 114, 124, 126, 154; Christopher Hassall, *Rupert Brooke: A Biography* (1972) pp. 117-120, 136-7, 145-51, 156-7, 176-7, 193-5, 204, 224, 242-6.
   For Brooke's early interest in Ibsen, see Brooke to St John Lucas, 13 Feb. 1908; to Katherine Cox, 22 Jan. 1911; and to Frances Cornford, 10-15 Feb. 1911 – Brooke's *Letters*, pp. 122, 275, 280-1. Cf. his notice of *Love's Comedy* in *Cambridge Review*, 28 Oct. 1909, p. 50.
89. Cf. Leonard Woolf's memoirs of Ibsen's impact on his colleagues at Cambridge in *Sowing: An Autobiography of the Years 1880-1904* (1960) pp. 163-4.
90. Brooke to Frances Cornford, 10-15 Feb. 1911, *Letters*, pp. 280-1.
91. Cited in Hassall, *Brooke*, pp. 377-9.
92. See Blatchford's defence of the 'true' or womanly woman in his articles in the *Clarion* referred to in n. 46.
93. Printed in Arne Kildal (ed.), *Speeches and New Letters by Henrik Ibsen* (1911) p. 65.
94. See, for example, most of the essays in Rodell Weintraub (ed.), *Fabian Feminist: Bernard Shaw and Women* (University Park, Penn., 1977).
95. In *The Quintessence of Ibsenism*, 2nd edn., pp. 127-39.
96. 'Shaw Reveals "Who Was Candida"', *Evening Standard*, 28 Nov. 1944, p. 6. Cf. 'Author's Note' in the programme of a production of *Candida* staged in Feb. 1937, repr. in Dan H. Lawrence (ed.), *The Bodley Head Bernard Shaw: Complete Plays with their Prefaces*, vol. I (1970) p. 601.
97. See Louie Bennett, 'Ibsen as a Pioneer of the Woman Movement', *Westminster Review*, CLXXIII (Mar. 1910) pp. 278-85.
98. For the most recent examples of this sort of criticism, see McFarlane, *Ibsen: A Critical Anthology*, p. 65; Maurice Valency, *The Flower and the Castle* (1964) p. 386; George Archibald Henderson, *Shaw: Man of the Century* (1956) p. 406. For a very rare dissenting view to this orthodoxy, see Eric West, 'Shaw's Criticism of Ibsen', *University of Colorado Studies*, IV (1953) pp. 106-27. Cf. also J. L. Wisenthal's introductory essay in his recent collation *Shaw and Ibsen* (Toronto, 1979).
99. See Hassall, *Brooke*, p. 377.
100. Ellis, in *To-day*, I, pp. 362-3; Dearmer, review of *A*

Doll's House in *Church Reformer*, XI (June 1892) pp. 141-2.

101. The first reference to Ibsen in Shaw's writings which I have found is in a letter to William Archer, 16 Mar. 1885, in Shaw, *Collected Letters*, vol. I, pp. 126-7. Before writing the lecture which became *The Quintessence of Ibsenism*, Shaw had already set down some of his thoughts on Ibsen in an unfinished article, 'From Dickens to Ibsen' (Shaw Papers, BL Add. MS. 50693, fols. 201ff), and in an unsigned review of the London première of *A Doll's House* in the *Manchester Guardian*, 8 June 1889, p. 8.

102. *The Quintessence of Ibsenism*, 1st edn, pp. 46, 56, 72, 122, 124, 159.

103. Ibid., p. 160. Cf. pp. 74-5, and the section 'The Technical Novelty of Ibsen's Plays' in the second edition, pp. 173-204.

104. *The Quintessence of Ibsenism*, 1st edn, p. 137.

105. Shaw Papers, BL Add. MS. 50661, fol. 22.

106. Published mainly in the *Saturday Review*, and collected in *Our Theatres in the Nineties*.

107. S. Webb to B. Potter, 14 Mar. 1891, in *Letters of Sidney and Beatrice Webb*, vol. I, p. 265.

108. Ibid.

109. Letters of 13 Sep. 1891 and 21 May 1892, ibid., vol. I, pp. 295, 413. Cf. S. Webb to Shaw, 29. Oct. 1911, ibid., vol. II, p. 376.

110. The play is not even mentioned in Louie Bennett's 'Ibsen as a Pioneer of the Woman Movement', *Westminster Review*, CLXXIII, pp. 278-85.

111. See Tsuzuki, *Life of Eleanor Marx*, p. 165.

112. Eleanor Marx to Shaw, 2 June 1885, in Shaw Papers, BL Add. MS. 50511, fol. 88v.

113. *Angels' Wings* (1898) p. 80.

114. See Rowbotham and Weeks, *Socialism and the New Life*, pp. 75-91.

115. 'Mr George Bernard Shaw', *Echo*, 9 Dec. 1890, p. 1.

116. 'Open Letter' to the editor of *Liberty*, Benjamin Tucker, published 27 July 1895, and repr. as *The Sanity of Art* (1908). See esp. p. 39.

117. Ibsen to Georg Brandes, 17 Feb. 1871, in McFarlane, *Ibsen: A Critical Anthology*, p. 79.

118. Ibsen to Brandes, 20 Dec. 1870, in Mary Morison (ed.), *The Correspondence of Henrik Ibsen* (1905) p. 205.

119. *The Quintessence of Ibsenism*, 1st edn, pp. 95-6.

120. Printed in McFarlane, *Ibsen: A Critical Anthology*, p. 104.

121. See James W. Hulse, *Revolutionists in London* (Oxford,

1970) pp. 78, 89-105, 109-10, 114-15, 118-22; Willard Wolfe, *From Radicalism to Socialism: Men and Ideas in the Formation of Fabian Socialist Doctrines, 1881-1889* (New Haven, Conn., 1975) pp. 131-44.

122. Manifesto of the Socialist League, printed in the *Commonweal*, Feb. 1885, pp. 1-2.

123. Shaw, 'The Fabian Society: What It Has Done & How It Has Done It', *Fabian Tract no. 41* (1892) p. 3. Cf. A. M. McBriar, *Fabian Socialism and English Politics* (Cambridge, 1962) pp. 9, 20-2.

124. See my Oxford D.Phil. thesis, 'Fabian Socialism and the Arts' (1978) pt III.

125. See Hobsbawm, 'The Fabians Reconsidered', in his *Labouring Men, passim*.

126. Preface to *The Pillars of Society and Other Plays*, pp. xxvi-xxvii.

127. *The Quintessence of Ibsenism*, 1st edn, p. 94.

128. *Fabian Essays in Socialism*, p. 105.

129. See Meyer, *Henrik Ibsen*, vol. II: *The Farewell to Poetry 1864-1882* (1971) pp. 181, 261.

130. Ibid., p. 68.

131. Ibsen to Andreas Isachsen, 1873, trs. and quoted in J. W. McFarlane and Graham Orton (eds), *'The League of Youth' and 'Emperor and Galilean'* (Oxford, 1963) p. 605.

132. See, for instance, Francis Adams, Preface to his *Songs of the Army of the Night* (1890) pp. 12-13; E. B. Bax to Shaw, 21 Aug. 1884, in Shaw Papers, BL Add. MS. 50510, fols 253-4; John Burns's diary, entry for 2 Jan. 1892 (comment on H. H. Champion), in Burns Papers, BL Add. MS. 46312, fol. 2; J. Bruce Glasier, 'Matthew Arnold, and "A Man's A Man For A'That" ', *Commonweal*, 29 Dec. 1888, p. 411, and *William Morris and the Early Days of the Socialist Movement* (1921) p. 29; Hyndman, *Further Reminiscences*, p. 211, and *The Record of an Adventurous Life* (1911) *passim*; F. W. Kitz to Shaw, 1888, in Shaw Papers, BL Add. MS. 50512, fols 74-7; Peter Kropotkin to Mrs Dryhurst, BL Add MS. 46362D, fol. 24; Tom Mann, *Memoirs* (1923) pp. 40-1, 57-8; Revd C. Marson, 'A Word for Fabians', *Church Reformer*, XII (Nov. 1893) p. 286; May Morris to Shaw, 19 Nov. 1885, and 22 Aug. 1888, in Shaw Papers, BL Add. MS. 50541, fols 49, 91; William Morris to Joseph Lane, 21 May 1889, in Burns Papers, BL Add. MS. 46345, fol. 103; Morris to Andreas Scheu, 16 and 18 July 1884, in IISH Scheu Papers, Box 1, folder 2; Elizabeth Robins Pennell, *The Life and Letters of Joseph Pennell*, vol. I (New York, 1929) pp. 158-9; Scheu to Shaw, 29 Dec. 1885, in Shaw Papers, BL Add.

MS. 50511, fol.154; Shaw to Hyndman, Apr. 1900, in Shaw Papers, BL Add. MS. 50538, fols 125-6; Shaw to Scheu, 26 Oct. 1884 and 7 July 1891, in IISH Scheu Papers, Box 1, folder 3; Beatrice Webb, *My Apprenticeship*, pp. 193, 321-2, 354, 404; Sidney Webb, 'The Way Out', lecture in Passfield Papers, VI.19, fols 10, 56-8.
133. Jackson, *The Eighteen Nineties*, pp. 244-5.

3 A Question of Method: Ibsen's Reception in Germany

DAVID E. R. GEORGE

I

'You know my methods in such cases, Watson.' Would that we literary sleuths could say the same: the focal issue of this conference and of all such enquiries into international reception remains that of methodology. The comforting confirmation of our expectations achieved by most studies in this field (the Expressionists loved Strindberg, Noh drama first appealed to the Symbolists, Chekhov was rediscovered after the Theatre of the Absurd) should not blind us to the fact that, even if the evidence is detailed, and the convictions assured, the methodology is not much advanced on I. A. Richards's famous judgement of literary theory as a whole: 'a few conjectures, a supply of admonitions, many acute isolated observations, some brilliant guesses, much oratory and applied poetics, inexhaustible confusion, a sufficiency of dogma, no small stock of prejudices'.[1]

On what evidence do we base the historical reconstruction of an author's reception? Precisely how does any critic 'represent' his times? How many footnotes are necessary to make a reliable statement about a decade of audiences - several thousand people? What makes a performance 'exemplary'?

And if we resolved such questions of evidence to our critical satisfaction: what could be the underlying cause of the judgements? The opinion-making role of critics? The inner logic of literary evolution? Socio-economic structures? Ideological blinkers?

In 1968, I published a book in German entitled *Ibsen in Deutschland - Rezeption und Revision*. The necessity of a further revision becomes clear when one surveys the work which has been done in the last fifteen years, a period in which reception theory has emerged as a challenge to virtually all branches of literary theory. One has only to think of the work of Gadamer, Riffaterre, Fish, Mandelkow, and, above all, the Konstanz School (Jauss, Warning, Iser), where a synthesis of formalist, phenomenological and Marxist attitudes has been attempted. The code is far from broken, but at least the basic question has been exposed: to what degree and in what ways can a work of literature be said to predict or predetermine its reception? Heidegger tells us that 'the proper way to preserve the work is cocreated and prescribed only and exclusively by the work'.[2] Barthes, at the opposite end of the spectrum, proclaims an infinite variability of appropriations.[3] The claim of the phenomenologist that the personal, private, relative meanings which readers will admittedly and inevitably add to the 'objective meaning' supplied by the text are not the proper subject of literary analysis is simply reversed by the Marxist, who argues that they are all that is significant in literature – provided that they can be explained not as private and personal readings but as reflections of ideologies, a claim acceptable to the psychoanalytical critic, provided such systems are in turn reduced to deep structures of consciousness. Whatever the variations, there is common agreement: that reception is not just a passive act of appropriation and that the history of literature cannot be approached simply as a sequence of works pregnant with inalienable meanings. But the emerging agreement that reception is the area to be investigated is not matched by any agreement about what are the relevant factors, let alone their priority. Some have sought to reconstruct literary horizons and norms, others have probed the coding of the texts, many have sought for extra-literary referents, predominantly in some concept of ideology, but there is not even agreement about the key terms 'norm', 'code', 'ideology'.

Perhaps the most comprehensive theory remains that of Jauss in *Literaturgeschichte als Provokation der Literaturwissenschaft*.[4] Jauss proposes that the entire history of literature needs to be rewritten as a series not of works but of dialogues between works and readers in which each new reception is influenced by all previous effects. But he too seeks for an 'objektivierbaren Bezugssystem der Erwartungen'[5] – a phrase which the English translation offers as 'definable frame of reference',[6] thus skirting the issue not only of Jauss's contribution but of them all: the very notion of some 'objectifiable reference system' to stem the opened floodgates of infinite, subjective relativity. In the course of his argument, Jauss proposes, but then is forced to abandon, first, recourse to the texts' innate

and unalterable guidance systems; then the average reader;
until he finally offers a heuristic model in which new works
break existing norms, only themselves to become automatised
and canonised – an idea owing much more to Russian Formalism
than to Marxism, the detente with which appears to be over
even before it began. A similar marriage, on the same shared
concern with reception, has been proposed by Frederic
Jameson in *Marxism and Form* (Princeton, NJ, 1971), where he
suggests that both phenomenology and Marxism could agree on
the common need to incorporate the act of cognition into any
description of cognition: a common return to Hegel, in other
words. Whatever the outcome of these and similar, hesitant
invitations to get together, this method of split-level
reading, of self-conscious criticism, of simultaneous
reception and search for the catalysts of that reception
appears to describe the most obviously agreeable basis upon
which to build. The theoretical edifice is far from stable,
but, as Warning writes, 'He who is willing to return to the
texts only when the theory is complete will hardly find any
readers left for these texts.'[7]

Meanwhile it seems clear that the answer for any particular work or author or period will obviously vary according
to the degree of the author's craft, the visibility of the
implied reader, the literary sensitivity of the particular
reader, the homogeneity of the society in which the book is
appropriated, the paradigmatic richness of the text, the
unanticipated connotations supplied by history, and so on.
But, whilst the aesthetic autonomy of literature at the
production end can be quite convincingly argued (for how
else can one account for the varied ways in which writers
have responded to the same dominant ideology?), the influence of extra-textual factors at the reception end appears
to be necessary to account for the changes in *normative*
interpretations from age to age. For these are not just the
acts of single, idiosyncratic critics, but widespread norms
of expectations with which one audience recognises certain
things (and overlooks others) which an earlier audience did
not even see.

Ibsen is the case in point in this paper; Stockmann is an
example: did Ibsen intend to show the fine line which separ-
ates anarchism from Fascism? Ignoring the siren calls of
the intentional fallacy and focusing only on the intention
realised in the text, it remains clear that a post-1945
audience could not but see Stockmann's advocacy of euthan-
asia, genetic engineering and state breeding-farms in quite
a different light from the audience at that performance
which Stanislavsky describes in *My Life as Art*: a performance of *An Enemy of the People* which coincided with the

massacre in Kazansky Square and which, in spite of the
censor's savage excisions and his presence in the auditorium, ended at the line 'One must never put on a new coat
when one goes out to fight for freedom and truth.' Pande-
monium resulted, and the performance had to be stopped.

Chekhov has been mentioned at this conference: the question has been asked whether his plays should be politicised.
But the historical fact that the Russian Revolution broke
out less than two decades after he wrote means that we who
read and see him now must read and see a minutely detailed
portrait not of late-nineteenth-century Russia but of a pre-
revolutionary society and, in consequence, hear that sound
of chopping wood with less ambivalent feelings, and refer
all that talk about a future society of selfless labour to
Marx and Engels rather than to the Tolstoy whom a
contemporary audience would have had in mind.

One is tempted to ask further: what happened to those
audiences? Did they go off and sharpen axes, or join one
party, or another? We do not even have the biographical or
statistical evidence. In spite of the fact that functional,
teleological definitions of drama form the predominant
theme of its 2000-year-old Western tradition, that passage
from ideas to convictions, from convictions to attitudes,
and then on through motives to acts cannot be our concern,
for we have no adequate psychological or literary theory to
apply to that extension. But we can and must ask about the
original passage of ideas from work to recipient or, deeper,
the transplanting of structures of perception: what causes
this to operate differently in different ages? It cannot be
only or all the craft of the writer, if for no other reason
than his inability to foretell which future events will
conjure up which unintended connotations in later readers.
Whatever his craft, the unanticipated but inevitable
additions and subtractions to the meanings of his words –
for these are only ever conventions – must escape his later
control. As Eco writes,

> Sometimes the addressee's entire system of cultural units
> legitimate an interpretation that the sender would have
> never foreseen. . . . Because of such unpredictable decod-
> ing, the text may be consumed at only one of its content
> levels, while the other (equally legitimate) levels remain
> in the background.[8]

One need not exaggerate: the variations will remain fin-
ite. *Peer Gynt* could never be a play about female incon-
stancy or the world's reliability, but it can be, and was,
regarded at different times as a play about bourgeois hypoc-

risy, male infidelity, lyrical irresponsibility, Silesian mysticism and even anti-semitism. One cannot argue the arbitrary infinity of equally valid interpretations, but one must recognise the variability of normative receptions – and seek to account for them.

In the book which I published in 1968, I adopted what I should now call an eclectic approach – with controls: a pluralistic correlation of critics, combined with an examination of creative writing, popular literature, classical canons, theatre productions, political, economic and social structures, philosophical issues, translations, national images. What was sought were the coherent factors, not aberrant idiosyncrasies.

W. H. Eller's *Ibsen in Germany 1870-1900* (Boston, Mass., 1918) had already assembled most of the critical judgements made about Ibsen between 1870 and 1900, but had not explained how these judgements acquired opinion-making significance. It is clearly not enough to do as Vodicka does, namely argue that critics have a 'duty' to reflect the literary norms of their age and hence do reflect them.[9] Successful critics undoubtedly do reflect in part the ideologies and tastes of their times – otherwise people would stop reading them – but it is difficult to identify precisely where they reflect their readers and where they argue only their own case. Temporarily and pragmatically, the solution adopted was to introduce a 'reputation factor', namely the prestige of the critic as indicated by the breadth of his readership and the degree to which later writers quoted him as an authority.

The second most obvious – but in literary analyses often overlooked – factor is that of productions. Here it seemed essential to establish first which plays were most popular during which years. For, as Van Tieghem had already noted fifty years ago, when an author crosses a national frontier, he very seldom brings his whole opus with him; more often only a particular work or a particular aspect provides inspiration.[10] To this statistical evidence there had then to be added the role of intermediaries, especially translators and, for drama, styles of direction and acting.

This emerging picture had then to be related to further possible factors which would have influenced the reception: above all, the state and direction of contemporary literature in the receiving country, both original literary production and contemporary literary criticism and theory – manifestos, salons, periodicals and so on. It was necessary to analyse further the literary canon of the age: to know which authors were held in high esteem, or were, apparently, fulfilling some need of the age, which other foreign authors

were being imported at the same time, and which philosophical issues dominated intellectual discourse. For it seemed
reasonable to suppose that placing the author in question
against the panoramic backdrop of the literary and intellectual activity of the age would suggest which aspects of his
work would appear most insistently.

Finally (though there was no hierarchy in these factors),
it seemed necessary to consider which political, economic
and social factors predominant at the time might have forced
a reader or spectator to make connotative connections which
might later be obscure.

II

The results achieved by applying this model were not startling. Brandes emerged as the first 'influential' critic,
the chief mediator: he had corresponded with Ibsen since
1866, knew both the man and the earlier work as yet untrans-
lated into German, and was, at the same time, highly respected in German literary circles, writing for many of the
leading periodicals. And what Brandes clearly did was to
present both Ibsen's personality and his early work as the
bases of his later 'social realism'. Ibsen's personality
is presented as aggressive and polemical, an enemy of all
groupings, be they state, family or marriage. Brandes's
Ibsen combines pessimism as regards the present with optimism for the future: he has his finger on the pulse of
modern life, specifically being concerned with the conflict of generations and 'class prejudices, especially the
difference between rich and poor, social influence and
social dependence'.[11] These elements are those which
Brandes locates even in the early work, thus effectively
cutting off interest in them as mere precursors of the more
developed social realism of the later plays from *Pillars
of Society* onwards.

Brandes had already called Ibsen *grundgermanisch*, and
this was taken up by the second representative critic, Leo
Berg, who belonged to the influential *Die Gesellschaft*
circle, for which he published articles and translations
of Zola's works; he was the founder of Durch and wrote one
of the earliest studies of Naturalism. His first essay on
Ibsen appeared in Berlin in 1887: *Henrik Ibsen und das
Germanenthum in der modernen Literatur*. The title heralds
the content: 'Now it is true that Ibsen is not a German
but he is Germanic: flesh of our flesh, blood of our blood'
(p. 4). His specifically 'Germanic' qualities consist in his

social criticism: 'German is his great and single-minded
love of truth and the courage to confess to it . . .
when the doll Nora says at the end, "I must find out who
is in the right: society or me", that only a German can
understand' (p. 5).

The same approach was then pursued in Berg's *Hebbel und
Ibsen - eine Parallele* (1889). Ibsen means for Germany
'a moment of self-reflection': the affinity between Ibsen
and German drama is seen as their common concern with using
literature as a means of social criticism - an interpretation which involves Berg in a wholesale, retrospective re-
interpretation of German nineteenth-century literature
itself.

In Brandes's and Berg's books, the overall emphasis on
Ibsen as a polemicist had involved consequential claims
about the typicality of his characters: Nora is a spokes-
woman for the emancipation of women, Stockmann a spokesman
for a new morality. With Otto Brahm, the alternative
approach to Ibsen's realism emerges: the emphasis upon his
acute psychological observation and detailed motivation.
Brahm was probably the most influential of them all in the
1880s and 1890s: a recognised literary scholar and publicist
who wrote for most of the more influential periodicals: his
essay on Ibsen, also of 1887, was copied by most later
writers.

Brahm recounts his first encounter with Ibsen, when he
had attended the 1878 production of *Pillars of Society*:

At once we received the first presentiment of a new poetic
world, felt ourselves, for the first time, face to face
with people of our own times, in whom we could believe.
And out of a comprehensive critique of contemporary
society we saw the ideals of freedom and of truth as the
pillars of society, triumphantly ascending. From that
moment on we belonged to this new art of reality, and our
aesthetic life had received its content.[12]

Brahm too saw Ibsen as 'Germanic'; he too focused on his
social criticism; he too finds parallels with Zola.[13] He
met Brandes in 1879 and then interviewed Ibsen in Rome in
1885; from the former he learned that the whole of modern
Scandinavian literature was dedicated to tendentious literature, but what he in fact emphasised in his own account was
less the representative nature of Ibsen's characters than
their depth psychology, an interpretation of particular
importance for *A Doll's House*:

Ibsen has not developed his Nora as a typical figure, into

whom he breathes his own feelings and nothing more . . .
he has given her quite unique, individual traits which
resist generalisation. Whoever would make the author
responsible for every word that Nora says would do him a
gross injustice.[14]

It was Brahm who then transferred this to the stage. Brahm
was the founder of the Freie Bühne, an institution which
some were to condemn later for distorting Ibsen,[15] but
which Brahm himself claimed was simply the necessary continuation of Ibsen's provocation.[16] The original founders,
Harden and Wolff, had resigned in opposition to Brahm's
demand for sole control over the choice of plays and the
style of productions: a style soon tagged the *Brahm-stil*,
one involving the total re-education of his company in the
techniques of psychological realism. It was the inability of
German actors and actresses to act realistically which he
had identified as the cause of the initial failure of *The
Lady from the Sea* and *Hedda Gabler*: his desire to present a
'psychologically realistic' as opposed to a 'polemical-
typical' Nora was hampered by the same inadequacy. In 1892
he had seen Barnay's production with Agnes Sorma in the lead
and criticised her for failing to bring out the subtle nuances in Nora's development and growth. Two years later, in
1894, he employed the same actress himself; Ibsen attended
the performance and is reported to have declared her the
best Nora.[17] In many ways, Brahm foreshadowed Stanislavsky's technique of total identification: he found his
best pupil in Kainz, but, though Brahm himself recognised
Mrs Alving as the central character in *Ghosts* and himself
directed the production, Kainz's virtuoso 'method-acting'
stole the show and thus distorted the whole theme.[18]

Finally, there was Paul Schlenther, co-director of the
Freie Bühne and editor of the first − and still the sole
authorised − translation of Ibsen's collected works into
German, for which he wrote the introductions to volumes I
and V-IX − introductions which (like those of Brahm) consistently stress psychological realism over representative
typicality.

All these representative and influential critics focused
attention on certain plays rather than others. Ibsen's
poems were − surprisingly enough − the first of his works to
be translated into German (1868). *Brand* followed in 1869
(published 1872); the first performance was of *The Vikings
of Helgoland* (1876). But he really broke into the German
theatre only in 1878, when *Pillars of Society* was performed
on five different Berlin stages within two weeks. *A Doll's
House* followed − translated in 1879, performed a year later

in Munich, Berlin, Hamburg, Dresden, Hannover. *Ghosts* was held up for five years (aside from two private performances in 1886 and 1887), but when it did appear on the stage, in 1889, the scandal assured Ibsen's arrival; and cemented the 'social realist' interpretation.

Clearly, reasons for this reception had to be found in the literary and intellectual climate of the 1870s and 1880s: the evidence was not hard to come by. During this same period, the Harts published their *Kritische Waffengänge* (1882), M. G. Conrad founded *Die Gesellschaft* (1885), Bleibtreu published his *Revolution der Literatur* (1886) and Bölsche *Die naturwissenschaftlichen Grundlagen der Poesie* (1887). In the same year as *Ghosts*, Hauptmann broke through with *Vor Sonnenaufgang* and Sudermann with *Die Ehre*. Zola, Tolstoy and Dostoevsky were imported, in distorted images; Hebbel and Ludwig were rediscovered.[19]

Darwin was in the air, with a new concept of fate and a new insight into biology; Taine, with a new concept of determinism through environment; Comte, with a new emphasis on observed detail. Politically, the socialists were on the move: from 124,000 members in 1871 to 350,000 members in 1874 and six seats in the Reichstag. They were banned in 1878; when the ban was lifted in 1893, they had 1,768,000 members and forty-four seats in the Reichstag. This is not surprising. Germany had been finally united in 1871, a date which, in retrospect, forms a watershed: traditional values and norms were soon to be radically questioned. A parliament had been convened: a decade of economic revolution followed, bringing with it urbanisation (between 1830 and 1882 the German population shifted from being only one-fifth urban to becoming three-fifths urban), a revolution in the position of women (in 1895, 1½ million of the 6½ million German workers were women) and profound changes in the very structure of German society. And here one must pause: one can see readily enough how Ibsen provided a dramatic reflection of some of these issues - notably the conflict of generations, the corruption of bourgeois values, feminism (one must recall that German women had no right of political assembly and could be - and were - banned from the theatre). But where are the slums, where are the strikes, the lock-outs? Ibsen 'failed' to offer any detailed treatment of the issues of urbanisation and industrialisation. No one at the time very much blamed him for that, and no one now does, for he had perhaps little experience of these issues; moreover, they did not interest him. Nevertheless, he interested the German theatre-going public. *Pillars of Society* was, apparently, made to fill this gap: Kummer reports that 'It was acted as a class-war play',[20] and Landsberg makes the exaggerated claim that 'the relationship between entrepreneurs and workers is unrolled with socialist colouring in its whole breadth'.[21] But this accounts for only one portion of one play: what is interesting here is not that Ibsen did not dramatise such issues but that the neglect of these issues in his plays does not appear to have hurt his popularity at the time. It is significant here that the socialists of the 1920s would dismiss Ibsen for neglecting such issues, and in no uncertain terms.[22] The answer for the 1880s and 1890s is tentative and speculative. Part of his success even at this first, heady stage may well lie in his offering no radical challenge to the economic base but only a contribution to the fashionable self-questioning of middle-class intellectuals, happily (or not) embracing the negative criticism of bourgeois life but spared the socialist alternative. Ibsen may have provided, in other words, the opportunity to indulge in self-criticism without the challenge to man the barricades – even then going up in Paris![23]

It was in Paris that the first version of the 'naturalist' Ibsen then took place. Lugné-Poe is the seminal figure here. He had put on *Pillars of Society* and *Enemy of the People* for the circle of anarchists with which he was associated, but it was not these plays nor any overt political reference which brought Ibsen his fame in France, but rather Lugné-Poe's direction of *The Lady from the Sea* in 1892: a play which, Lugné-Poe claimed, Ibsen wanted to be his first French production, but which in fact was Lugné-Poe's own choice.[24] The play was performed in a half-light, the decor was allusive, suggestive, ambiguous, the language intoned as in a psalm. Ellida was acted by Georgette Camée, the interpreter of Maeterlinck: Maurice Denis's lithograph shows her as a phantom in long white veils. This 'Maeterlinck connection' had been found by the Belgian dramatist himself[25] and appeared to be confirmed by Ibsen's own later plays, also produced by Lugné-Poe. Their success seems to prove that his choice met the wishes of his audience: whereas *John Gabriel Borkman* was performed 116 times in fifteen months, *A Doll's House* was performed only once – in Mme Auberon's salon. It was not for want of trying: Antoine had preceded Lugné-Poe with a production of *Ghosts* at the Théâtre-Libre in 1890; Tissot, Sarolea, Ossip-Lourié and others had presented Ibsen as a social realist, but this interpretation, which had ensured Ibsen's success in Germany, aroused little interest in France. Antoine's second production was already 'enveloped in symbolism which is like the reflection of the pale Norwegian sun'.[26]

Part of the reason for this probably lies in Paris's

satisfaction with its own, national brand of 'social realism': the plays of Dumas *fils*, Augier and Sardou, whose combination of 'naturalistic' scandal elements with the traditions of the well-made play offered the French audience the sort of watered-down version of Naturalism which they could readily accept. Part of the reason must also lie in 'cultural images' or 'mirages'; to the French, Norway was not a nation of Aryan cousins, but a land of heavy mists, mystical and mysterious.[27] But neither of these factors can explain how this new Ibsen then swept across the Rhine. For that one must seek explanation, once again, in the parallels between his work and the new literary climate: the reaction against Naturalism and the evolution of a literature of myth, allegory, mysticism and symbolism, one which could and would find in the later plays a neo-Romantic symbolist to supplant the earlier social realist.

Leo Berg exemplifies this shift. His essay of 1901, *Henrik Ibsen*, offers a re-evaluation of Ibsen from the perspective of the later plays. Instead of Hebbel, the new connections are with Maeterlinck and Nietzsche; instead of *A Doll's House*, the key-work is now *The Master Builder*, both in its form and in its content. Berg calls it 'the conscience-drama of modern man', handling the problem of the Nietzschean Superman (p. 29). Instead of being 'Germanic', Ibsen is now *nordisch*: 'the specifically Nordic element in Ibsen is . . . his form of mysticism' (p. 34).

If Berg documents the course, Hermann Bahr was the pilot. He was responsible for introducing French Symbolism into Austria, and then into Germany, had declared the demise of Naturalism as early as 1891 and could point back to his 1887 essay on Ibsen as already heralding the hidden mystic soon to emerge. True, in that first essay, Bahr had also paid his respects to Brandes, had called Ibsen the most modern European, enemy of tradition and convention in literature and art, but he had singled out *Brand* and *Peer Gynt* as the crucial works, 'the true seat of his gifts'.[28] They are more romantic than realistic, and Bahr's theory, as early as 1887, was that this synthesis of Naturalism and Romanticism is the true task of modern literature. The later plays he sees as adding the patina of realism, but they remain for Bahr essentially dramatisations of ideas, an interpretation which enabled him to present Nora, Bernick and Stockmann as ideological constructs rather than as realistic people.

Bahr was a man of the theatre more than a literary critic, and doubtless one reason for this interpretation was the inadequate state of 'naturalistic' acting methods at the time. Rather, however, than seeing the resolution, like Otto Brahm, in the improvement of realistic acting techniques to

bring out Ibsen's realism, Bahr saw this as revealing that
the true Ibsen never was a realist, a claim confirmed by the
later plays. In the volumes of his theatre criticism, Bahr
went on consistently to single out *Peer Gynt* for special
emphasis and to condemn the new naturalistic acting as
unsuitable, for – as Stanislavsky was also to discover – it
did not 'work' with Ibsen's later plays, any more than for
Maeterlinck or Hofmannsthal. For Bahr, Reinhardt, not Brahm,
is the true director, and Duse the ideal actress:

> Duse's Hedda Gabler, which we saw last year, first enabled
> us to sense the other Ibsen which the traditional present-
> ation of Berlin Naturalism hides. They do not notice that
> his people, however everyday their behaviour may be,
> always have something almost mystical about them, some-
> thing fabulous, imaginatively monstrous, as from a
> fantasy-world of giants.[29]

The revision was confirmed by Alfred Kerr, possibly the
main arbiter of theatrical taste in the two decades around
1900. Kerr belonged to no particular group, but if anything
appealed to him as a literary and theatrical ideal it was
the synthesis of Naturalism and Symbolism – and that is what
he found in Ibsen. In *Das neue Drama* (Berlin, 1912) he
compared Ibsen with Hebbel but a Hebbel now also re-
interpreted as combining psychological realism with 'the
mystical flight into the infinite' (p. 13). The most telling
comparison is, however, again, with Maeterlinck (p. 16). One
should also mention Max Nordau's *Entartung* (Berlin, 1892),
in which Ibsen is seen as documenting the decadent mysticism
of the *fin de siècle*. If one then assembles all the essays
of the period 1890-1910, one discovers that four key terms
now emerge as predominant: not 'modern', 'realistic' and
'Germanic', but 'mystical', 'symbolist', 'romantic' and
'Nietzschean'.

They affected the productions too. Duse brought a new
Ibsen to the German stage, beginning in Vienna in 1892,
where she opened to half-empty houses but closed, nine days
later, to a converted public. Her Nora is described as
'passionate, sickly, neurasthenic, self-involved',[30] a
version which won over both Reinhardt and Hofmannsthal and
foreshadowed her more famous Hedda Gabler.[31] Duse then
took this new Ibsen on a triumphant tour of Germany in 1906-
7. From the statistics it emerges that the most popular play
in the German repertoire in 1904 and 1905 was *The Lady from
the Sea*. Reinhardt supplanted Brahm as the new director,
devising a style which emphasised the symbolism, and employ-
ing Edvard Munch as stage-painter. The interpretation was

carried on by Carl Heine's touring Ibsen theatre, whose placard says it all:

On the left top the head of Ibsen peers out of a black background. . . . On the right, the thunderous sea; snakes, a Norwegian symbol, encircle the sea and the figure of a woman who gazes with yearning out of her earth-bound misery into that invisible ideal realm which is to bring mankind salvation.[32]

Of course, this whole revision could be accounted for by Ibsen's own artistic evolution; except that, in addition to the later plays, it was *Peer Gynt* which now emerged as Ibsen's major work.[33] So that the most obvious explanation must lie in Ibsen's appropriation by the new literature — by Maeterlinck, by Hauptmann, who had also moved on to neo-Romanticism with *Der versunkene Glocke* with its reminiscences of both *Peer Gynt* and *The Master Builder*, and, above all, by Hofmannsthal, whose essay on Ibsen, published in 1893, presented all his characters as variations on one single type: the artist, the *fin de siecle* poet. To Hofmannsthal, they are all egoistical epicureans, aesthetic hedonists, sensitive decadents.[34] Obviously, Hofmannsthal was thinking as much of his own *Der Tor und der Tod* as Ibsen, but the parallels between that play and Ibsen's *Peer Gynt* cannot be overlooked.

And so one finds a second Ibsen, one whose emergence owes something to an alternative cultural mirage, more to the coincidence of his own artistic development after *Enemy of the People* and *The Wild Duck* with the parallel reaction of German dramatists and audiences against Naturalism. That does not mean that some more 'faithful' or 'objective' account of his work now began to emerge: the new interpretation was not content simply to deny his affiliation with Naturalism, but eager as ever to exploit only those elements of his work which connected him to the new wave. To the pleasure of burying the 'old' Ibsen along with Naturalism was added the joy of his own apparent resurrection as a Romantic.

In 1906 Ibsen died, and any subsequent re-interpretation of his work cannot, therefore, be explained in terms of his own development but must be explicable in other terms. And there were at least two important subsequent revisions: Ibsen the neo-classicist and Ibsen the Expressionist.

There were two neo-classical movements in late nineteenth- and early twentieth-century Germany: the first, in the 1870s, dominated by the Schiller epigones; the second, in the first decade of the twentieth century, led by the Hebbel

epigones: Paul   Ernst,   Wilhelm   von   Scholz   and   Samuel
Lublinski.

The first movement had already rebelled against the
'naturalistic' Ibsen – both the one-sided interpretation of
the man and the concentration upon some of his plays:
instead they attempted to establish a case for *Brand*, *The
Vikings at Helgoland* and *The Pretenders*. It was this last
play which Wildenbruch – the foremost Schiller epigone of
the 1870s – alone exempted from his damnation of Ibsen.[35]
The same case was presented by Heinrich Bulthaupt, another
neo-classical dramatist, whose *Dramaturgie des Schauspiels*
(Oldenburg and Leipzig, 1881) enjoyed thirteen editions in
the next thirty years. Bulthaupt judged *The Pretenders* comparable with the work of Shakespeare: 'a work of genius of
the first order and in my estimation one of the greatest
plays of world literature' (p. 25). Only one other play drew
the same praise, *Brand*:

> And just as it reconciled the poet with his homeland and
> brought him fame, gold and honour, so too, I am convinced,
> it will still live on in the literature of the world when
> Ibsen's other products with their vulgar ephemeral
> interests and their own pathological defects are long
> gone. (p. 39)

This first wave was, however, dashed by the Naturalist
interpretation which swept away not only this possible alternative version of Ibsen but also the whole neo-classical
revival on which it floated. No matter how enthusiastically
these critics championed the earlier, historical plays,
their irrelevance for Germany's own literary development is
demonstrated conclusively by the fact that, though many had
appeared in German translation before the social-realist
plays, they were very soon forgotten, in spite of the fact
that they had even been performed on the stage by the
Meininger, the foremost classical company of the times. No
doubt this Ibsen was an interesting, even sympathetic
phenomenon, but as a neo-classicist he had nothing particularly original to offer the development of German drama.
This demonstrates quite convincingly that it is not enough
for a foreign author simply to match the literary production
of the importing country – a point which will be taken up in
more detail later.

The second wave of neo-classical interpretations was set
off by Max Martersteig, director and literary historian,
producer of plays by Wildenbruch, Grillparzer, Kleist and
Grabbe but above all responsible for the rediscovery of
Hebbel, and of Ibsen as a neo-Hebbelian who 'followed the

demands of classical aesthetics'.[36] Martersteig rejected the later plays and claimed that the misinterpretation of Ibsen as a Naturalist would not have occurred if Germany had first seen Ibsen's earlier, 'classical' plays.[37] But *Brand*, *The Vikings* and *The Pretenders* had all appeared first in German: if Ibsen could achieve prominence in Germany as a neo-classicist it could only be as a creative impulse and thus not in the pre-Naturalist phase but in the post-Naturalist reaction. Here Paul Ernst is the seminal figure: himself an early socialist and Naturalist who moved on to neo-classicism, and tried to carry Ibsen with him. His first essay on Ibsen had also appeared in 1887 and had criticised Ibsen for not presenting socialist solutions to the sickness of the times, offering instead only negative criticism breeding pessimism.[38] By 1904, Ernst had changed his whole direction, and in his new interpretation offered in *Henrik Ibsen* (Berlin and Leipzig, 1904) he no longer criticises Ibsen's lack of socialism or praises the social-realist plays: instead he singles out *The League of Youth* as 'a masterpiece', and *The Pretenders* as Ibsen's 'most significant play' (pp. 30, 52).

Wilhelm von Scholz and Samuel Lublinski made much the same contribution,[39] but the conclusion one must draw from this strange episode is that mere similarity can never ensure a foreign author a place in a country's literary development but, rather, some unpredictable combination of familiarity and innovation.

As the century progressed, Ibsen's irrelevance for the continuing development of German drama was apparently increasingly confirmed. Two courses are eventually open in the history of any reception: either the author is seen as a purely historical figure whose time has passed, or his situations, characters and themes become invested with universal and eternal significance. One way or another, he becomes a 'classic'.

Both things happened to Ibsen. The young Expressionist revolt against both Naturalism and neo-Romanticism expressed itself as a revolt against Ibsen. Such an attitude is evident in Kasimir Edschmid, the leading theoretician of the new Expressionist generation and in Franz Werfel, Wolfgang Paulsen, Bernard Diebold and others. In Pörtner's comprehensive collection of Expressionist manifestos, *Literatur-Revolution 1910-1925* (Mainz, 1960), Ibsen is scarcely mentioned at all. He had been replaced by Strindberg, Nietzsche and Wedekind, all three of whom had themselves rejected Ibsen in no uncertain terms: Strindberg calling him a 'coward' and a 'charlatan',[40] Nietzsche a 'typical old spinster',[41] Wedekind a charlatan who wrote 'charades'.[42]

One can, of course, still fish out parallels between
Ibsen and the new drama (for instance, Werfel's *Spiegel-
mensch* and *Peer Gynt*) but what emerges here in historical
terms is the picture of a generation which had been born
when Ibsen was being hailed as the great social realist, an
identification whose combined literary and extra-literary
supports made it almost impregnable: the deficiencies of
Naturalism are identified as the faults of the Norwegian.
Thus both Toller and Sorge had enjoyed Ibsen in their youth
but came to reject him as and because they grew.[43] The
happy coincidence of Ibsen's plays with the literary, philosophical and ideological climate of the 1880s and 1890s
seems to have indelibly stamped him with now unrevisable
slogans.[44]

'They cry Ibsen's twilight', wrote Diebold during the
Ibsen centenary of 1928, and indeed essays appeared entitled
'The Twilight of Ibsen', 'What's Henrik Ibsen to Us?',
'Should We Still Play Ibsen Today?", 'Has Ibsen Still Anything to Say to Us?' and 'Does Ibsen Still Have Value for
Our Times?'[45] - rhetorical questions answered in the
negative. This literary questioning was complemented by a
number of works on Ibsen from professional (i.e. thematic)
perspectives, written by medical men, lawyers, sociologists
and psychologists.

But there were also views of Ibsen from a religious perspective, sympathetic accounts by Lutherans, Catholics,
theosophists, Freemasons.[46] If any play of his was to
survive this twilight, it had to be a play with a strong
religious, predominantly mystical, component, for the immediate post-war years in Germany saw a major religious
revival; thematically it had to present a search for
identity in a fragmented society; formally it had to be a
'station drama'. And it was found: between 1913 and 1933,
the literature on *Peer Gynt* far exceeds that on any other
Ibsen play.[47] Statistics indicate that it was by far the
most popular of Ibsen's plays in the German repertoire. In
1916-17, of the 578 performances of Ibsen in German
theatres, 119 were of *Peer Gynt*.

It was helped by an adaptation, that of Dietrich Eckart,
whose 1911 version, first performed on 18 February 1914,
was in the course of the next two years performed over 100
times at the Königliche Schauspielhaus in Berlin alone. Once
again, this cannot be put down as the contribution of a
single idiosyncratic reader but must be seen as somehow
representing the needs of an age.

Eckart later joined the Nazis, and his adaptation of *Peer
Gynt* brought out not only the religious-mystical,
'Expressionist' elements of the play but also Eckart's own

racist feelings, offering a combination of parallels to
Angelus Silesius and anti-semitism.[48] This was achieved by
presenting the Jews as the epitome of materialism, an
interpretation confirmed and supplemented by Paul Schulze-
Berghof, who used *Peer Gynt* also to castigate Anglo-American
materialism, recommending that, in the fourth act, Peer
should be played in the 'cold, leathery, peace-parchment'
mask of President Wilson.[49]

The other successful adaptation of Ibsen to the new wave
can be found in Dusseldorf in the productions of Dumont and
Lindemann. Between 1915 and 1932, they presented seventeen
of Ibsen's plays 601 times: a mini-history in which the
early social-realist productions with which Dumont exploited
both Nora and Mrs Alving as pleas for feminist emancipation
were replaced by a more religious interpretation which again
shifted the emphasis to *Peer Gynt*. Otto Brües summarises:

> If in the generation of the *Sturm und Drang* the term could
> be coined 'Germany is Hamlet', so now, in spite of his
> Norwegian figure, Peer Gynt was Germany, namely the
> Germany that had been too loud and unruly, too addicted to
> thoughts of power and fear, so that the yearning grew in
> the heart for the peaceful and spiritual homeland, a
> yearning to return home to it just as Peer Gynt after the
> mistakes of his life returned to Solveig.[50]

III

In 1968 I was content to stop there, keeping the conclusion brief, content simply to observe that the conventional
division of Ibsen's own life-work into four groups - neo-
classical history plays, allegorical lyrical dramas, social-
realist and then symbolist dramas - is paralleled by the
four receptions, each of which singled out one group for
major emphasis, and none of which were able to embrace the
totality of his work. I should have liked more information
on audience-composition, a closer look at the semantic
shifts caused by translation, more detail on the design of
book-covers, typesetting, binding, posters - but not too
much, for a topic which threatened, like any Ph.D., to
dominate one's life. But now, after a decade of research
into other areas - predominantly the relationship between
Asian and Western drama - the unresolved questions of that
early study return with ever-greater urgency. For the
question why Ibsen ceased to exert any real influence after
the 1920s pales by comparison with the neglect by

Western writers of Chinese and Japanese drama for centuries;
the distortions suffered by Ibsen when his work was transplanted a few hundred miles south seems inconsequential compared to the misrepresentations of Balinese drama by Artaud
and of Noh by Yeats; the difficulty of reconstructing a
historical period is doubly compounded when a whole culture
needs to be pieced together. East–West comparisons not only
exceed in their complexity intra–European comparisons, but
challenge the whole accepted methodology of comparative
literature. The traditional approaches through influence,
theme, period and genre simply fail with two phenomena
which have no identifiable *rapports de fait*, but which
nevertheless reveal profound convergencies of structure and
function, forcing one in the end to abandon all causal
explanation for purely analogical comparisons and functional
phenomenologies. Such a procedure assumes, however, that one
is able to analyse and then compare phenomena without subjective or cultural bias – an assumption which must make one
pause. Gadamer has proposed that the real value of investi-
gations into historical reception is the way they force the
reader to recognise his own susceptibility to such bias, his
own historicity; East–West comparisons highlight the
reader's or critic's own cultural confinement. Retrospec-
tively we may and do smile at the recognised narrow vision
of late nineteenth–century interpretations of Ibsen, and of
Noh, but is our assumption of our own freedom from similar
time– and place–bound blinkering not the real issue? Can we
be so sure that their biased interpretation is not further
biased by our interpretation of their interpretation? Are we
right to feel confident of our own freedom from bias both
with regard to the work and with regard to critics of that
work? Our adventures with implied, competent, average,
ideal and super–readers should not blind us to the fact
that such readers are invariably only generalisations of
ourselves.[51]

When, if ever, is it possible to reconstruct an author or
his reception without any bias by our own reception? Conven-
tionally, the term 'classic' is presumed to cover such a
stage. A 'classic' is a work which we can approach with a
firm belief that it has transcended mere ephemeral popularity and temporal relevance and achieved some trans-
historical status which is supposed, in turn, to protect the
work from further acculturation. We can thus happily accept
Jan Kott's as a polemical vision because we believe that the
'real' Shakespeare is sufficiently protected to permit such
recognisable adaptations. History nevertheless continues to
surprise us. Who would have thought before Jane Fonda that
A Doll's House could still speak polemically a hundred years

later? Utitz had declared in 1921 that Nora was a historical figure.[52] Who would have anticipated how effectively
Günther Grass could turn Shakespeare against Brecht, who
thought he had already exploited the contemporary relevance
of *Coriolanus*? Only utter irrelevance, it seems, can protect
an author from continuing historical distortion, so that the
term 'classic' comes to overlap with the term 'irrelevant'.
Small wonder that our children are bored by our selections
and clamour for a relevance we know must involve a distortion. Those who would seek such 'value-free' status for
their favourites must face the danger that their selection
of 'masterpieces' may have no value.

The children, of course, do not understand: the most sin-
ister 'relevance' of the 'classics' is precisely their
apparent documentation of that which is timeless and un-
changeable in 'human nature', unalterable in the 'human
condition'.[53] That is, in the end, the thrust of much
Marxist criticism of literature: the recognition that it has
such power to confirm its public in the passive acceptance
of unalterable human characteristics and predicaments which
no new social order can change – and which the addition of
Asian examples threatens to universalise. Returning, for
exemplification to Ibsen, must one not account for the popularity of such a work as *Ghosts* to an audience of middle-
class intellectuals by recognising that its underlying
message is that the world is as you fear it may be, that you
are right to feel alienated from it, but right also to sit
still in your seat, for you can do nothing about it – a dual
confirmation of the correctness both of the alienation and
of the passivity? This is only one example of the way in
which one could suspect and perhaps fear that literature is
far more able to confirm existing orders than campaign for
their reform – especially drama, which has progressively
confirmed the passive status of its audience.

The as-yet unformulated theory of the degree to which
literature can go beyond the transfer of ideas to the activ-
isation of motives mentioned above looms again as a press-
ing task of modern theory.

Meanwhile, we must restrict our enquiries to the purely
literary provocation; and here both the old Ibsen material
and the new enquiries into Asian drama unearth a puzzling
conundrum. On the one hand, any successful transplanting of
a foreign work must depend on the cultural assimilability of
the import into the evolving national corpus. It must therefore conform to the evolution of the receiving country's own
literature. But, on the other hand, for it to be necessary
to import it at all, it must also supply something which is
not available at home and is therefore in some way recognis-

ably different from the internal corpus. But not too different: in spite of Artaud, we still have no magical drama of
transcendent gesture comparable to the Balinese; in spite of
Yeats, we have no theatre of mystical illusion comparable to
the Japanese. They have yet to become 'assimilable' and will
presumably remain so until their cultural strangeness is
sufficiently muted to permit their provocative relevance to
emerge. For this combination of assimilability and yet novel
provocation is clearly a fine mix, and here again one must
pause. Is it only works which provoke but do not overturn,
which excite but do not disorient, that can be appropriated?
In which case, the tentative hypothesis offered above that
literature may not exceed a certain degree of welcome confirmation would seem to be further supported. The solution
to this paradox in the case of Ibsen is the evidence that
the early Ibsen before *Pillars of Society* had in some sense
recapitulated the earlier history of German drama, bringing
it to a point in his own development which was roughly the
point it had reached in Germany's own literary history but
then pushing it forward in a way no German dramatist apparently could. The evidence is supported more by analogy than
by direct influence: the ransacking of library catalogues,
letters, diaries, the repertoire in Bergen, the dubious
testimony of such as Paulsen force one to search for anal-
ogies between *Catalina* and the *Sturm and Drang*, between *Lady
Inger* and Romantic fate tragedy, *The Vikings* and Hebbel; to
note the Hegelianism of *Emperor and Galilean*, the Faustian
qualities of *Peer Gynt*, and so forth. But the point can be
reached where *Pillars of Society* can be seen as the logical
continuation not only of Ibsen's own work but of German
literary history as a whole. This raises the question: why
him, why not Hebbel, or Buchner, or Ludwig, or Anzengruber?
The answer appears to be that none of these other possible
catalysts of a social-realist drama had successfully translated new techniques of characterisation by environment
and heredity into a new, modern concept of fate or a new
vehicle for social criticism. The 'realistic' elements in
these authors' plays were designed, it seems, not so much
to create a new drama as to prop up an old drama. They
are comparable, therefore, more to the series before *Pillars
of Society* than to the series after. In neither Hebbel's
Judith nor Gutzkow's *Werner* nor Ludwig's *Erbförster* or
Anzengruber's *Das vierte Gebot* does heredity figure as a
force of fate or as a biological concept. In Hebbel's *Maria
Magdalene*, Büchner's *Woyzeck* and the plays of Anzengruber,
environment similarly is employed as a technique of characterisation, not as a new form of fate or a principal medium
for social criticism. Ibsen did make this transition, serv-

ing thus as a sort of 'missing link', able thus to spawn a
whole brood of epigones.[54] Part of the reason for this
must be not his own exceptional ability alone but also the
fact that his work was not shrouded and obscured by a
'classical' interpretation in the way Hebbel would have been
obscured by a German reader. It was only after and because
of Ibsen that Germany became able to discover these things
in her own writers.

One chapter, therefore, in the reception of a foreign
writer is always the retrospective rewriting of the importing country's own literary history. In Ibsen's case, this
was a provocation repeated more than once as each new wave
rewrote his contribution.

The logic of this process appears as a simple dialectic in
which original distortion received corrective bias until the
pendulum, like any dialectical motion, reaches a stage of
exhaustion, however temporary. In practice, this picture is
complicated – and its momentum in part explained – by a further factor, namely the existence of contradictions within
any consensus. Even during the heady days of Naturalism,
there was dispute as to whether Ibsen's agreed-on realism
consisted more in his psychological profundity or his social
criticism, a dispute centring on the question whether Nora
is typical or unique, Bernick's final speech psychologically plausible or a rhetorical, authorial tirade. In other
words, in any period, there are not only divergencies
between major and minor versions but also contradictions
within the major consensus. Here we discover the most fruit-
ful overlap between reception and ideology, for the more
recent work on ideology has proposed that it too requires
description not as a coherent philosophy of an age but as a
'hegemony' or a 'homology': a construct which ignores the
contradictions but evolves and strengthens itself by
shifting ground and emphasis to prevent contradictions
from becoming divisive or even visible. In which case, the
explanation of reception in terms of ideology looks much
more interesting than earlier crude models of reflection
which, as Raymond Williams writes, 'was itself specialized
to crude stimulus-and-response models, adapted from
positivist physiology'.[55] The value of ideology is that it
recognises that consciousness is itself part of the deter-
mining apparatus, but essentially a false consciousness, one
which buries the real contradictions of the social order,
above all by perpetuating myths of its innate unchangeabil-
ity. So that, returning now to the question, what one can
observe happening through Ibsen's introduction into Germany
is a series of partial insights into the contradictions
of his age which do not, however, disturb the ideological

core. That is, essentially, the 'vulgar Marxist' attack on all nineteenth-century bourgeois writers, but it is one which overlooks Engels's notion of the essential opacity of ideological constructs:

> That the material life conditions of the persons inside whose heads this thought process goes on, in the last resort determines the course of this process, remains of necessity unknown to these persons, for otherwise there would be an end to all ideology. . . . The real motives impelling him remain unknown to him, otherwise it would not be an ideological process at all.[56]

Or, as Terry Eagleton puts it, the function of ideology is to 'ensure that the situation in which one social class has power over the others is either seen by most members of the society as "natural", or not seen at all'.[57]

Here Marxism joins psychoanalysis. What evolves is a general theory that both authors and readers are subconsciously determined by deep structural patterns of thinking even where man supposes himself to be most free – in the imaginative creation of fictive worlds. It is a holistic model in which partial insights into structural inconsistencies are paid for by the increased opacity of their ideological core. This, in turn, creates that balance of confirmed alienation and impotence referred to earlier. The model is very tentative, faltering on the threshold of application, for, if it is essential to the definition that an ideology differs from a deliberate political lie in being unconscious, how can one be sure that the identification of this conditioning in others is not itself undermined by one's own, also essentially unconscious, ideological determination? In a land that invented boomerangs one has reason to be aware of one's own vulnerability.

This is not the place to resolve this question. The purpose of this extension is only to suggest that this may be a programme for the future. Three areas appear to emerge to claim our attention. The first is to decide the primary factors in any reception – political, economic, philosophical, literary and so forth – and either arrange them in a hierarchy, or refer them all to the umbrella term 'ideology'. The second is to decide whether one can quantify (for any particular case, or more generally), the complementary ingredients of familiarity and novelty in any reception. (This too may be integrated with ideology in the form of some equation which relates familiarity to buried mystification and novelty to partial insight.) The third is both a historical and a theoretical investigation into whether literature can ever go far beyond provocation to actual intervention. (This too relates to ideology as a legitimising construct in which the unearthed contradictions encourage partial disaffection, but not total rebellion.)

It may not do to wear a new coat when one goes out to fight for truth, but, unless we patch our theoretical robes, our present ragged array is certain to trip us up.

NOTES

1. *The Principles of Literary Criticism* (London, 1924) p. 6.
2. M. Heidegger, *Poetry, Language, Thought* (New York, 1971) p. 68.
3. *On Racine* (New York, 1964) p. ix.
4. German text in R. Warning (ed.), *Rezeptionsästhetik* (Munich, 1975). English text in *New Literary History*, vol. II (1970).
5. Warning, *Rezeptionsästhetik*, p. 130.
6. *New Literary History*, vol. II, p. 11.
7. Warning, *Rezeptionsästhetik*, p. 39. Unless otherwise indicated, all quotations from German and French in this paper have been translated into English by the author.
8. U. Eco, *A Theory of Semiotics* (Bloomington, Ind., 1976) p. 141.
9. Quoted in Warning, *Rezeptionsästhetik*, p. 75.
10. P. Van Tieghem, *La Litterature comparée* (Paris, 1931) p. 25.
11. G. Brandes, *Moderne Geister* (Frankfurt a. M., 1887) p. 446.
12. O. Brahm, *Kritische Schriften* (Berlin, 1915) pp. 447f.
13. Cf. ibid., pp. 127, 76, 35, 459.
14. Ibid., p. 230.
15. For example, Carl Heine, 'Mein Ibsen-Theater', *Velhagen und Klasings Monatshefte*, vol. XL (Bielefeld, 1925-6) p. 423.
16. Brahm, *Kritische Schriften*, pp. 453f.
17. J. Bab (ed.), *Agnes Sorma* (Heidelberg, 1927) pp. 54, 64.
18. Cf. H. Richter, *Kainz* (Vienna and Leipzig, 1931) pp. 49, 56, 57; G. Wethly, *Henrik Ibsens Werk und Weltanschauung* (Strassburg, 1934) p. 58.
19. For documentation of this, cf. D. E. R. George, *Henrik Ibsen in Deutschland* (Göttingen, 1968) pp. 26f., nn. 41 and 42.
20. F. Kummer, *Deutsche Literaturgeschichte* (Dresden, 1922) vol. II, p. 278.

21. H. Landsberg, *Ibsen* (Berlin, 1904) p. 77.
22. For example, Kurt Hiller, *Das Ziel* (1915) vol. I, p. 187.
23. Cf. Ian Britain's argument in the present volume that Ibsen's ideas and his art exercised a peculiar fascination for the English socialists because of the way in which these things served to crystallise their own emotional dilemmas and to dramatise their self-conflicts as 'middle-class revolutionists'.
24. Cf. A. F. Lugné-Poe, *Henrik Ibsen* (Paris, 1937) p. 30; but cf. a letter from Ibsen to Prozor, dated 3 Mar. 1891, in which he proposes that *The Wild Duck*, *Hedda Gabler* and *An Enemy of the People* should be the first works to be performed in France.
25. Cf. *Le Figaro*, Paris, 2 Apr. 1894; M. Maeterlinck, *Le Trésor des humbles*, 4th edn (Paris, 1916) pp. 196f.
26. Cf. *La Plume*, Paris, 15 May 1891.
27. Cf. George, *Ibsen in Deutschland*, p. 47, n. 14.
28. H. Bahr, *Henrik Ibsen* (Vienna, 1887) pp. 64f.
29. H. Bahr, *Glossen* (Berlin, 1907) pp. 350f.
30. F. Winwar, *Wings of Fire* (London, 1956) p. 140.
31. Cf. *Magazin für Literatur* (Vienna), LXI (1892) no. 11; B. Harding, *Age Cannot Wither* (London, 1949) p. 72; H. von Hofmannsthal, *Gesammelte Werke: Prosa II* (Berlin, 1950) p. 60.
32. Heine, in *Velhagen und Klasings Monatshefte*, vol. XL p. 425.
33. J. Bab, *Der Mensch auf der Buhne* (Berlin, 1906) p. 275: supporting statements documented in George, *Ibsen in Deutschland*, pp. 58f.
34. Cf. Hofmannsthal, *Gesammelte Werke: Prosa II*, pp. 100, 106, 109.
35. E. von Wildenbruch, *Das deutsche Drama* (Leipzig, 1906) p. 37.
36. M. Martersteig, *Das deutsche Theater im neunzehnten Jahrhundert* (Leipzig, 1904) p. 603.
37. Ibid., p. 602.
38. 'Ibsen und Björnson', *Die Neue Zeit* (Stuttgart), VII (1887) p. 129.
39. Cf. George, *Ibsen in Deutschland*, pp. 72f.
40. Cf. A. Strindberg, *Samlede Skrifter*, vol. XIV (Stockholm, 1918) pp. 13ff., and *Brev*, vol. II (Stockholm, 1948-56) p. 353.
41. F. Nietzsche, *Gesammelte Schriften*, vol. XXI (Munich, 1928) p. 221.
42. F. Wedekind, *Gesammelte Werke*, vol. IX (Munich, 1921) pp. 340ff.
43. George, *Ibsen in Deutschland*, pp. 77f.

44. Cf. ibid., pp. 78f.
45. Ibid., p. 80.
46. Ibid., p. 83, n. 24.
47. Ibid., p. 84, n. 26.
48. D. Eckart, *Bühnenbearbeitung des 'Peer Gynt'* (Munich, 1916), *Ibsen, Peer Gynt, der grosse Krumme und Ich* (Berlin, 1914), and *Das Wesen des Peer Gynt* (Munich, 1919).
49. P. Schulze-Berghof, *Zeitgedanken zu Ibsen's Peer Gynt* (Leipzig, 1918) pp. 47f.
50. O. Brües, *Louise Dumont* (Emsdetten, 1956) p. 91.
51. Cf. A. Fowler , 'The Selection of Literary Constructs', *New Literary History*, VII (1975) p. 45.
52. E. Utitz, *Die Kultur der Gegenwart* (Stuttgart, 1921) p. 3.
53. Cf. Maria Shevtsova's paper on Chekhov in the present volume, which documents the similar universalisation of Chekhov in recent productions.
54. Cf. D. E. R. George, 'Ibsen and German Naturalist Drama', *Ibsenårbok* (Oslo, 1967).
55. *Marxism and Literature* (Oxford, 1977) p. 34.
56. Ibid., p. 65.
57. *Marxism and Literary Criticism* (London, 1976) p. 5.

4   Chekhov in France, 1976-9: Productions by Strehler, Miquel and Pintilié

MARIA SHEVTSOVA

I

The history of the director begins at the turn of the century. Since that time, when the director established his primacy in the theatre – as Antoine did in France and Stanislavsky in Russia, for instance – directors have been a powerful influence in the theatre, particularly in the evolution of the *mise-en-scène*.

Today's directors must contend not only with the traditions of direction, but also with the tasks of renewal and innovation. Throughout the 1970s in Europe, novelty, originality, and uniqueness were qualities much sought after in stage presentation. The director was commonly regarded – by himself and by his public – as a star.

The three directors who are the subject of this paper – Lucian Pintilié, Giorgio Strehler, and Jean-Pierre Miquel – have all responded to the challenge of novelty. Each aims to achieve uniqueness in his productions, yet none pursues uniqueness simply for its own sake. I shall examine in turn Pintilié's production of *The Three Sisters* (1978-9); Strehler's production of *The Cherry Orchard* (1976-7, from its original Milan season, 1973-4); and Miquel's *Uncle Vanya* (1976-7 and 1977-8). Each of these productions, I suggest, can be seen as an attempt to test and elaborate particular theatrical principles, and particular attitudes to Chekhov and the Chekhovian universe.

II

Productions of Chekhov in France can be described in the first instance, and paradigmatically, by Pintilié's

words on his objectives for Chekhov: 'magical realism'.[1]
This phrase illuminates his own methods in *The Three
Sisters*.[2]

Pintilié's wish to escape a mundane, simply imitative
representation, which goes under the name of naturalism in
France, is shared by Miquel, whose *Uncle Vanya* draws on the
poetic rather than the realistic resources of Chekhov's
text.[3] To translate these into visual terms, Miquel
required an elliptical mode instead of a mimetic one, or, as
Miquel formulates it, a 'dispositif plus symbolique que
vrai'.[4]

In his preference for an alternative to discursive
structure, Miquel recalls Strehler, who noted, as he was
preparing *The Cherry Orchard* at Milan's Piccolo Teatro, that
his major problem in interpreting Chekhov was finding the
correct symbol, a correct evocative-plastic-poetic image for
the physical object, the cherry orchard itself, with which
the actors' work in space could meaningfully co-ordinate.[5]
Strehler feels that the difficulty of adequate metamorphosis
is a fairly representative one for directors staging Chekhov
today.

Three years later, Strehler and the Piccolo took *The
Cherry Orchard* to Paris.[6] Paris had already enthusiastically acclaimed their *Il Campiello* during the Odéon's 1975-6
season (returning in 1976-7). Chekhov was as magnanimously
received as Goldoni.

There are plastic similarities (as we shall see) between
Miquel's *Uncle Vanya* and Strehler's *The Cherry Orchard*. The
ideational kinship between Miquel and Strehler cannot be
explained, however, simply in terms of chronology. Nor is it
really a question of cultural memory, borrowing, or one
director's influence on another. The impact of the Italian
performances on Parisian audiences and stage professionals
is to be understood, in part, in terms of a sociology of
reception, which examines the specific social conditions
that allow a given work to be felt as important. It is
also to be understood in terms of a sociology of artistic
production – in this case, of theatrical production: here we
would need to examine the conjuncture of socio-cultural conditions out of which emerges a particular, historically
recognisable vision, which cannot be confused with the
vision of another time and place, and of another group or
class.

Strehler, Miquel and Pintilié are concerned, from a
present-day standpoint, with both a valorization of theatrical processes and a reassessment of the Chekhovian universe,
whose historical genesis is in late nineteenth-century
Russia and whose stage genesis lies with Stanislavsky and

Nemirovich-Danchenko. The premises of realism, accentuating, as they do, psychological and social verisimilitude, are mediated in the theatre by precision of acting and the veracious detail of narrative, sequence and decor behind the now famous 'fourth wall'.[7] Stanislavsky's and Nemirovich-Danchenko's direction yields its proper sociological explanation concurrently with one released by Chekhov's texts. The explanation available for Chekhov, however, need not necessarily coincide at all points with the first.

Uncle Vanya is subtitled 'Scenes from Country Life'. While life in the provinces can be viewed as drama or comedy – Chekhov's terms for *The Three Sisters* and *The Cherry Orchard* respectively – it occurs for Chekhov, not in *any* world, but in a Russian world.

III: Pintilié's *The Three Sisters*

Our directors construct their productions at a distance from this world, the distance varying significantly in each case. In his production of *The Three Sisters*, Pintilié only partly eschews the Russian world, and that mainly at the level of conceptualisation and textual interpretation. At a visual level, he relies on a recognisably Russian environment. Costumes and setting are historically descriptive, even sumptuously metropolitan – not so much encapsulating provincial existence as reinforcing the illusion of Moscow in the minds of Olga, Masha and Irina.

Act I opens onto a large room, combining two adjoining shapes, a square and a rectangle. Almost the size of the stage, its walls are lined with imposing, ornamented French windows through which birch-trees are visible and through which enters the brilliant light outside. The birch-trees are brought into the room by their forest-like repetition on a backdrop whose intricacies of light and shade suggest depth, adding to an already optically busy ensemble.

Perspective is used less for placing action on a number of levels than for its pictorial effects. An important exception occurs towards the end of Act IV, where action is distributed on several planes. Natasha appears with her lover at a high window while, below, Andrey wheels his second child in a pram. Vershinin appears from a lower level again, beneath stairs, to bid Masha farewell. As personal fates are being decided, the military prepare to leave town; and both private and public matters are carried out in a subdued mood. Electronic dissonances replace what would otherwise have been the activity and noise of actors playing an imminent departure, during which the aspirations of three sisters collapse into ruins. Music, too, in Pintilié's Chekhov, has an illustrative purpose.

Although the performance ends with the impression that space has been made elastic, its characteristic feature is the concentration of activity on a limited surface: the middle of the room with which the performance begins. Act III, when the town is on fire, shows how this very area is a synecdoche for the whole production. All characters gravitate towards it, now the sisters' bedroom. Beds, tables and chairs are arranged towards the centre, restricting space, while keeping clear the contours of the room surrounding it. A room within a room, the composition closes movement. As if to stress this closure, the act's critical scene, that in which the sisters' disappointments and tensions erupt, is mediated through images of stasis. Masha and Olga, for instance, deliver their most important lines while lying horizontally on their beds, face and feet towards the audience.

While Pintilié heightens Chekhov's scene-directions, even as he follows them carefully, his use of space is somewhat unadventurous, traditional. The result is that decor and props have a larger responsibility in transmitting Chekhov's concentration on his heroines' wasted lives than do acting techniques, the use of body and voice. The accumulation of objects (the white lace-covered table in Act I, with its numerous glasses and other household goods, a huge white cake on a trolley, massive flowers set here and there, a piano, the neo-classical balustrade of Act IV) in a brilliant setting produces a visual splendour worthy of the adjective 'magical', in a spectacular and technologically oriented sense of the word.

Pintilié, then, takes realism into hyper-realism whose visual-spatial point of departure is the Moscow Art Theatre. Stripped of its intentional exaggerations, which serve as a commentary on Stanislavsky's theatre, past and present, *The Three Sisters* would look like Oleg Yefremov's projection of Chekhov – like *Ivanov*, premièred at the Moscow Art Theatre in 1976.

Excesses are to be seen, equally, in the actors' performances, especially in those of the female characters. Where Chekhov writes 'she weeps' or 'she speaks through her tears', the women over-respond, creating a falseness which has little to do with theatricality (Meyerhold, Tairov) or didactic parody (Brecht) and much more to do with a stereotyped notion of the 'Russian temperament'. Emotional Russia – a crude archetype at its best, in its transnational versions – finds her way all too frequently into Pintilié's work with his actors.

Masha has a particularly sensitive position in the production. She is its cornerstone. For Parisian spectators,
she is, moreover, the principal entrance into a foreign
terrain, a terrain that Paris can penetrate fully provided
it unhesitatingly accepts both the entrance and the edifice
– that is, the production's emotionalism. As if to counter-
act the impact of an atmosphere whose foreignness is not
altogether strange (and cannot be, since it feeds on an
archetype), Pintilié introduces sobriety by having the women
read Chekhov's directions at the beginning of each act in a
normal speaking voice. An alienation effect, in the manner
of Brecht, this meta-theatrical procedure does not quite
succeed in anchoring the production's overall socio-psycho-
logical direction.

The difficulty is in Pintilié's idea of the sisters as
three faces of the one woman, the mythological woman who is
at once mother (Olga), child (Irina) and erotic female
(Masha). Realised physically through close grouping of the
sisters throughout the performance, this conception is not,
however, elaborated through the individual characters. Olga
is only a mother, Irina just a child, and Masha sheer
eroticism. Each, then, is cut off from the other two, and
the intended effect – that each is a different face of the
same woman – is correspondingly diffused.

Absence of nuance in the theatre need not be a drawback
or, necessarily, an obstacle to sense, innovation, excite-
ment, and so on. In *The Three Sisters*, simplification of
each woman forces each into role-playing (Olga as mother,
for instance) and forces her into it without the whole production showing that this is precisely the intention.
Another consequence of simplified interpretation is the
emotionalism mentioned earlier. Character-giving emotion is
Pintilié's aim, as his use of the term 'realism' suggests.
But, because this particular kind of emotion is not
adequately built into the production and, consequently, is
not supported from within, it veers towards histrionics.

Pintilié's conflicting processes – one emblematic, the
other inherited from psychological theatre – do not find
their resolution on stage. They approach it in Masha, in
whom they are most interesting and potentially most reward-
ing.[8] In her, Pintilié gives an example of savage, because
repressed and displaced, sexuality. If Masha flaunts her
sexuality in sections of Acts III and IV, her hair loosened,
her body released, she does so in rage against a milieu
which stifles her libido and in defiance of men incapable of
understanding, or freeing, her imprisoned drives. Natasha
parallels her erotic aggression and becomes her rival in a

hidden struggle for sexual emancipation from which both Olga and Irina are excluded. Since the male characters are presented as ineffectual, their weakness shifts interest, once again, to the women.

By focusing on frustrated sexuality, rather than on any other Chekhovian frustration, Pintilié reorients Chekhov, situates him post-Freud and steps away from Russia into the vicinity of a France sensitised by the women's movement of the seventies – its mid-seventies phase in particular – and by Lacan's psychoanalytical theories. His psychoanalytical approach to Chekhov marks out Pintilie's particularity. The conflicting processes cited originate in his dual system: Pintilié takes his interpretative principle from modern France and its technical implementation from pre-revolutionary Russia. The same coupling is at work in *The Seagull*. There again Pintilié's emphasis is psychoanalytical and falls on one woman, Nina (instead of the ensemble of characters), whose sexuality withers where Irina's never begins.

IV: Strehler's *The Cherry Orchard*

In Strehler's *Cherry Orchard*, Russia is transposed into an ethereal dream dimension whose whiteness (Damiani's set-design is of an amazing beauty) is peopled by aristocrats reminiscent of Visconti's, their passions flamboyant and vibrating and recalling the Piccolo's work on Goldoni. Towards the end of Act II, an over-Russianised (in the sense that he is over-picturesque) peasant-like tramp, to whom Ranevskaya gives her money, brusquely unbalances the elegant composition as if to flash out of this nowhere – Ranevskaya's nowhere – into the years immediately preceding 1905.[9]

By means of this cumbersome, expository intrusion upon an otherwise symbolic whole, Strehler crystallises the elements of social history contained in Chekhov's text. (The tramp's accent, likewise, is heavily Russian, in contradistinction to the other actors' normal Italian.) Ranevskaya and Gaev, bankrupt gentry; Varya and Anya, impoverished next generation; Lopakhin, merchant; Trofimov, 'eternal student' and/or revolutionary; and Firs, emancipated serf – all are on stage. The intrusion is all the more striking because social distinctions are made to be of minor relevance throughout the production. They are absorbed, rather, into the homogeneity of a plastically bewitched ensemble.

The moment's seemingly contradictory nature is designed,

none the less, for several specific purposes. It comments on
Ranevskaya's evasiveness in the face of financial and
personal crisis; anticipates the drastic solution to these
crises in Lopakhin's purchase of her cherry orchard (and
thus, structurally speaking, foreshadows the end of Act
III); reflects back on Trofimov's speeches about Russia's
need for change, simultaneously affirming his position and
undercutting it just enough to make it look a little too
like comfortable intellectualising; and reminds the audience
of encroaching historical change – the revolutions of 1905
and 1917 – not as if Chekhov foresaw them, but rather by
hindsight from the present day.

Notwithstanding this sudden spotlight upon history, the
whole act puts into focus Ranevskaya's present, showing
that she lives it ahistorically, on two counts. She lives
her present from the viewpoint of what is objectively an
increasingly remote past, and she does so solely through her
own, subjective memory. Furthermore, she lives even the
present as if it were already the past and in her memory,
this temporal ellipsis showing that she does not live the
present at all.

Where Ranevskaya's own past is concerned, her memory
floats between two phases: one, her early adulthood,
imagined to be serene (whereas it is riven with vexation,
especially over her son's death); the other, her childhood,
which may or may not have been as idyllic as she now claims.
The set for this act is organised as if it had been dictated
by the images of Ranevskaya's double memory, in which
sequences from the past tend to fuse into one and fuse again
with the present. The set's unifying principle – whiteness –
articulates both the nature of this memory and the images it
processes.

Some details will illustrate my point. The act takes place
on a white rhomboid rising to the back of the stage. The
actors' white or pale-beige costumes all but disappear into
it, whether their bodies are curved into it, as if in a
mould, or sitting, or standing at different points on its
surface. When the actors stand at the top of the slope they
blend into the white back wall. Space seems to extend endlessly, the actors forming in it a relation of numerous
geometric shapes, as in an abstract painting.

In one sequence Ranevskaya lifts her white parasol,
whirls it in the air or on the rhomboid, leaning towards it
in various positions while her parasol turns towards the
audience. Trofimov stands on the edge of the rhomboid,
twirling his straw hat, his legs an angle and a straight
line. Lopakhin paces upwards, his back to the audience, and
turns abruptly towards Ranevskaya. Since the actors move

continually, their geometric shapes change rapidly. When the
actors hold a position longer, they emphasise, by the contrast of their relative stillness, the fast pace at which
they move in general.

Whiteness is made more translucent still by stark lighting, which conveys the heat of that summer's day even as it
retains Chekhov's seasonal indication at the opening of Act
I, when Ranevskaya returns to Russia from Paris in spring,
the cherry-trees in bloom, 'but in the orchard there is
morning frost'. Seasonal and temporal changes are pre-
empted by the enormous white veil held high above a quarter
of the stalls and swooping downwards in a low curve, to be
caught above the acting-space. The veil remains in its
position throughout the preformance. Autumn leaves, which
are gathered in generous quantities over the veil, flutter
down as the audience enters the theatre. Some continue to
drop onto the lowered forestage, also a rhomboid, or fall
further back, as if blown by wind. Their fall in Act II
foreshadows the end of summer. Ranevskaya is about to be
dispossessed; and to leave Russia forever.

The veil, Strehler's abstract image for the cherry
orchard, is also his image for Ranevskaya's memory – a
dream, a fantasy, into which she merges her present,
forgetting and at other times ignoring the fact that trains
cross the countryside, telegraph-poles spread along its
horizon, dachas are being built as cherry orchards are being
destroyed, as her own will be destroyed. Ranevskaya's
fairy-tale attitude towards Russia's present and future, as
well as her own, is ingenuously captured in the movement of
a whistling toy train which encircles her group as she,
sophisticated lady, chats, laughs, flirts with Lopakhin and
Trofimov, poised gentlemen, and Varya and Anya, graceful
maidens.

The exquisitely built train passes in front of
Ranevskaya, unnoticed. The actors are situated upwards and
across the rhomboid slope, giving the illusion of elongating
it in two directions at once: out into the wings and away
from the audience, whose view is already lengthened by the
intervention of the rhomboid dip which is the forestage.
Placed towards the back, at various distances from each
other, but all a long way from the front of the stage,
and further away, still, from the audience, the actors look
like pictures from a child's storybook, they are small,
vulnerable people living out their tale in a world they have
made imaginary.

The one character who is neither sitting nor leaning while
the train runs is Lopakhin. As the train passes right in
front of Ranevskaya, Lopakhin's squat body is standing

towards the audience. All their bodies are now towards the
audience. And Lopakhin - who has just tried to convince
Ranevskaya to confront the reality of her situation and
build dachas in the place of her cherry orchard - watches
the train, the only one who actually sees it, the only one
with practical sense.

Viewed from the stage, where Lopakhin's physical distance
in relation to the train is like that of the other characters (except Ranevskaya when the train brushes her),
Lopakhin's stance suggests his command of the whole situation. Viewed from the audience, his position is subject to
the production's distancing and diminishing processes, so
that his mastery of reality also appears small. This visual
placing implies a value placing internal to the production:
namely, that Lopakhin's view of reality is not to prevail.
Nor can it, in fact, given that the entire act is constructed from Ranevskaya's point of view, which is engag-
ingly presented to the audience, in this way directing its
attitudes towards her and in her favour. The general effect,
like the specific instance of the toy train, is a minimis-
ation of encroaching historical reality.

Strehler's open space gives a sense of unlimited possibilities for movement in space, which his actors materialise
in their extraordinary plasticity. Their wide vocal range
resounds in their mutual space as they create rhythms to
correspond with, and extend, their body-rhythms, the whole a
complex notation, as if a musical score. The quality of
music is palpable throughout. Even when space is scattered
with objects, as in Act I, rhythms and sounds continue,
unhampered.

Act I, in fact, opens in the key in which most of the
performance will be played. Its opening is as significant a
micro-structure of the whole act as the train-scene is of
Act II. The two micro-structures coincide at all semiotic
levels. Ranevskaya moves vivaciously through her old, white
nursery, then opens a tall cupboard to the side, from which
fall piles of toys. She sits on the floor to fondle and
gather them, like a child. A little later, she and Gaev
momentarily sit at white, children-size desks and benches,
or on tiny chairs belonging to a doll's house. Every character is in motion; Charlotta's poodle stands on its hind
legs. But Ranevskaya's memory of her childhood dominates
the scene in its each and every detail, including her words.
As she relives her past, Ranevskaya appears to be still a
child, an enchanting one, who becomes at times an alluring
woman and yet is essentially a child in body and mind.
Valentina Cortese, slim and buoyant, is a perfect choice for
this interpretation.

Ranevskaya's infantile innocence communicates itself to her friends, each of whom adopts and adapts it in his or her own fashion. By the end of the performance this collective innocence appears a little sickly, decadent even, like the autumn tones of the falling leaves. Actors and scenography provide a plastic-poetic beauty whose gentle allusions to the decay of a given society maintain a perspective on history, but whose power is so great that it considerably narrows that very perspective. Strehler noted that the problem of treating Chekhov was to be likened to that of three interlocking Chinese boxes. The first box contains the real (to avoid ambiguity here we should call this 'the concrete situation'); the second, history; and the third, life.[10] It is this third, the box of the '"eternal" parable', to cite Strehler, which encompasses his *Cherry Orchard*.[11] Strehler's term 'history' includes the notion of a history specific to one epoch. His production shows him to be well aware of the difficulty of transcribing both 'history' and history in a symbolic form.

A short parenthesis would be useful here for comparison and contrast. When Anatoly Efros staged *The Cherry Orchard* at Moscow's Taganka Theatre (1974-5), he approached it from the angle of a question similar to that asked by Strehler: how to synthesis set-design and interpretation in a symbol or a metaphor.[12] Efros's solution is to have a mound at centre-back on which are placed several wrought-iron chairs and crosses and two gravestones and cherry-trees, with a bough in bloom also hanging above the front of the stage. The set is white and serves for the whole play. Costumes are graceful and predominantly white, and there is white light from the wings, where white curtains float, or billow in the wind. There are no local details: no colourful cloths, samovars and so on. The actors' exploitation of space, rhythm, speed, gesture and voice springs from a principle of plasticity not unlike the one guiding Strehler's production.

While the sign-systems of Efros's and Strehler's production are comparable, they operate in terms of two very different sub-textual readings of Chekhov. In Efros, the thrust of these signs is not a parable and not a circumscribing universal statement. They specify a historical period, but, rather than extend it into a metaphysic of the eternally human, narrow it by bringing it closer to a contemporary social world whose problems are concrete.

The action of making concrete and contemporary statements via a particular period of the past and within a metaphorical structure depends on how the actors interpret the characters. Between them the two interpretations considered here form a thickly textured interrelationship of markedly

different points of view, so that, although Efros's scenic
metaphor is derived from Ranevskaya, her view is not
privileged. Ranevskaya's vision of the world ceaselessly
connects with and disconnects from the other characters',
but collides seriously with the tough-minded ideas of
Lopakhin and Trofimov. This collision of three forces is the
axis of Efros's stage interpretation of *The Cherry Orchard*'s
sub-text.

Let us now consider how Efros treats the same scenes as
we have detailed for Strehler. At the beginning of Act I,
Ranevskaya comes running in, an elegant dancer incarnating
a refined Parisian who has lost all traces of her Russian
origins and education. Efros de-Russianises her to point
out that she returns as a foreigner to a strange land.
Ranevskaya's past and present are completely severed, a
fact made clear by the way she countlessly repeats 'my
little cupboard' (which is not on stage) in different tones
and inflections, which establish the numerous levels at
which she thinks and feels throughout the performance.
(Efros occasionally extends Chekhov's text by the repetition of a key phrase.) Not that Ranevskaya has forgotten
past sorrow. It is all too alive in her nervous, restless
activity; and the gravestones on the mound are a constant
reminder to the audience of its pressure.

Ranevskaya's past as such is not stressed. In this production it is the consequences of past that matter. Her
vivacious behaviour tips and tilts continually, to show that
it is a symptom of various anxieties. Her rejection of
Lopakhin's advice, which he offers almost as soon as she
arrives, stems from her inability to grasp social and
economic phenomena, least of all in their significance for
Russia, from which she has been absent too long. Just as
important, her refusal comes from a desire not to hear what
she is told. Attractive and well-meaning, Ranevskaya is
also a broken woman.

The precise dimensions of Ranevskaya's condition are
measured in relation to Trofimov and Lopakhin, who love and
wish to help her. By the time the nursery scene is over,
Lopakhin emerges as a morally solid, sensible man who is as
sensitive to personal issues as he is conscious of social
ones. Later in Act II, when Lopakhin exhorts Ranevskaya,
once again, to build dachas, his genuine concern for her is
paralleled by his interest in Russia's present and future
development. But his attitudes to Ranevskaya and Russia are
controlled by the actor, the scene and the entire production
so as to prevent any deterioration of his image into a
simplification or even a caricature of love or ethics,
capitalism or politics.

Similar processes of complexity and control are at work in
the creation of Trofimov. One crucial example is Trofimov's
long speech on Russia, shortly after the dialogue between
Lopakhin and Ranevskaya in Act II (alluded to above). As
Trofimov delivers his speech, he moves right up to the foot-
lights and addresses the audience. The actor's workmanship
is extremely fine. Zolotukhin presents Trofimov as being
worthy of respect and worth hearing, but at the same time
detaches himself just enough not to appear to be over-valu-
ing him; he specifies the problems of Trofimov's society
and, through his position, posture, gestures and voice, has
the audience understand that he is asking it questions about
its world even as he asks what it thinks of Trofimov's.
Between them, though with Ranevskaya as the essential
intermediary factor, Lopakhin and Trofimov synthesise the
production's argument, close an epoch and open onto Soviet
Russia.

V: Miquel's *Uncle Vanya*

Historical specification and, therefore, Russia too are
eliminated altogether in *Uncle Vanya*. Miquel says of his
approach to Chekhov: 'It is not only a given type of society
which is called into question, but each and every society.
It is not only a given type of social individual who is
called into question, but each and every individual.'[13]
And of his view of *Uncle Vanya*'s characters: 'their
historico-politico-social situation is of little consequence
in their painful and ironic search' - that is, in their
search for how to relate to themselves, let alone to each
other.[14] Miquel's adaptation of three extant French translations shows, as does his production, a deliberate and
assiduous de-Russianisation whose aim is a number of universal statements. When they are materialised in the language,
attitude and behaviour of characters, these statements are
to bring Chekhov closer to a French audience, making him
directly accessible and explicitly modern at one and the
same time. Miquel's conviction that Chekhov cannot be read
today without our thinking of writers from Fitzgerald to
Pinter, is the motor force of an *Uncle Vanya* treated as the
internal, lonely odyssey of isolated psyches.[15]
Miquel makes about eighty deletions in his adaptation of
Chekhov's text. These concern directions for scenic settings
and interior decoration, props (samovars, for example),
emotion and behaviour (tears, embraces, intonations, hands
hiding faces, manner and place of entrances and exits) and

sound-effects (for instance, a watchman knocking and then calling at the end of Act II). Miquel completely deletes patronymics and surnames (which in Chekhov introduce important social and psychological nuances) and reduces the use of Christian names. He removes names of villages, remote towns and provinces and other socio-national and geographical references (for instance, izbas, kulaks – translated simply as 'peasants' – and government inspectors) or cultural allusions (Astrov on Turgenev, Act IV), all of which locate the play's themes and narrative. Proverbs, jargon, vernacular expressions and other indications of locale are removed or, as in the case of slang, translated into racy, modern French.

Suppression of details Miquel calls 'picturesque' or 'folklorical' is absolutely essential for his denuded, ideogrammatical stage. Of greater importance still to his thematic configuration are the cuts, extensive at times, to speeches carrying 'historico-politico-social' weight. This is of course consistent with his de-Russianising in the cause of universalisation. Meanwhile, the 'social individual' recedes considerably as the existential individual replaces him. One revealing example is when Elena speaks to Sonia about Astrov (Act II). She says 'a man of talent' where Chekhov's text has 'a man of talent in Russia', and then leaves out details relevant to the nature of Astrov's medical work as well as its difficulties (the enormous distances, the peasants' brutishness and backwardness). Shortly before, Astrov speaks of poor conditions in 'this provincial life', but the qualifying phrase in Chekhov (which describes it as Russian and evaluates it as such acerbically and for a number of precise reasons) is suppressed, as are Astrov's scathing remarks on Russian intellectuals.

Nowhere are Miquel's universal-existential motivations more evident and more consequential than in his cuts to Astrov's speeches, particularly in Acts III and IV. Deletions (or, in some cases, changes) are of an informational, analytical and critical kind: those in which Astrov talks about disease, illiteracy and starvation, the decimation of villages, the destruction of the natural environment and its ecological repercussions, how and why these numerous forms of deterioration occur and what should be done about them. Astrov's most important exhortations to Vanya's household on the need to work and be socially constructive instead of passive and narcissistic are deleted, as are his major criticisms of himself in the same context. The scientist and social reformer in Astrov are given restricted play and meaning by Miquel's reformulation of him.

Astrov, in Miquel's production, is first and foremost a
philosopher who has abandoned his usually energetic participation in the material world at large and now contemplates
it from within the warmth of Vanya's household. The smaller,
domestic world, whose pleasures penetrate him, is none the
less an object of contemplation, lazy irony or mockery and
is also inscribed in his meditation on how 'Life sucks one
in' (Act I). Each character, from a seductive, languorous
Yelena, a pampered Serebryakov and a misguided Vanya, to a
Sonya on whom all burdens fall, glides into this life as if
into the sand, mud and marshes evoked by the characters'
words and existing beyond their house. For this life, the
image is sand beneath a long, low footbridge leading to the
back of the stage, where it forks out in two opposite
directions and disappears into the wings.

Despite the dialogue between them, the actors, who move in
and out of their characters, now to portray them (realism),
now to estrange them (theatricality), utter words that be-
long, rather, to solitary meditation (Astrov, Vanya, Sonya)
or egoistical monologue (Yelena, Serebryakov, Mariya), each
of which is of a different tonality but adds to the all-
pervasive poignancy of the whole. Silence is used to shape
solitude; piano fragments of Rachmaninov to intensify it; a
slow acting tempo to fix it in language and space.

The stage's luminous quality creates an atmosphere for
reflection and/or self-absorption. Light projected upwards
from beneath the back of the stage illuminates more often
than not the white back wall and a tall poplar at the inter-
section of the three footbridges, which casts its shadow on
the wall. Another poplar just upstage of centre stage-right
is in shadows. Oblique lighting on the horizontal and
vertical lines governing the stage (marked by the bridges
and trees) is used - especially during Acts II and IV - to
create a subtle interchange between areas of light and
shade. Contrast of this kind physically translates the
internal climate of Astrov, Sonya and Vanya, whose transit-
ions into darkness are seemingly imperceptible but none the
less real, or surge out into violence, as happens with Vanya
at the end of Act III. Vanya's attack on Serebryakov is
treated, however, in a comic, near-farcical vein to juxta-
pose his habitual introspection with his sudden mobilisation
of himself into action, for which he is shown to be singu-
larly untalented.

Light and space are principles of isolation. Act I opens
onto the architectural sparseness and simplicity described
above. A deep brown desk is placed towards the front of the
stage, but at some distance from the foot of the bridge
behind it. Three brown chairs are separated from each other

and from Vanya sleeping in a chaise-longue in a strip of
light near the darkened poplar. Later on Yelena,
Serebryakov, Sonya and Telegin enter, walk at a distance
from each other at a leisurely pace and are photographically
stilled. Yelena stands alone, her body to the audience, her
head to the wings, from which she has just appeared; Sonya
stands closer to Serebryakov. Both are nearer to the inter-
section and Telegin, who is slightly to its other side.
Their backs are to the audience. These three characters are
in shadow, while Yelena, also in white, is in a patch of
light. She sways in her approach to the audience along the
central path, as she will do afterwards when she talks with
Astrov or is kissed by him in Act III, in a scene which
shows to its maximum her curious indifference and her ambiguous sensuality arising out of boredom, but verging on
androgyny. Yelena frequently sits away from the others, with
her legs crossed and a cigarette in her hand.

At the beginning of Act II, when Serebryakov is ill and a
storm breaks, the back wall shows white clouds. The poplar
appears dark, mysterious in its isolation. Another image at
front of stage is superimposed onto the surrealistic image
held at the back: the absurd vision of Serebryakov, who
could have stepped out of Molière's *Malade imaginaire*. As
Yelena, Sonya and Vanya enter successively, they brush past
each other, but do not take position in direct relation to
each other. The actors move as in a dream-sequence and in a
low muted light against which their candles flicker, deepen-
ing the shadows of the props used for Act I and now
rearranged to draw in space.

Narrowed or not, however, space does not provide a line of
communication between the characters. Sonya alone makes the
effort to penetrate the other characters' solipsism during
this act and the rest of the play. Her delicate efforts are
like an invisible thread binding the production together.
Her gentle warmth gradually and consistently unites it,
while every other theatrical principle in it accentuates
dislocation. At the end of Act IV, when Vanya and Sonya sit
down at the desk to work on their accounts, Sonya's quiet,
calm voice envelops the scene. A candle illuminates her face
as she systematically works through the accounts, her carefully measured silences in counterpoint with her words and
Vanya's reading of figures. It continues to shine on her
face as she gazes at an indeterminate point between the
wings and the audience and slowly, movingly recites the poem
which ends the performance. Sonya's soliloquy hangs strangely in the air, like the map of Africa, which hangs unseen by
the characters during the act and symbolises a familiar yet
unknown continent, an everywhere and a nowhere in one and

the same instant.

Françoise Bette's remarkable Sonya, who is poised between fragility and endurance, limpidity and grief, emerges as an indirect commentary on Astrov on the one hand (played with haunting diffidence by Miquel himself) and Vanya on the other (Henri Virlogeux's performance is a combination of humour, petulance and nostalgia). Where the two men's love for Yelena is shown to be nurtured by the loneliness, elusiveness and frustration of existence, Sonya's love for Astrov is shown to grow from a desire to take a hold on existence. Like theirs, her love is out of reach. Unlike Astrov and Vanya, who are presented as imagining love or toying with the idea of it, Sonya loves, is locked in by love, and through this very fact is confined to a solitude greater than any other in this *Uncle Vanya*.

VI

I shall not attempt here to move beyond analysis of the semiotic organisation of the productions discussed and fully enter into a sociological explanation for that very organisation of interwoven semiotic levels: the actors' bodies; phonetic, rhythmic and semantic properties of language; the meaning of words; sets and objects; music, light and, of course, acting space, which is not an abstraction - space *per se* - but a particular and concrete phenomenon formed by the relation of acting methods to the placing of objects and the play of light.

My synopsis of each production's organisation indicates some explanatory elements of a sociological order, though only within the framework of cultural formations. What I have called Miquel's principles of isolation and dislocation, for instance, take their full significance from Existentialism, France's cultural product, whatever may have been its ramifications abroad or, for that matter, its subsequent transformations in France in the last decade.

My introduction referred to contemporary directors' search for stage uniqueness; to the difficulty, also, of this task given the existence of theatrical tradition (the history of theatre) and the exigencies of a social present which performances must mediate if they are (a) to have an audience, and (b) to contribute to the processes of history (theatrical history included). I should like to state, now, that the productions discussed presuppose an important, and necessary, principle: that there is no such thing as one text, *the* text, Chekhov's or any other writer's; there is, instead, a new text, created by the production itself, in terms of which the production is to be viewed, understood and analysed - which, in short, is to be read as a text in its own right.

This principle contains, at its very heart, an inescapable problem, that of the respect to be shown to the written text (as distinct from the performance as text) which the director uses as his starting-point. For Pintilié, Strehler, Miquel and Efros, however, 'respect' for Chekhov does not mean reconstructing Chekhov as if he were still being performed in his own time. It means capturing from the viewpoint of today those components in Chekhov which give access to history - that is, to the socio-historical conditions in which Chekhov's texts were produced and from which they derived their meaning. Simultaneously, it means opening a road into the history of the present, into the different socio-historical conditions in which the performance is to be received and, indeed, has its own genesis. It is this last, the present socio-historical nexus, which is accentuated by each of our directors - rightly, moreover, for otherwise theatre performances would be museum-pieces.

This said, we must still take into account another factor related to the problem of showing 'respect' for Chekhov when the production is 'a text in its own right'. We have seen that each director approaches Chekhov on the assumption that what is taken from Chekhov for metamorphosis, through the semiotic system particular to each production, is none the less substantially true to Chekhov, *is* Chekhov, and not, say, Molière. The de-Russianising processes we have noticed to a lesser or greater degree in each production also testify to the assumption that a 'Chekhovian' particularity exists, which is not dismantled but, rather, is validated by a reading from within the social codes specific to the genesis of the performance. These codes are themselves mediated by all the semiotic levels of each production.

NOTES

1. Cited in the journal of the Théâtre de la Ville, Paris, Nov. 1978. Pintilié used this phrase for all Chekhov play-texts, his presentation of *The Seagull* (Théâtre de la Ville, 1975/6) and for his objectives in general, to which he feels Chekhov (along with Gorky) gives him the best access. All translations in this paper are my own.
2. Presented at the Théâtre de la Ville, Paris; French version by Marie-France Ionesco and Lucian Pintilié;

director, Lucian Pintilié; design, Radu and Misuna
Boruzescu; music, Costin Mieseanu; assistant director,
Alain Tartas. With Nelly Borgeaud, *Olga*; Sabine
Haudepin, *Irina*; Marthe Keller, *Masha*; Étienne Bierry,
Chebutykin; Maxime Dufeu, *Tusenbach*; Rémy Carpentier,
Soliony; Dominique Marcas, *Anfisa*; Rellys, *Ferapont*;
Michel Auclair, *Vershinin*; Roland Bertin, *Prozorov*;
Georges Wod, *Kulyghin*; Julian Negulesco, *Fedotik*; Luc
Florian, *Rodé*; Nathalie Baye, *Natasha*.

3. Presented at the Théâtre de l'Odéon, Paris; French
version by Jean-Pierre Miquel; director, Jean-Pierre
Miquel; design, Henri Oechslin; costumes, Dominique
Borg; assistant to the director, Pierre Romans. With
Denise Noel, *Marina*; Jean-Pierre Miquel, *Astrov*; Henri
Virlogeux, *Vanya*; Hubert Gignoux, *Serebriakov*; Xavier
Bouvier, *Teleghin*; Nicole Garcia, *Elena*; Marcelle
Arnold, *Maria*; Françoise Bette, *Sonia*; Daniel Roman, *a
servant*.

4. Miquel's note to his adaptation of *Uncle Vanya*, in the
programme book of the Centre Dramatique de Reims (1979)
p. 32.

5. *Per un teatro umano* (Milan, 1974) p. 269.

6. Presented at the Théâtre de l'Odéon, Paris; Italian ver-
sion by Luigi Lunari and Giorgio Strehler; director,
Giorgio Strehler; design, Luciano Damiani; music,
Fiorenzo Carpi. With Valentina Cortese, *Ranevskaya*;
Monica Guerritore, *Anya*; Giulia Lazzarini, *Varya*; Gianni
Santuccio, *Gaev*; Franco Graziosi, *Lopakhin*; Piero
Sammatro, *Trofimov*; Enzo Tarascio, *Pishtchik*; Claudia
Lawrence, *Charlotta*; Gianfranco Mauri, *Epikhodov*; Marisa
Minelli, *Dunyasha*; Renzo Ricci, *Firs*; Cip Barcellini,
Yasha; Vladimir Nikolaev, *tramp*; Armando Benetti, *guest*.

7. The Russian sense of the word 'realism' has, in France,
come increasingly to be attached to the term 'naturalism', which also bears the pejorative sense outlined at
the beginning of section II of this paper. The interchangeability of the terms 'realism' and 'naturalism'
and, therefore, the ambiguity in France of 'naturalism'
can be traced back first to Zola, and then to Antoine.
Contemporary Soviet Russian directors make a clear
distinction between 'realism' and 'naturalism', which
they see as a vulgarisation and degradation of the
former.

8. Marthe Keller's performance has moments of powerful
beauty which, unfortunately, do not square with her and
other performers' melodramatic scenes. This is all the
moreunfortunate in that Marthe Keller, who principally
works in the cinema, is an actress of no mean talent.

9. Chekhov wrote *The Cherry Orchard* between 1901 and 1903. It was produced by Stanislavsky and Nemirovich-Danchenko at the Moscow Art Theatre in January 1904.

10. *Per un teatro umano*, p. 260.

11. Ibid., p. 261.

12. Presented at the Taganka Theatre, Moscow; director, Anatoly Efros; chief artistic director of the theatre, Yury Lyubimov; decor and costumes, Valery Leventhal; music, G. Pyatigorsky. With A. Demidova, *Ranevskaya*; N. Cub, *Anya*; T. Zhukova, *Varya*; V. Sternberg, *Gayev;* V. Visotsky, *Lopakhin*; V. Zolotukhin, *Trofimov*; F. Antipov, *Pishchik*; M. Politseymako, *Charlotta*; R. Dzhabrailov, *Yepikhodov*; T. Sidorenko, *Dunyasha*; G. Roninson, *Firs*; V. Sulyakovsky, *Yasha*; V. Korolev, *tramp*.

13. *Uncle Vanya* programme note, p. 32.

14. Ibid., p. 31.

15. Ibid., p. 32, for Miquel's references to Fitzgerald and Pinter.

5 Splinters of a Shattered Mirror: Experimentation and Innovation in Contemporary Soviet Theatre

KYLE WILSON

Vsevolod Meyerhold gave his last public speech at the first all-Union conference of theatre-directors in Moscow on 15 June 1939. This conference was a final step in a campaign to establish as complete a control over the theatre as possible. Meyerhold was the one remaining recalcitrant obstinately refusing to conform to the new aesthetics of 'socialist realism'. There is disagreement about the content of his speech: some say that it was suicidally courageous; others that, in fact, Meyerhold, like his pupil Eisenstein before him, recanted, and passed from the scene, absolutely broken in spirit. What we now know of this period, the late thirties, makes the second version far more probable: there was no glorious defiance. However, there is evidence to show that in his creative work he remained an unrepentant radical, spurning the new doctrine of socialist realism: his final production, *A Life*, an adaptation of an early classic of the New Art, *How the Steel was Tempered*, was suppressed before final rehearsal, and was not even mentioned in the Soviet press until the seventies; but eyewitnesses confirm that it was utterly heretical. As a consequence, Meyerhold's reputation as fiery opponent of all old forms, passionate advocate of new ones, as feverish experimenter and innovator, remains unblemished. As such is he remembered today.

Meyerhold's name was hardly ever mentioned in the Soviet press until after Stalin's death. (It did make an appearance in official publications during the notorious 'anti-cosmopolitanism' campaign of 1948, where it was synonymous with all that is undesirable in art.) However, many of his actors

99

and students survived Stalinism: Garin and Martinson, who
played Khlestakov in his *Revizor*; Ilinsky, the original lead
in *The Bedbug* and *The Magnificent Cuckold*; and, among directors, Ruben Simonov, who continued to work at the Vakhtangov
Theatre while Okhlopkov took over one of Meyerhold's old
theatres, renamed in honour of Mayakovsky. Boris Ravenskikh,
who still directs at the Maly Theatre, was a student of
Meyerhold, though his productions seldom give any indication
of this. So, while the man was destroyed, his image could
not be obliterated from people's minds, and throughout the
dark ages of Stalin's later career, when Soviet theatre
reached its nadir of pious conformity to official strictures, Meyerholdian techniques actually continued to be used
in productions. Alexander Galich relates that students at
the Vakhtangov acting-school mounted a production using
Meyerhold's ideas and devices in 1940: unfortunately, this
was an example of *Meyerkhol'dovshchina*, 'Meyerholditis', the
indiscriminate application of his ideas to socialist-
realist material, and the audience was bewildered and indig-
nant when a Greek chorus, Japanese Noh masks and *commedia
dell'arte* were used in a play about record-breaking production on a Communist Youth building-project.[1]

Nikolay Okhlopkov, one of the most radical talents of the
thirties, survived into the seventies, but only at the price
of his artistic originality. Herbert Marshall relates how he
encountered Okhlopkov in the late fifties.

> He was heartbroken. I could see that there was no soul
> left. He'd achieved all his great things in the Golden
> Days of the thirties. Now he'd become a member of the
> Supreme Soviet, a Hero of Socialist Labour, loaded with
> honours, but the heart had gone out of him.[2]

In 1956 Meyerhold was, to use the eerie Soviet euphemism,
'posthumously rehabilitated'. The choice of this particular
term is significant, for it implies not that the victim was
innocent, but that the sentence was perhaps excessive, an
unfortunate consequence of the cult of personality, for
which the Party should not be held responsible. Nor does
rehabilitation imply exoneration, the return of a prodigal
son. For there was that in Meyerhold's art which causes
Soviet critics even today to treat him gingerly. The most
notable thing about Meyerhold's productions is that they
were all startlingly innovative: his ideas were always in
flux, his art regularly and radically renewed itself. His
theatrical credo, with its key tenet of continuous change,
of an endless quest for new and better forms, smacks dis-
tastefully of Trotskyism. The two words most commonly

associated with his theatre, *uslovnost'* (or stylisation) and *eksperimental'nost'*, had, by 1956, acquired a distinctly pejorative connotation, for both are interpreted as heresy against that new artistic truth first revealed by Zhdanov in 1934, socialist realism. According to this doctrine, the true functions of any work of art are to instruct, to inculcate the ideological creed of Marxism—Leninism, and to glorify it together with its prophets, founders, interpreters and repositories. Again, the point is that Truth has been revealed – therefore any new interpretations are automatically heretical and will be persecuted as such. As a Russian proverb has it, *pravda odna* – there is but one truth. This truth is based on a dogmatically materialist view of reality: any work of art that expresses, in no matter how cryptic a form, the idea that phenomenal reality is not all, any reinterpretation of reality on non-materialist principles, is rightly perceived as sedition: not only was Meyerhold's constant experimentation Trotskyist, but his stylisation and grotesquerie were perversions of the truth. He who is not with us is against us, any experiment is counter-revolution, and so he had to go. It is paradoxical that only under totalitarian regimes is the theatre given its full due, its great power recognised. We have no such martyrs in our theatres in the West.

Meyerhold's rehabilitation was a concomitant of the post-Stalinist reforms instituted by Khrushchev. Limited and cautious as they were, their significance cannot be over-emphasised, for they initiated a process of schism and liberalisation that has become the key characteristic of the development of the arts in the Soviet Union today. Despite reactions against this process, in 1956 and again in 1964, there can be no retracing of steps: the gains that have been made could be nullified only by the most extreme measures; and the consequent erosion of the dogma of socialist realism has gone so far as to render the term meaningless in much of actual practice. None the less, officially the doctrine remains sacrosanct, and, though its boundaries are crossed with great caution, no one will risk a frontal attack; a certain lip-service is paid to terminology in an attempt to camouflage innovation. When asked if his highly unorthodox production of Ibsen's *Brand* conformed to the tenets of socialist realism, the director of the Rainis Theatre in Riga, Arnold Liniņš, replied: 'Everything is socialist realism, so long as it is called socialist realism.'

One might have surmised that with the resurrection of their leader and in the conditions of new liberalism in the theatre, Meyerhold's actors and students would attempt to salvage his theatrical methods and ideas. Alas, chastened by

their experience of Stalinism, most have turned their backs
on him to become pillars of the theatrical establishment,
members of a tenured elite with exclusive rights to choice
roles in those very museums of embalmed culture they once
despised. It is paradoxical that Igor Ilinsky, once Meyerhold's leading actor, has directed and starred in a production of Ostrovsky's *The Forest* at the Maly Theatre which
represented the absolute antithesis of Meyerhold's. The set
would have been considered conservative in 1900, there was a
Stanislavskian score of crickets, woodpeckers and babbling
brooks, and so orthodox was the production that it was
awarded a state prize. (It is possible, however, that
Ilinsky - whose guile is attested by his very survival and
chameleon-like ability to adapt to circumstances - outrage-
ously parodied the ossified Maly style. If so, the deception
was audacious, but of considerable subtlety. Further, in
his interpretation of Shchastlivtsev, Ostrovsky's mournful
and downtrodden wandering actor (with a highly developed
instinct for survival: the parallels become increasingly
ironic), Ilinsky appeared to quote, mimetically, the biomechanics of Meyerhold's production of the same play.)
    Others of Meyerhold's supporters had remained faithful,
and in 1961 they began to publish the materials they had
collected: Ernst Garin, in his reminiscences, included
detailed descriptions of Meyerhold's teaching-methods, and
of the productions of *Woe to Wit* and *The Government
Inspector*. A. Gladkov and A. V. Fevral'ski produced detailed
material on other productions, including the revolutionary
constructivist production *The Magnificent Cuckold*. This sal-
vaging process reached its climax in 1968 with the publication in two volumes of Meyerhold's collected letters, speeches and, most important, theoretical writings. Meanwhile,
directors were among those enjoying one of the great gains
of the reforms, the reappearance in print of suppressed
Russian writers and access to some of the most innovative
twentieth-century Western writers: Babel', Bulgakov,
Platonov, Mandel'shtam, Tsvetaeva and Bunin were rehabilitated; long-banned Western writers were published in translation - Faulkner, O'Neill, Albee, Brecht, even Ionesco. And
for the first time there appeared in Moscow some of the best
European and American theatres: directors could now see the
fruits of their own transplanted Russian tradition, and
some of the best of them - Lyubimov, Efros, Yefremov,
Tovstonogov - freely admit their debt to Peter Brook, Jean
Vilar, Roget Planchon and to Giorgio Strehler. These developments combined to fertilise, enrich and stimulate the
regeneration of Soviet theatre that began with Khrushchev's
de-Stalinisation.

The revival moved in three main directions, in direct
parallel to developments in prose: the repertoire changed
drastically – in particular, many Western playwrights came
to be represented; dramatists began to examine social
conditions more critically, to hint at the contradictions
between the official view and their perceptions, and to re-
evaluate the events of the immediate past (*pereotsenka
proshlogo*). This new direction in writing has been slotted
into the doctrinal system as 'critical' realism, i.e. as a
variant of socialist realism. Finally, in the area of form,
of production style, non-realistic devices began to appear,
while stage-designers initiated a new, richly metaphoric and
expressionist style recently labelled 'grotesque realism'.
It is this experimentation, this tentative search for new
forms, that is implied by the metaphoric formulation 'the
Meyerhold tradition'. This brand name is used cautiously,
generally in private conversation by a small group of directors, designers and critics which represents the liberal
camp in the theatre and which is characterised by an ambition to increase the variety and depth of Soviet theatre
through free experimentation, access to all possible
creative influences and, above all, by the use of non-
realistic means of expression. One perceives a furtive note
in their use of Meyerhold's name, for the ostensible ideological monopoly of Party doctrine remains; in this pantheon
you will find Stanislavsky and Nemirovich-Danchenko (for it
is their 'psychological realism' that alone among the
various approaches of the 1920s found favour with the Party
– largely because of its accordance with the tenets of
Leninist materialist philosophy – and which is still
jealously preserved and constantly eulogised as the only
valid theatrical style). In this pantheon one finds, by a
strange quirk of fate – namely, Stalin's espousal of him –
the poet and playwright Mayakovsky; but no Meyerhold. Moreover, the conservative camp of critics remains in unchal-
lenged ascendancy, and they are vigilant, always ready to
raise the spectre of 'modernism'. 'Meyerholdian' is a word
that remains synonymous with 'modernism', with 'formalism',
and, according to the inverted logic of Soviet word-usage,
whereby synonyms have an ability to become antonyms,
'modernism' is 'decadence' or 'revisionism' (the Soviet
writer Vassily Aksenov has coined a useful term for this,
'terminological switching'; Orwell's 'Doublethink' is
perhaps more apt). If there is to be progress, then the
advance must be cautious if a conservative counter-reaction
is to be avoided.

So the term does not imply a sudden regeneration of form
on the model of Meyerhold, but it does imply the same thing

on a very small and limited scale, a process of recovery and
rejuvenation through experimentation and innovation that is
at least proceeding. Nowhere in the Soviet Union will you
find a theatre to match this description taken from the
Moscow Theatre Almanac of 1935:

> The theatre is avant-garde and experimental. In con-
> structing his productions, the director strives for the
> utmost precision, rigorousness and logicality of form
> deriving directly from the profound ideas latent in the
> text. Thus, in its most brilliant and characteristic
> productions, the theatre endeavours to manifest its maxi-
> mum expressive force in a combination of text, gesture,
> music, sound, objects and light. Every character has his
> own particular rhythm of movement, every gesture and every
> word is carefully considered and stands in its exact
> place in relation to the whole. Every movement has its own
> motivation, linked with the overall conception of the
> play, every figure has his own rhythmical image. The
> theatre demands of its actors great precision, clarity and
> expressiveness of movement, a complete conscious mastery
> of body and voice in its efforts to sway and convince the
> public.
>
> (*Teatral'naya Moskva*, 1935)

Thus Meyerhold's theatre described by an obviously well-
intentioned critic in 1935. To find a theatre with a similar
credo, which consistently creates productions comparable in
richness of style with Meyerhold's *The Government Inspector*,
The Forest or *The Magnificent Cuckold*, one must look to the
Germany of Peter Stein, to Brook and Strehler (both of whom
have had productions mounted in Moscow), to Patrice Chéreau
or to the modern Polish masters. For in the Soviet Union no
such theatre is possible at present. The paternalistic concern of the multifarious organs of state control of the arts
about what is suitable for Soviet audiences and their high
level of efficiency in ensuring that their 'advice' is
followed guarantees that innovation, experimentation and the
methods of theatrical expression that smack of non-Marxist-
Leninist, heretical interpretations of reality are kept to a
minimum. The farcical plots of the forties and early fifties
of the girl-meets-tractor type have largely disappeared, but
the majority of Soviet plays are still concerned with
problems of production, and the archetypal plot still
centres on some corrupt villain in academia or industry
whose machinations wreck the career and love-life of the
hero, a dedicated young scientist or engineer of flawless
ideological orientation, until the local Party secretary,

alerted by a faithful elder colleague of the hero, arrives in time to set all wrongs right. There has appeared since 1956 a small number of talented and daring dramatists (Volodin, Rozov, Kazantsev, Shukshin), and at long last the anti-hero has appeared, treading the boards of the Moscow Arts Theatre in 1979 in Aleksandr Vampilov's *The Duck Hunt* - but the key point about Soviet dramaturgy is that, unlike poetry, no experimentation with non-realistic devices will be countenanced by the censorship; all plays, no matter what their content, must be firmly keyed into the realistic mode. It is for this reason that those productions which do bear comparison with those of the above-mentioned European directors - and they have begun to appear - are almost invariably of pre-Revolution Russian classics such as Gogol or Dostoyevsky, or of foreign plays. Even these may not escape the concerned attention of conservative critics and cultural watchdogs, as Anatoly Efros's career shows.

To summarise: a small number of directors are cautiously experimenting with form, and they are held to be the representatives of a reappearing 'Meyerhold tradition'. In its broadest sense this formulation is a metaphor for any experimentation, any challenge to official dictates on style; in its narrowest, the use of forms of theatrical expression reminiscent of those of Meyerhold, Tairov, Eisenstein and Okhlopkov. These directors' success represents a limited victory for the liberals in the divided camp of Soviet theatre and bears witness to a cautious liberalisation.

The establishment in Moscow in 1963 of the Theatre on the Taganka under Yury Lyubimov and, more, its survival through sixteen years of constant controversy and attacks by conservative critics is the most striking indicator of a new direction. Some informants date the onset a year earlier, when Georgiy Tovstonogov astounded audiences in Leningrad with his highly stylised and 'publicistic' (i.e. inference-loaded) production of the most venerable of Russian classics, Griboyedov's *Woe from Wit*. The production began with the cast introducing themselves - a device which has since become a cliché, but remains effectively non-socialist -realist. Throughout the action the hero Chatsky would repeatedly address his lines to the audience, particularly when a parallel could be drawn between the text and contemporary social problems. A famous example, 'molchaniye blazhenstvuet na svete' ('Secure is he who keeps his mouth shut') was actually shouted into the auditorium. By thus emphasising certain textual ideas and by reintroducing long-proscribed devices, such as endowing objects with overt symbolic values, Tovstonogov was appealing for reform, for a more flexible official attitude to art. In general, however,

he is not considered a radical innovator, but, rather, by
far the best of that smaller number of directors who
restrict themselves largely to a traditional, realist
approach and yet constantly produce theatre of remarkable
quality. Tovstonogov's productions bear comparison with
those of any theatre of similar approach in the West.

Lyubimov is not a realist, illusionist director. He is
in fact a theatrical heretic and the survival of his theatre
appears at first glance the great enigma of Moscow theatre
life. When asked by a Western correspondent his opinion of
the Taganka, the Minister for Culture, Demichev, replied
testily, 'The Taganka is not a *Soviet* theatre.' A constant
line of attack by conservative critics focuses on Lyubimov's
apparent contempt for the work of Soviet dramatists, for
among the twenty-two productions in his current repertoire, not one is the work of a Soviet playwright. Of those
that have disappeared from the repertoire, one was by
Yevtushenko, another by Brecht, another an adaptation of
Lermontov's *A Hero of Our Time*. Of the numerous works for
which permission for production was refused, again not one
was a Soviet play. This situation is absolutely unique – it
is the stated policy of the Soviet Ministry of Culture that
at least 30 per cent of any theatre's repertoire must consist of works by Soviet dramatists. Here, a particularly
vicious attack on Meyerhold published in *Pravda* on 17
December 1938 is relevant:

> The situation in Meyerhold's theatre regarding plays by
> Soviet dramatists is lamentable: not only has not a
> single Soviet play remained in the repertoire, but none of
> those he has produced has been taken up by other Soviet
> theatres. In other words, Meyerhold's work with Soviet
> playwrights has been fruitless. In all its long career the
> theatre has not presented a single play that has entered
> the Soviet repertoire. Obviously Meyerhold cannot and does
> not even want to understand Soviet reality, to portray
> those problems which concern all Soviet citizens, and he
> refuses to join the ranks of the workers in Soviet art.
> Repeatedly, when confronted with these criticisms Meyer-
> hold has replied 'There are no suitable Soviet plays' or
> 'but our theatre is not suited to the staging of these
> plays'. Thus this theatre, ignoring the Soviet themes, and
> the method of realism, which is the road of development of
> all truly Soviet art, has isolated itself from Soviet
> drama and the Soviet public.

This could equally well apply to Lyubimov's Taganka Theatre,
75 per cent of the repertoire of which consists of stage

adaptations of prose works. Of these, only two are of works praised as models of Soviet socialist realism. Further, only one production of a Russian classic is currently (1979) in repertoire and this is by a guest director (I refer to Efros's *Cherry Orchard*). Finally, it is Lyubimov who, after four years of stubborn campaigning and lobbying, managed to obtain permission to present a stage adaptation of Bulgakov's novel *The Master and Margarita*, which is the very antithesis of socialist realism. Lyubimov's method is to take a work of literature, almost always one which has been criticised by the literary establishment as 'problematical' or 'complex' - these being euphemisms for 'ideologically suspect' - and to stage it in fast-moving, graphic style, using all manner of non-realist devices. The acting-style is avowedly non-Stanislavskian, more like that known as Brechtian, in which actors appear to 'play themselves', or at least repeatedly step out of character to address the audience. And not only is form non-realist: as Meyerhold did, Lyubimov tends to style himself the author of his productions, the scripts of which he constantly alters, depending on the political climate, and he is a master of what is called Aesopian language, of criticism by hint, suggestion, parallel and inference. Moreover, his actors are in the habit of interpolating their own comments, often ingeniously inserting quotations from critical attacks on a production into that very production to lampoon the critic.

How can one account for the survival of a theatre in which a non-realist production method is used to satirise social conditions, and the policies of the Ministry of Culture are largely ignored? Some hold that patronage among the Party elite is the explanation, that in fact Brezhnev's children, enthusiastic supporters of the theatre, intercede on behalf of its delinquent director. There is probably some truth in this - certainly Lyubimov enjoyed a warm relationship with the previous Minister of Culture, Madame Furtseva, who was generally liked by theatre people; but a more probable explanation is that the Taganka is a *vitrina*, a piece of window-dressing of considerable propaganda value which can be paraded when Western critics raise a cry about lack of creative freedom and suppression of criticism. Further, the Taganka is also an example of a peculiarly Soviet phenomenon, the 'safety valve', a policy of permitting the small number of disaffected intellectuals to indulge their tastes while carefully ensuring that potentially pernicious works reach only a tiny minority of the public. Thus abstractionist painters are now regularly permitted to hold closed exhibitions, and modernist composers are less frequently allowed to play their unorthodox creations in the hall of

the Composers Union Building. The Taganka seats only 414 and
tickets are almost unobtainable for the average Muscovite.
Thus it fulfils its functions without exerting any corrupt-
ing influence on the masses. The boat is gently rocked with
one hand and steadied with the other: at least this is what
happens in theory. In practice, however, the influence of
the Taganka Theatre has been enormous, for at least three
generations of the directors who are seen as leading figures
in the emerging movement have served their apprenticeship
under Lyubimov; and, then, the Taganka continually establishes precedents which are proving particularly fecund.

One of the most talented, yet least known, of this new
rank of directors, is Pyotr Fomenko. Between 1966 and 1968
he worked with Lyubimov staging two productions based on
poetry-readings, both owing much to the style of Meyerhold's
and Mayakovsky's co-operation on *The Bathhouse* and *The
Bedbug*. Both productions, *The Living and the Dead* and *Listen
Here*, are daring in their satire and starkly simple in their
staging. Their satirical thrusts are aimed at bureaucrats,
moralists and above all at conservative critics. Fomenko's
next production was of Peter Weiss's *Die Ermittlung*, translated into Russian as *Doznaniye*. At the dress rehearsal
Furtseva told Lyubimov that performance was out of the
question. The reason is interesting. Weiss's play is based
on the Nuremburg trials. It examines the rise of Fascism in
Germany and the fascist outlook as it develops in individuals. Now, in the Soviet Union the transcripts of the
Nuremburg trials are held only in so-called *spetskhrany*,
'closed holdings', and are available only to trusted
researchers, perhaps because they are felt to contain too
many potentially embarrassing parallels. Soviet readers and
theatre-goers have a highly developed sensitivity to such
parallels, and moreover a tendency, strengthened by their
isolation, to relate all that is unfamiliar to their own
situation. And, experience has shown, dissident or critical
messages may increase in aesthetic power when perceived by
inference. Weiss's message that what occurred in Germany
could happen anywhere, and that every person has the seeds
of a fascist outlook in his nature, may be too close to the
bones of recent Soviet history.

Fomenko's staging was utterly unadorned and stark, shorn
of the elements of fantasy and improvisation which had
already become trademarks of the Taganka style. The text was
what mattered. The very small number of actors, clad in
sombre, nondescript dark suits, seldom moved, delivering
their lines without vivid expression or emphasis, without
mime, without gesture, occasionally exchanging roles, so
that a judge could become the accused, or *vice versa*:

according to informants, the significance of this was not
lost on the audience that saw the rehearsals – we are all
both victim and tormentor. As noted, Soviet audiences tend
to perceive even the plays of such as Shakespeare, Ibsen,
or indeed any other who is concerned with social problems,
in terms of their own, and the Taganka makes a habit of
exploiting this feature of its audience's character. In
Lyubimov's adaptation of Gorky's *The Mother*, two czarist
soldiers, symbols of oppression, remark, 'Russians only need
a little freedom. Too much is not good for them. Freedom
here must be kept within sensible limits.' In this context,
Fomenko's own remarks about his Weiss production are
intriguing:

Of course, one cannot equate our Soviet public with that
in Weiss's homeland. Nevertheless, cast your eyes around,
without hypocrisy or pharisaism and you will find un-
pleasant traits among our own people: petty bourgeois
materialism, gratuitous nastiness, unscrupulousness, big-
otry, a love of interfering and hostility to independent
thought and action, all of which is incompatible with
communist morality and humanity which characterises our
society. Such faults are not, of course, fascism, and
never will be; but focusing upon them, magnifying them is
the moral duty of every artist. My production is designed
to convince everyone of the need to be vigilant.

(From unpublished notes by Fomenko)

After the banning of his production, Fomenko left the
Taganka, a black mark against his name, and in the ten years
since has staged only a small number of productions in various theatres. Among the best have been *The Death of Tarelkin*
by Sukhovo-Kobylin – this, ironically in Meyerhold's old
theatre, now named after Mayakovsky; a highly stylised *Dead
Souls* at the Pushkin Theatre in Leningrad; and recently
Lyubov' Yarovaya, a Soviet classic of the twenties, in, of
all places, the very conservative, orthodox Maly Theatre in
Moscow. The choice of Fomenko to direct in this theatre is
symptomatic of recent attempts by the Ministry of Culture to
breathe some life into a theatrical waxworks. The *mise-en-
scene* was indeed stylised and unconventional, and certain
textual ideas were expressed by non-textual, plastic means.
That the production enjoys critical acclaim can only be
grounds for optimism.

In an article in *Theatre Quarterly* Spencer Golub points
out that the Taganka's theatrical style differs from Meyerhold's in one fundamental way: it tends to uniformity.[3]
Despite Lyubimov's efforts – and he struggled for four years

to obtain permission to stage two of his most recent productions, Bulgakov's *Master and Margarita* and Brecht's *Turandot* – and despite the periodic injection of new talent such as a set-designer of genius, David Borovsky, Lyubimov's productions tend to repeat each other, to the extent that *Master and Margarita* is largely a synthesis of much that has gone before, with many devices taken directly from previous productions. 'Very interesting, but we've seen so much of this before' is a frequent reaction to this production.

The inspiration of Anatoly Efros, however, remains vital, and, while he experiences more failures than Lyubimov, his finest productions are widely considered to be masterpieces. These tend, like Meyerhold's best, to be arresting re-interpretations of Russian classics. His *Three Sisters* is often described as the finest Chekhov production seen in Moscow since the days of Nemirovich-Danchenko. Efros's career has been punctuated by clashes with the conservative camp; on two occasions he has been dismissed from theatres for ideological errors, and so he has compromised, regularly staging model socialist-realist plays which even his talent cannot enliven. He remains a venturesome innovator who has studied Meyerhold's legacy assiduously, and occasionally borrows directly from him. His three finest current product-ions are *The Cherry Orchard*, Gogol's *Marriage* and Turgenev's *A Month in the Country*. Certain aspects of these productions are peculiarly Meyerholdian, some indeed springing directly from Meyerhold's scenographic lexicon.

A key feature of Meyerhold's method was to devise a sensationally original yet flexible set which was often itself metaphorical, or at least lent itself to the striking of vivid metaphors; and scenography is the one aspect of theatre art in which the Soviet theatre is second to none. As an example, Danil Lider's design for a recent production of *Arturo Ui*: Ui and his thugs crawl up from the sewers onto a metal platform, through manhole covers which later become tables and bar-stools. The set may also be used for *Macbeth*, in which case the forest of telegraph-poles, traffic lights and wires is cleared away, the witches emerge through the holes, the covers become shields. The rise of the set-designer to a position of equality with the director is a crucial feature of the new tradition. The importance of this 'plastic direction' as it is called is apparent in Valery Leventhal's partnership with Efros in *The Marriage*: the *mise-en-scène* centres on, and is informed by, the set.

The proscenium arch is cunningly covered with material so that it resembles an ancient picture-frame. Deep backstage this frame is duplicated in miniature. The audience is aware of rows of slats, or rather screens, flanking the stage,

coloured nondescript green, grey, blue. Herbert Marshall
relates just how important music and musical rhythms were
for Meyerhold – so they become for Efros. Against the dark
tones of the Orthodox liturgy, in low light, a portrait
group, the wedding-party, glides slowly out of the upstage
frame towards us. They are toylike, dolls, childlike –
their faces express quiet joy. The box set with its greens
suddenly becomes a church interior, an iconostasis. Abruptly, startlingly, a gong sounds, the screens reverse through
180 degrees, the cast turns and stares in silence at the
screens: they now depict a nineteenth-century street-scene
in Petersburg, with a number of running figures. The cast
stare mournfully at these figures and two key images have
been established and juxtaposed: the first, of what all hope
for; the others, of the shattering of their hopes. The
screens clatter back to their original position – the cast
disperses – the shutters have closed on hope. The gong and
the screens recall Meyerhold's gong and famous eleven doors
in his *Government Inspector.*

Invention of this high level occurs throughout: one of
the most interesting devices is that of the introduction of
a new character on the model of Khlestakov's double in
Meyerhold's *Government Inspector.* At three separate points
a huge, bearded and forbidding figure lurches onto the
stage, advances on a fear-struck Agafiya Tyukhanova, and
whips a grotesque outsized hand from behind his back, raising it above her as if about to strike. The other characters
do not ignore this apparition, but simply look on vacant-
eyed. The girl's fears of what marriage may bring are thus
startlingly embodied, the dramatic texture vividly enriched.

Efros's treatment of Turgenev's *A Month in the Country* is
almost as inspired as his *Marriage.* Richly detailed ensemble
acting, ingenious stage business, subtly controlled rhythms,
and unerring use of stage metaphors combine in a production
which goes far towards realising Efros's stated ambition of
combining the best of the opposed schools of Stanislavsky's
'authentic emotion' and Meyerhold's 'stylised representat-
ionalism'. The latter is most tellingly employed in the
finale. The heroine, Nataliya Petrovna, is alone on stage,
deserted, abandoned. Her self-delusion and egocentric
intriguing have alienated friends and lovers, who decamp in
Chekhovian fashion, leaving her, a wounded survivor on a
battlefield of the emotions, facing desolate middle-age.
Here Turgenev's text concludes, and precisely here Efros
manages a *coup de théâtre* by creating a huge pause. In place
of the traditional tranquil finale, suffused with a certain
elegaic, sweet sadness and resignation, Efros gives us the
crazed desperation of the heroine, her horror, her guilt,

her fear for the future. Soap-opera hysterics are avoided, because the role is played by Olga Yakovlevna, one of the best contemporary Soviet actresses. She leans against the proscenium arch, weeping convulsively; in the distance we hear Mozart's G Minor symphony, which has been used through-out to punctuate scenes. Abruptly this is interrupted by harsh grating and crashing sounds - stagehands have appeared and are dismantling Efros's acting-machine, the composite metal lacework arbour-*cum*-carousel which is the effectively symbolic set. Finally, one stagehand approaches the actress, who is spotlit, and takes from her grasp the kite she is clutching, the play's symbol for childish innocence, which she has destroyed. The carousel, the centre of the unreal frivolous world of illusion she has created, self-destructs before our eyes. The grating, muffled crashes immediately evoke the axes at work in Ranevskaya's cherry orchard. The disintegration of Natalia Petrovna's world of illusions is expressed by the dismantling of the theatrical illusion. In my view this experiment works, for theatre is an unpredict-able animal. Others doubtless find the device excessively contrived and obtrusive. The point is its daring; it is innovative, it is anti-traditional, and, in this broad sense, it is Meyerholdian.

Efros and Lyubimov are seen as the two vigorous talents wearing the mantle of Meyerhold and regenerating Soviet Russian theatre in Moscow. A young man called Mark Rozovsky might well have become their fellow had he not fallen under suspicion because of his very first production, with a scratch student group at Moscow University. The play, entitled *Our House*, was an audacious satire on the values of the emergent Soviet middle class, staged in a manner highly absurdist, recalling *The Bald Prima Donna*: characters were dehumanised, automatons, grotesque representations of particular Soviet attitudes, prejudices or vices. Such unequivocal formalism, clothing clearly seditious themes, was immediately vilified by conservatives as a fantastic distortion of reality, showing a complete misunderstanding of Soviet reality, and the group was disbanded forthwith. Rozovsky then became a freelance script-writer and director and now has a number of famous productions to his credit, including an adaptation of Tolstoy's short story *The Ostler* at Tovstonogov's Dramatic Theatre in Leningrad, and a celebrated *Crime and Punishment* at the Theatre of Russian Drama in Riga, Latvia, where he now works regularly. His choice of domicile is significant, for the atmosphere in Riga is far more conducive to experimentation.

Cultural policy in the Baltic republics is clearly more liberal than elsewhere in the Soviet Union. The reasons are probably political, reflecting official attitudes to the troublesome 'nationalities question', the problem of relations between non-Russian peoples and the central government in Moscow. The latter's attitude would appear to be that potentially rebellious minorities must be treated with caution and indulgence: Russian and Soviet artistic traditions must not be imposed on peoples whose traditions have more in common with Western European cultures than with Russian or Slavic. A cursory glance at the repertoire reveals plays by such anathematised Western writers as Pinter, Ionesco, Wesker and Beckett, and plays by Soviet Russian authors not permitted production in Russia proper. Indeed, Riga has become a sort of testing ground for problematical Russian plays, which, after an interval of two or three seasons, may appear in Moscow or Leningrad. Examples of this are Aleksandr Vampilov's *The Duck Hunt*, which features the first true Soviet anti-hero, and Victor Rozov's *Gnezdo Glukharya*, a fierce attack on corruption and malpractice among high-ranking government officials.

Content is not the only difference: style, unemcumbered by socialist-realist strictures and prohibitions, is infinitely more eclectic and rich; unadulterated 'modernism' is what one repeatedly encounters in Riga, Tallin and Tartu. Up until 1972 Lithuania, too, boasted a fine theatre, in Kaunas; then a young dissident immolated himself in a city park and the KGB, applying a tested formula for short-circuiting emergent nationalism, simply transferred almost the whole of the town's intelligentsia to distant parts, among them the staff of the national theatre. The Lithuanians do have, however, the only Balt playwright of note, Marcinkiavicus, of whose great historical trilogy, *Mindaugas*, *Kathedral*, and *Marshvidas*, only the first part has been translated into English. Its central theme, incidentally, is the futility of violence! It is in Latvia and Estonia, however, that one finds innovative directors of great stature. Moscow theatre-critics urged me to see the productions of Lininš and Tooming, particularly the former's fabled *Brand*. In 1977 Lininš's Rainis Theatre toured Moscow. As is the practice — another camouflage device — he brought two safely realist productions of accepted Russian classics, *The Seagull* and *Enemies*, together with the highly unorthodox *Brand*. Theatre-goers, in a rare display of civil disobedience, stove in the doors of the theatre in their efforts to see *Brand*, as a result of which an extra performance was scheduled. The results are already apparent: Lininš was invited by Oleg Efremov to come to Moscow to produce *Peer Gynt* at the Arts Theatre.

Lininš was vastly impressed with the Brook/Scofield *King*

Lear and one can discern elements of that production in his Ibsen; but his theatre is a collective enterprise, and its success owes much to a small number of other men of great talent: Ilmar Blumberg, his set-designer; Juris Strenga, his male lead and co-director; Morderis Tennison, a victim of the Kaunas purge and famous for his choreography and staging of crowd scenes; and Liniņš's wife Aina, who has studied the teaching methods of both Mikhail Chekhov and Riszard Cieslak and applies her knowledge in the theatre's acting-courses. The set-designer, Blumberg, is a taciturn intellectual, an ascetic, who travels to Germany and Poland to study development in set-design. His stature can be judged from his 'plastic direction', his solving of problems posed by *Brand*. On the floor of a bare, black box of a stage, the audience perceives, in a murky half-light, the menacing geometric bulk of Blumberg's trapezoid platform. Constructed by the designer, who has studied engineering and applied mathematics, it rests on a central pivot or fulcrum, so delicately balanced that two actors can revolve the platform at considerable speed using only their forearms. The platform is multi-symbolic. It defines Brand's world, it evokes the bleak landscape of the play's setting, it crystallises the character of Brand himself; its relentless, almost cruel angularity creates an image of his fanatical obduracy.

It appears inflexible, yet its versatility is astonishing: its slow hypnotic movement through the vertical plan establishes a grandiose rhythm of great expressive power, its furious revolutions in Acts IV and V mirror Brand's frenzy. In scenes of confrontation it is a yawning gulf between antagonists. In Act V, Scene ii, in which his followers, disillusioned and chastened, turn on him shrieking for his blood, Brand stands craglike, Christlike, on one edge of the construction, his figure sweeping towards and away from us at frightening speeds, as the platform is rotated by some eerie and unperceived force. His followers, brilliantly trained by Tennison to function as a single unit, stand in the pit of the theatre and, as one, charge the platform as Brand sweeps towards us, only to fall back as he hurtles away. The right-of-stage front extremity of the platform is established as the area of death, and it then becomes a vast, barren altar on which Agnes and Alf are sacrificed, victims of Brand's fierce fanaticism. Here Agnes is laid out, feet towards the centre, while the chorus wheel slowly about, opened hands held high as if carrying her coffin. Here too Brand finally sinks, with Strenga's long angular figure draped over the edge as the platform slowly, awesomely, rises to create a symbol of ultimate salvation. The production moves at great pace and its textual rhythms are

both subtle and yet almost mesmerising. The four-hour epic,
so often condemned as unstageable, was here triumphantly
vindicated. The production, though respected, is not popular
in Riga. The local audience, Liniň says, prefers lighter
entertainment.

An important element of the Soviet theatre scene is the
so-called *malaya stsena*, or alternative stage. Most theatres
have a second space either backstage, below stage or in a
foyer, where productions not for general consumption may be
presented, and where much experimentation takes place,
perhaps yet another manifestation of the 'safety valve': the
alternative stage of the Taganka is an exclusive club of
trusted persons. This *malaya stsena* is already a long-
established practice in Russia, said to stem from Reinhardt.
It is on the alternative stage of the Vainemuine Theatre in
Tartu that two young Estonians, Jaan Tooming and Evald
Hermaküla, stage their experiments. Here they have recently
presented two plays, Ibsen's *Little Eyolf* and Strindberg's
Dance of Death, which represent the most advanced, overtly
formalist productions of the last few years. My own application to visit Tartu was refused, but the productions were
described to me in detail by a member of the company. I
shall just mention some features: Hermaküla's Strindberg is
unequivocally anti-illusionist and richly eclectic. He
broadens the play's focus to make it an impassioned anti-war
statement. This theme is signalled by pistol and machine-gun
fire punctuating the action. Other military motifs are given
prominence: upstage-centre, a huge and menacing black military cape hangs on a coat-rack, eerily resembling a decapi-
tated body. The floor of the set is littered with shattered
and rent objects, the wreckage of human conflict and violence. Much of the action proceeds in near darkness, the
faces of the speakers illuminated by candles. These are held
by a stagehand who bears an uncanny resemblance to Edgar,
and who is, we realise, Edgar's double, a younger, more
handsome Edgar. An even more daring stroke is the dupli-
cation of Kurt, one actor representing him as Alice sees him
– handsome, dashing, not unlike the 'young' Edgar; the other
as Edgar sees him, older, a senior officer like himself, a
comrade-in-arms. Alice addresses only 'her' Kurt, Edgar only
'his'. In the finale of this version both Kurts join forces
with Alice to bundle Edgar into the gaping, open coffin
which, resting on a low catafalque, occupies centre stage.
The production's graphic, symbolic use of candles and
doubles, and its savage imagery combined with highly controlled stylised acting, go far beyond the cautious experiments of Lyubimov and Efros. Soviet informants maintained
that this was the most advanced theatre in the USSR. They

proceeded to describe another production, in the same
theatre, of *Little Eyolf*, staged by Hermokuila's colleague
Jaan Tooming.

Tooming's style, like Hermokuila's, has nothing whatsoever
in common with pseudo-Stanislavskian socialist-realist
method - and is just as eclectic. This eclecticism, the bold
juxtaposing of widely varying dramatic styles, is perhaps
the key development of recent years in production technique
in progressive theatres elsewhere, but is largely unknown in
Soviet Russia, where it is automatically proscribed as
'formalism': that Tooming should be permitted to adopt it is
an indication of the degree of freedom enjoyed by artists in
Estonia. His spectacular and symbol-laden use of light,
sound and colour recalls the anthroposophical theatre of
Rudolf Steiner; a dominant device in the production is the
mimetic expression of textual ideas and themes in rhythmical
sequence on a stage dwarfed by massive white geometric
structures (evoking glaciers and icebergs), both of which
elements were characteristic of the style of Tairov (who
favoured an action style approximating to interpretative
dancing on a stage divided by huge squares, cubes, cones and
ramps); finally, the acting techniques in which Tooming
drills his actors owe much to Meyerhold's biomechanics and
the exercises developed by Grotowski and Cieslak. Allmers,
Rita and Asta, dressed in colours with symbolic significance, act out their fates in a series of complex mimetic
sequences alternating with naturalistic delivery of dialogue, while Borghejm perches upstage-centre behind a
battery of drums on which he beats out rhythms regulating
and regulated by events downstage. This is punctuated by
subtly contrived light-and-sound interludes described by the
director as 'dream and/or vision' sequences. A feature of
the performer's technique is 'eye-acting': in Act I Eyolf
seems to grow out of Allmers's back as the latter staggers
towards the audience (while Asta appears to fly at one side
of the stage and Rita, in lurid crimson, lies in convulsions
opposite), and the audience is immediately struck by the
little boy's huge, strangely haunted and tragic eyes. Later,
both Rita and Allmers appear to take on the physical traits
of Eyolf, in particular these remarkable eyes. On stage
there is but one prop, a large, black rocking-chair which,
after the Ratcatcher has vacated it, becomes a 'throne of
death', the focus of mimetic 'dance-of-death' sequences.
Tooming has rearranged Ibsen's text, interpolating quotations from modern Estonian poets and adding a finale: the
final pages of *Faust II*. This extremely brief list of a
number of elements may serve to indicate the richness of
texture and startling originality of Tooming's production.

The success or failure of these radical interpretations is not in question here: the point lies in their overt anti-illusionism and stylisation. For here is a theatre whose productions are clearly subversive, in that they challenge the legitimacy of officially approved style and thus, by inference, the whole social system. In Moscow or Leningrad such theatre would be political dynamite, and thus it is not to be found on the stages of their theatres.

It does occur, however, in their so-called 'underground' theatres (*podval'ny teatr*). These are small groups of dedicated actors, exasperated by the poverty of the officially sanctioned repertoire, who risk persecution by staging proscribed works in secret, in cellars, warehouses, private flats, wherever they can. The group whose work I was fortunate enough to see included actors from the Taganka and Satire theatres. Their repertoire consisted of Pinter's *The Caretaker* and *The Dumb Waiter*, Ionesco's *Les Chaises* and Shakespeare's *Richard III* (the latter is not, of course, proscribed, but here it is produced with absurdist elements). The group had recently obtained copies of the plays of Beckett and Handke and were translating them for performance. Another such group of young actors from one of Moscow's most venerable and traditional 'academic' theatres were in 1978 secretly staging a serialised adaptation of another 'proscribed work', the Bible; one of Moscow's leading, though officially unrecognised, song-writers, Yuly Kim, was rehearsing an 'underground' production of Goethe's *Faust*. The state authorities were undoubtedly aware of these activities, but, apart from the dismissal of the director of the first of the above-mentioned groups from his position as a television producer, there has thus far been no persecution. The organs of control would thus appear to be biding their time and awaiting developments, meanwhile applying a 'safety-valve' policy.

The achievements here documented notwithstanding, the Soviet theatre in general remains an artistic backwater, offering little to those concerned with new developments in theatre. Apart from the obstacle to advance constituted by the government's policy of strict political control, directors and playwrights remain cut off from the early Soviet experimental tradition, a caesura effected by Stalin's subjugation of the arts in the thirties. Other factors also impede change, such as the intense conservatism of the ruling group and the conventionality of public taste. Original productions will continue to appear, particularly on the periphery, in the Baltic republics in Georgia (the most recent example is the Rustaveli Theatre's *Richard III* directed by Robert Sturuya, which has enjoyed great success in

Edinburgh and London); meanwhile in Moscow and Leningrad a stubborn struggle to push back the boundaries of the permissible in style and content continues.

NOTES

1. Aleksandr Galich, *General'naya repetitsiya* (Posev, 1974) pp. 79–81.
2. 'Eisenstein and Others', *Listener*, 29 Mar. 1973, pp. 413–15.
3. 'The Theatre of Anatoly Efros', *Theatre Quarterly*, VII (Summer 1977).

6 Visions of Absence: Beckett's *Footfalls, Ghost Trio* and *. . . but the clouds . . .*

MARTIN ESSLIN

Not I and *That Time* are plays of total stasis, with the light focused on a fragment of the human body suspended in space. In the three plays which follow, movement is reintroduced. But, while *Not I* and *That Time* still contain remnants of the discursive, story-telling element, the three later plays increasingly concentrate on an image pure and simple.

Footfalls, which shared a triple bill with *Play* and *That Time* in the evening staged for Beckett's seventieth birthday at the Royal Court Theatre in London (13 April 1976), also concentrates on a part of the human body: feet, but these are seen relentlessly pacing up and down, from right to left and from left to right on a dimly lighted strip of the stage; feet belonging to an aging woman, May, 'dishevelled grey hair, worn grey wrap hiding feet, trailing'.[1] Out of the darkness another voice is occasionally heard, belonging to May's mother, now aged ninety or thereabouts. The mother is bedridden and, from time to time, it appears, in need of ministrations from May: injections, straightening of pillows, change of drawsheet, bedpan, warming-pan, dressing of sores, sponging down, moistening of lips, praying with and praying for. The mother in turn is asking whether May will ever stop pacing up and down, revolving 'it' all in her poor mind.

In the second section of this tripartite play – after each section there is darkness, the next one is opened by a faint chime – the mother's voice is heard giving what seems the history of May's affliction : at a time when other girls of her age were out at lacrosse, she was already confined in

119

her home walking up and down. And, what is more, the motion
was not enough, she 'must hear the feet, however faint they
fall' (p. 35). In other words: May needs the *sound* of her
steps as an evidence of her existence. The event she is
revolving, only referred to as 'it', clearly was a experience of loss of self, as May herself later, in the third
part, says, in a pause of her relentless pacing up and down,
'A little later, when she was quite forgotten ... when as
though she had never been, it never been, she began to
walk' (p. 36). She used to pace up and down at night in a
little church. May's speech contains one or two glimpses of
the world, the world of that church, the candelabrum with
its flaming candles, and also, quite abruptly and without
transition, a brief reference to 'that poor arm' (p. 36).
That this refers to the arm of the crucified Saviour in
the church becomes clear when it is realised that in the
American edition, published earlier than the English one,
the passage reads, 'His poor arm'.[2] This is also the reading in Beckett's own typescript of the play. The suffering
Saviour on the cross (already present in *Waiting for Godot*)
thus reappears in this later work.

After this there is an abrupt transition in May's speech.
Like so many of Beckett's characters, May is a kind of
novelist; she is writing a story about 'Old Mrs Winter, whom
the reader will remember'.[3] Old Mrs Winter was sitting, in
May's story, with her daughter Amy at supper and referring
to something strange that happened during Evensong that day.
But Amy replies that she observed nothing strange at all: 'I
saw nothing, heard nothing of any kind. I was not there' (p.
37). Although Mrs Winter, her mother, saw her sitting there,
and uttering the responses, Amy insists she was not there.
And then the fictional story and the story we are seeing
clearly coalesce: in the play's last words, when May, in her
story, relates how the mother calls Amy in exactly the words
with which May was called by her mother, 'Will you never
have done? [*Pause.*] Will you never have done ... revolving
it all? [*Pause.*] It? [*Pause.*] It all. [*Pause.*] In your poor
mind. [*Pause.*] It all. [*Pause.*] It all' (p. 37).

It may be noted in passing that the name of Samuel
Beckett's mother was May. What seems to me, however, much
more significant is the fact that the anagram of May used in
the 'fiction' that May spins, Amy, can be read as *Am I*?

Footfalls thus presents an image of the loss of self, when
suddenly the question 'Am I?' is answered by a resounding
negative. All sense of selfhood is lost and the sound of the
footsteps relentlessly pounding the floor becomes the only
evidence of actual existence. Hand in hand, throughout
Beckett's work, with the loss of self goes the loss of the

world, which seems to have died or receded in *Endgame*, *Happy Days* or in the musings of characters who have lost their world in *Texts for Nothing*. But, whereas in these pieces the world was still lost to an identifiable self (Hamm, Winnie), in *Footfalls* the self itself is no longer there.

Yet all these thoughts still derive from the text of the piece, which, as it were, constitutes a last remnant of a narrative, discursive element. Yet in Beckett's own view that element has become secondary.

Shortly before rehearsals were due to start for *Footfalls* I was talking to Billie Whitelaw, Beckett's favourite actress, who was to perform the part of May at the Royal Court. She had written to Beckett, in some despair, as she failed to understand what the text of *Footfalls* was about. Beckett had replied to her in a note in his somewhat difficult handwriting and she asked me to help her to decipher it. It said something to the effect that she should not worry too much about the text, what mattered in the piece was its tone, pace and rhythm; the words were merely 'what pharmacists call the excipient'.

Quite clearly therefore, Beckett is more and more concentrating on the image, the poetic metaphor rather than the discursive or intellectual content of the texts he writes. From one point of view *Footfalls* could be described as a clinically accurate account of a compulsive schizophrenic, compelled to walk up and down at a certain pace, counting his steps in either direction. That would certainly be correct, but it would also be irrelevant. For the clinical symptoms have here been transmuted into a metaphor, or rather a cluster of related metaphors, which stand for a highly concentrated distillation, an alembic of the human condition itself: do we not all measure out our days by relentlessly scurrying to and fro, always moving, and always essentially remaining in the same place? And, for all our illusions of individuality and self-important selfhood, in the last resort does it not in the end amount to exactly what Amy/May feels: that we might just as well not have been there at all?

This is summed up in the final image of the play. After her last words darkness descends on the stage. The chime that has announced each section is heard even fainter than the last time. The light fades upon the strip of floor where May had been pacing up and down, but it has become even fainter than before. And there is '*No trace of* MAY' (p. 37). For ten seconds we can look at the empty strip. Then total darkness descends and the curtain falls.

Footfalls represents an important step in Beckett's development towards what I feel is really a radically different

type of drama, almost a new art-form. *Not I* and *That Time*
still contained sufficient narrative elements to link them
with traditional drama based on character and action. In
Footfalls, where the words really have become no more than
what pharmacists call the excipient, and where it has become
quite impossible for the audience in the theatre to make
sense of the words, what remains is a pure image, the poeti-
cal metaphor concretised into a picture, a moving and sounding picture, but essentially a picture nevertheless. This is
a theatre of visions, of images as one might receive them in
a dream, images to which our subconscious mind responds more
directly and more immediately than our consciousness. This
is the world, really, of surrealist painting: Marx Ernst,
Dali, or photographs by Man Ray or Moholy-Nagy. Except that
here the images are moving and sounding. But our relationship to these images, as an audience, is much nearer to that
of those contemplating such surrealist paintings or photographs. We are given no pointers how to relate, let alone
identify with, the characters portrayed, in so far as they
can still be called characters. And we are asked to respond
to what we see first by a gut-reaction to the whole image,
followed by attempts to decode it, exactly in the same way
as surrealist paintings are first perceived as wholes and
then gradually yield to a scrutinising and interpreting
intellectual effort.

It is quite clear that Beckett's imagination contains the
whole image in its full visual detail, not just the words
he puts down on the page. Hence it has for him become
increasingly important to be able to put the whole, visual
and aural, image onto the stage. His increased involvement
in the production of his works testifies to this need. He
himself directed *Footfalls* at the Royal Court, so that what
the audience eventually saw corresponded exactly to his
original vision.

Yet stage productions are ephemeral. It is surely significant that Beckett's next two plays were written for television, where, indeed, the original vision of the poet can
be fixed permanently on videotape or film. I feel that, in
fact, this new art-form – poetic visions, painterly moving
metaphors half-way between poetry and visual art – is
peculiarly suited to the televisual medium. (What a paradox:
the most vulgar, unpoetic medium as it is used today, may
potentially be the most poetic, the most complex of all
possible art-forms.)

Beckett wrote the two television plays *Ghost Trio* (originally titled *Tryst*) and ... *but the clouds* ... for one of
BBC2's arts programmes (producer: Bill Morton) intended as a
somewhat belated tribute to Beckett's seventieth birthday.

(It was, in fact broadcast in April 1977, about a year
later.) Both plays are extremely short and were screened
together with a television version of *Not I*, which, in some
ways, became a new and perhaps definitive form of that play.
It was performed by Billie Whitelaw with the moving mouth
constantly held in close-up. As a result the second character, the mysterious figure of the Auditor, who at certain
points in the stage version of the play makes a deprecatory,
despairing gesture, was eliminated. The effect of having the
mouth – lips, throat, teeth and tongue – held in close-up
for the entire duration of the play was almost unbearably
powerful: the moving mouth became terrifyingly alive, highly
obscene, a kind of *vulva dentata* in incessant and frantic
motion with the snakelike tongue darting and striking out in
a most menacing way. Beckett was enthusiastic about the
result – a sign perhaps that he was recognising the power of
the concentrated – and permanently fixed – televisual image.
The two other plays, which he had specially written for the
occasion, were in a far more elegiac mood, grey in grey, and
far more static.

   In both these plays the image predominates. There is in
each of them a voice which comments on the action, but it
does not, in either play, directly proceed from the visible
character speaking at the time. In *Ghost Trio* the voice is
female, although there seems no profound reason why it
should be. That voice has a touch of Beckettian self-irony.
After having asked the viewers not to adjust their set, as
the voice is supposed to be very low, it comments on the
picture we are seeing: 'The familiar chamber' (p. 41), and
points out the familiar Beckettian chamber's familiar
features, the pallet on the floor, the bare walls, the
single door, the single window and, finally, 'sole sign of
life a seated figure' (p. 42). This is the figure of an old
man, his face invisible as it is bent over an unidentifiable
object. Music (from the Largo of Beethoven's Fifth Piano
Trio, the Ghost) is heard and then ceases. The voice tells
us that 'He will now think he hears her' (p. 43) and
continues briefly to comment and describe the action as the
man, his face still invisible, moves to the door and window,
obviously hoping for a sign of the approach of the longed-
for female visitor. This sequence of actions is repeated
several times. By now the voice no longer comments, it is no
longer needed; the third section of the play proceeds without the spoken word. The old man goes through the motions of
listening, opening the door, etc. As he opens the window, we
see that it is dark outside, with dense rain falling. He
closes the window and goes to the mirror; briefly we
glimpse, for the first time, his face in the mirror. Then,

as he has settled back, bowed over the object he holds, which we now guess is a cassette-player, the source of the Beethoven music, faint footsteps are heard outside. There is a faint knock at the door. The door opens, revealing a small boy dressed in black oilskin, with hood, glistening from the rain. The boy looks up at us - and, we presume, the old man - and shakes his head in a gesture of 'no' - twice - then turns and disappears down the long dark corridor outside the door. The door closes. The music grows louder, the camera moves into close-up of the old man's still lowered head, until the end of the Largo. In the silence the old man now slowly raises his head; we see it again, but this time longer than the first time, when we glimpsed it in the mirror. It is the worn, lined face of a man who has suffered much. The camera recedes to a general view of the familiar chamber and the picture fades.

Ghost Trio is terrifying in its starkness and simplicity. The self-ironic voice of the opening sections is, in fact, it seems to me, not addressed to the audience so much as to the author; he is speaking to himself. Wearily he diagnoses his vision as simply another one of that familiar room, where all his heroes, Molloy, Malone, Krapp, Hamm, have spent their weary days. But here all individuality has become eroded; the man no longer has a name, not even that of the Unnamable. He is merely labelled F for 'figure'. Like the heroes of *Waiting for Godot* he is waiting for someone; as to them, the messenger bringing the news that the awaited person is not coming, is a little boy, as, indeed, in *Endgame* it is the appearance of a little boy outside the window which to Hamm signals the end. The figure crouched over an object which is revealed in the end to be a cassette-player (cf. Beckett's fascination with mechanical recording-devices in *Krapp's Last Tape*) is the last reduction into an image of utmost conciseness and economy of all the Beckettian protagonists: the *image* in its purest form, after all inessentials have been pared away. It is no longer important who the man is, what his name might be or, indeed, who it is he is waiting for. Again we are in the realm of what I am tempted to call visible poetic metaphor, fixed in a permanent form - by the author himself, for he supervised the production very closely, albeit Donald McWhinnie signed as the professional director for it. The play, if play it can still be called, only lasts a few minutes, but its power, in all its grey austerity, is immense and unforgettable.

... *but the clouds* ... which seems to have been written after *Ghost Trio* - it is not contained in the US edition of *Ends and Odds* (Grove Press, 1976), but is included in

the British edition, by Faber & Faber, dated 1977 – is a
variation on the same theme. Here the acting-area is not
even as concrete as that familiar room, but merely a circle
of light in total darkness. The protagonist of the piece is
again an old man, very much like the one in *Ghost Trio*
(played by the same actor, Ronald Pickup) and now it is his
voice that comments on the action:

> When I thought of her it was always night ... No, that is
> not right. When she appeared it was always night. I came
> in ... having walked the road since the break of day,
> brought night home, stood listening ... finally went to
> closet ... shed my hat and greatcoat, assumed robe and
> skull [i.e. skull-cap] ... vanished within my little
> sanctum and crouched, where none could see me, in the
> dark. (p. 53)

As the voice describes the actions we see them. The outside
world of the roads is on the left (the West), the sanctum at
the apex of the circle of light (the North), the closet
where he changes his clothes at the right (the East). At
rest we see the Man (M) in a crouching position. As he
explains, he is soundlessly begging for 'her' to appear to
him. Having established the pattern we see it again and
again: the man entering in hat and coat, crossing the
circle, reappearing in nightrobe and skull-cap and then
crouching: the endless circle of man's routine, rising and
going out and returning for the night and its dreams, summed
up in a single all-powerful, terrifyingly simple image.
    The voice now resumes and comments on the different out-
comes of his begging for the appearance of the woman's
image: one, she appeared but the images dissolved almost
immediately – and we now see the woman's face (eyes and
mouth mostly) for two seconds; or she lingered for a little
longer (five seconds is the indication in the script) 'With
those unseeing eyes I so begged when alive to look at me'
(p. 55). The third, obviously the most favourable case,
however, is when she appears and after a moment her lips
are seen to move, soundlessly, while the man's voice is
heard murmuring the words, '... but the clouds ... of the
sky ...'.
    Having established the pattern the voice can cease and the
action/image can be repeated. Of course, the voice wryly
adds afterwards, there was a fourth case, or rather case
nought, the commonest, 999 or 998 times out of a thousand,
when nothing happened at all, and all the begging was in
vain. The play ends with a repetition of the pattern of
entering, disrobing, crouching, and finally the woman's face

briefly appears and the voice repeats over her soundless lip
movements a fuller version of the quotation from Yeats's
poem *The Tower*: '... but the clouds of the sky ... when the
horizon fades ... or a bird's sleepy cry ... among the deep-
ening shades ...'.   The last image is of the man crouching
silently. Then the picture fades, into darkness.

As always, Beckett is allusive. The full quotation sheds
more light on the situation of the lonely figure in the
play:

> Slow decay of blood,
> Testy delirium
> Or dull decrepitude,
> Or what worse evil come —
> The death of friends, or death
> Of every brilliant eye
> That made a catch in the breath —
> Seem but the clouds of the sky
> When the horizon fades;
> Or a bird's sleepy cry
> Among the deepening shades.[4]

The face of a dead or lost love conjured up after long and
frequently fruitless efforts is a persistent Beckettian
topos: the whole of the radio play *Words and Music* centres
upon such an effort by an imperious old master, Croak, who
is bludgeoning his servants Words and Music to improvise on
the theme of love — until after many failures the face he
has been longing for appears in the embers of the dying
fire.

Ghost Trio shows failure, ... *but the clouds* ... at least
a partial success of an analogous endeavour. It is surely
not without significance that, while the *music* (Beethoven's
Ghost Trio) fails to achieve the desired result in the first
of these plays, the words (Yeats's poem) in the second do
actually conjure up the longed-for face.

Both television plays are structured on an analogous
principle: the voice-over commentary and descriptive text
rehearses, as it were, the sequence of images until the
viewer has grasped its pattern and significance. Once that
is achieved the image itself takes over altogether and
begins to operate autonomously, freed from the text. What
struck me, rereading the texts in their published form after
I had seen the performances of the plays a year or two
earlier, was in fact that I had forgotten the words and
merely retained the memory — a very detailed and accurate
memory — of the images. Here the text is, as it were, merely
there to introduce the image and then to fade away into the

background. The primacy of the image over the words is unquestionable. Moreover, the printed texts are so diagrammatic and technical that a reading of the two television plays by themselves will hardly produce even an approximation of what the plays look like in performance, as they have been permanently fixed on the film.

Footfalls still has the quality of a play-text which can stand up to reading. The two television plays, in their printed form, have been reduced to the status of mere blueprints and have, as such, lost the status of literary works. They stand in relation to the finished products, rather as a recipe stands in relation to the full flavour of the prepared dish when eaten.

Beckett's work has thus entered an area were only the performance itself can be regarded as the work of art, where the script is no longer a work of literature that can stand on its own. In this Beckett's development seems to me to converge with tendencies in the contemporary theatre that started out from completely different premisses: the performance art of painters and sculptors who have moved into quasi-theatrical forms – people such as Robert Wilson, Peter Schumann and other pioneers in this border-area between the visual arts and theatrical performance.

Thematically the three plays I have been discussing are, as is not surprising with a poet now in his seventies, concerned with the themes of death and loss of loved friends and companions. The loss of self suffered by May/Amy in *Footfalls* is an anticipation of death itself: when the sense of self is gone there is only the body left to make a noise of endless footfalls; and the dying Saviour on the cross, whose poor arm is briefly glimpsed and twice alluded to, presages the death of the body itself.

The two television plays, even more concentrated in their imagery, focus on the loneliness and isolation of an old man, who, however – as so often in Beckett's work – also stands for the whole of humanity in its ultimate loneliness and isolation, the endless routine of rising and retiring, day and night.

A short theatre-piece recently published (in the *Kenyon Review*, Summer 1979) which Beckett wrote at the request of the American actor David Warilow, who had asked him for a monologue on death, resumes these themes and shows how Beckett, even in his latest fragment for the stage, retains his intense preoccupation with the visual image. This soliloquy, which Beckett entitles *A Piece of Monologue*, shows a white-haired man, in white nightgown and white socks, standing 'off centre downstage audience left' about two metres distant from a 'standard lamp, skull-sized white globe,

faintly lit'. At the other end of the stage the foot of a
pallet bed is visible. We are thus in the world of ... *but
the clouds* ... (white night-gown) and *Ghost Trio* (the pallet
bed).

The monologue the old man delivers relates – in the third
person singular, 'he' – the story of someone (obviously the
speaker himself): 'Birth. Birth was the death of him. His
life, all two and a half billion seconds of it, was a
progress from funeral to funeral of ... he all but said of
loved ones.'

These remembered figures (always referred to in the above
deprecatory manner as people whom he almost but never quite
can bring himself to refer to as loved ones) had, at one
time, their photographs pinned on the wall at which he – the
speaker – stares when he gets up in his nightgown and white
socks in the dead of night, lighting the wick of the lamp
with a match on his buttock as his father taught him. Now
the wall is bare. He – the speaker? – has ripped them off
the wall one by one and swept them under the bed. A number
of motifs reappear in the monologue; they are combined and
regrouped on the structural pattern of a musical composition. The ritual of lighting the lamp. The bare wall. An
image of a funeral in the rain with dripping umbrellas. A
life of two and a half billion seconds, thirty-thousand
nights, is summed up in the last words of the monologue:

> Ghost light. Ghost nights. Ghost rooms. Ghost graves.
> Ghost ... he all but said ghost loved ones. Waiting on the
> rip cord. Stand there staring at that black veil lips
> quivering to half-heard words. Treating of other matters.
> Trying to treat of other matters. Till half hears there
> are no other matters. Never were other matters. Never two
> matters? Never but one matter. The dead and gone. The
> dying and the going. From the word go. The word begone.
> Such as the light going now. Beginning to go. In the room.
> Where else? Unnoticed by him staring beyond. The globe
> alone. Not the other. The unaccountable. From nowhere. On
> all sides nowhere. The globe alone. Alone gone.

And the stage direction: 'Lamp out. Silence. Speaker, globe,
foot of pallet barely visible in diffuse light. Ten seconds.
Curtain.'

The striking feature of this monologue seems to me, in
fact, that the speaker is concentrating on describing visual
images. The stage image we see is the primary set of images;
the images that are described by the speaker whom we see,
are, however, images of a higher order, images that conjure
up the mood, the poetic power the author tries to implant in

his audience's imagination. It almost seems as though the speaker of the monologue was trying to compose a scenario for a televisual pattern of images, but, in the absence of access to that medium, had to make do with mere descriptive writing, literature in the traditional sense.

A Piece of Monologue is, I believe, a fine piece of writing, a fine piece of poetic prose. But somehow I sense that it is literature striving to transcend itself, trying to reach the stage of pure, wordless image.

NOTES

1. Samuel Beckett, *Ends and Odds: Plays and Sketches* (London, 1977) p. 33.
2. Samuel Beckett, *Ends and Odds: Eight New Dramatic Pieces* (New York, 1976) p. 46.
3. Beckett, *Ends and Odds*, London edn, p. 36. All subsequent quotations from this edition.
4. *The Collected Poems of W. B. Yeats* (London, 1950) pp. 224-5.

7 To End Yet Again: Samuel Beckett's Recent Work

L. A. C. DOBREZ

Today we have no Delphic oracle, no intimate voice like that which spoke to Socrates – unless we except the daimons that find utterance through some of Beckett's obsessives – but, if we had, I expect it would tell us that there is no wiser man in the world than Samuel Beckett, since of all men Samuel Beckett is the one most conscious of his failure where wisdom is concerned. When I spoke to Beckett in 1977 he suggested that his productive writing phase began when he became aware in himself of what he termed not ignorance but nescience, ignorance as it were positively oriented. I want to focus on this element of Unknowing in Beckett's work, with particular reference to two plays written in recent years, *That Time* and *Not I*. Looking back on the long career which produced theatre of the calibre of *Godot*, *Endgame* and *Happy Days* and the poetic prose of *Murphy*, *Watt*, the novellas, the trilogy and *How It Is*, one might be excused the temptation to seek for signs of artistic decline in the seventies. But, since small masterpieces such as *Lessness* and *The Lost Ones*, the output of fine writing has continued. *That Time* and *Not I* are minute plays, each eight pages long in the Faber edition, yet they merit comparison with the best of the earlier work and surpass anything else written in English since Joyce. Like so much in Beckett they recall that stylish, elegant forgery, Joyce's craftsmanship, and the gentle note of Joycean sentiment, but without its emotional amplitude, as if the spring of inspiration were now wound tight about an infinitesimal point, gaining in intensity what has been lost in breadth. The mood is at times bitter in the extreme, yet Beckett's world does not allow for the expression of passion. If the Beckett protagonist is on fire, he burns quietly, like Dali's giraffe, in a landscape of stillness. Anger, in *That Time*, is kept bound in a straitjacket, to give a final effect of resignation, of

an elegy in a country of churchyards. In *Not I* the *memento
vivere* becomes a cry of panic, but one uttered with some
detachment. We have, in each case, a putting into practice
of the old Geulincx dictum: *ubi nihil vales, ibi nihil
velis.*

I intend to examine *That Time* and *Not I* in turn, beginning
with *That Time*. On the occasion I saw him, Beckett commented
on the ambiguities of translation, using the title *That Time*
as an example. 'Time' in English carries implications which,
in French, are divided between *temps* and *fois*, as they are
in Italian between *tempo* and *volta*. Of course 'that time'
may, and ought to be, read in several ways. The play illustrates the contemporaneity of three distinct moments of
consciousness. On stage is the face of an old man, the
Listener, who has no lines to speak. Voices, labelled A, B
and C, come to him from three sides, each recalling a
particular course of events in a pattern of precedence which
alters as the play proceeds. The result is a discreet
orchestration of motifs, each separate, each thematically
and linguistically related to others. A describes a sentimental journey, a visit to a place associated with childhood, B a lovers' meeting, C the wanderings of a tramp. The
tone is one of reverie, worthy of the Nausicaa or Penelope
episodes in *Ulysses* or of their counterparts in *Finnegans
Wake*.

A Opens:

> that time you went back that last time to look was the
> ruin still there where you hid as a child when was that
> ... grey day took the eleven to the end of the line and on
> from there no no trams then all gone long ago that time
> you went back to look was the ruin still there where you
> hid as a child that last time not a tram left in the place
> only the old rails when was that

— followed by C:

> when you went in out of the rain always winter then always
> raining that time in the Portrait Gallery in off the
> street out of the cold and rain slipped in when no one was
> looking and through the rooms shivering and dripping till
> you found a seat marble slab and sat down to rest and dry
> off and on to hell out of there when was that

— and B:

> on the stone together in the sun on the stone at the edge
> of the little wood and as far as eye could see the wheat

turning   yellow   vowing   now and then you loved each other
just   a murmur not touching or anything of that nature you
one   end   of   the   stone she the other long low stone like
millstone no looks just there together on the stone in the
sun   with   the   little   wood behind gazing at the wheat or
eyes closed all still no sign of life not a soul abroad no
sound (pp. 9-10) [1]

Each   of the three voices heard by the Listener sketches a
situation   which is characteristically Beckettian and recurs
more   or   less   throughout   Beckett's work from the thirties
onwards.   There is the solitary,   eccentric child who grows
into the later visitor, a figure reminiscent of Sapo-Macmann
in *Malone Dies*.   There is the unspecified ruin which appears
and   reappears elusively   in   *Mercier   and   Camier*,   *The
Calmative*,   *Molloy*,   *Lessness* and, most recently, *For to End
Yet Again*.   Here Beckett's   pseudocouple faced one of their
moments of truth:

Now we must choose, said Mercier.
Between what? said Camier.
Ruin and collapse, said Mercier.
Could we not somehow combine them? said Camier. (p. 101)

More than   twenty   years later,   *Lessness* returns us to the
same landscape: 'Ruins true refuge long last towards   which
so many false time out of mind' (p. 7).
The image is   one of a disintegrating   world and,   in particular,   of a   disintegrating   personality, Molloy's   'the
thing in ruins,   I don't know what it is,   what it was,   nor
whether it is   not less a question of   ruins than the indestructible chaos of timeless things   ...   a world collapsing
endlessly   ...   a world at an end ... ' (p. 40). Clearly, in
Beckett's   universe   collapse   is the one stable ontological
factor. It characterises personal development in a long line
of misfits   and tramps,   from Belacqua,   Murphy and Watt to
Vladimir and Estragon and,   finally,   the protagonist of the
third   story of   *That Time*,   who wanders in search of warmth
from   Portrait   Gallery   to   Post   Office to Public Library.
Equally it characterises human relationships. The lovers who
sit away from each other, gazing dumbly at all that ripening
wheat,   recall   the   Proustian round of love frustrated in a
thousand varied   ways   in   the course of Beckett's   fiction,
from the never-to-be touch of fingers in *Happy Days*,   or the
never-to-be kiss of Nell and Nagg in *Endgame*,   to the sweet-
sour memories of Krapp's tape, to that affection which,   when
requited in   *Murphy*,   makes for a short circuit (p. 7), and
which   mercifully   remains unrequited in the unequal contest

of Watt and the one-breasted Mrs Gorman, to the passion
which horribly animates the idyll of Mac and Moll in *Malone
Dies*, or which prompts Molloy to declare 'a mug's game in my
opinion and tiring on top of that' (p. 56), to, in the end,
the violent communion of *How It Is* and the creatures
'making unmakable love' (p. 37) in *The Lost Ones*. Beckett,
perhaps more obviously than most writers, returns over and
over to the place of his original inspiration. Even so, each
excursion into the old territory is entirely new, since each
represents a new attempt at definition, and always *from the
beginning*. *That Time* plays the old tune but it does so without repetition.

It should be stressed that the presentation of Beckett's
three situations, those of the sentimental traveller, the
lover and the tramp, is not static. *That Time* is a dramatic
piece of considerable force, with a threefold development
towards a point of climax which is, in its subtle way,
completely convincing. The chronological sequence of this
development is possibly indicated by the two ten-second
pauses which divide the play into three parts. The first
comes after voice B, the next after A and the work as a
whole ends on the note of C, so that we pause with the
lover, the traveller and the tramp in that order. In any
case this is the sequence one would wish to adopt in any
discussion of the components of the play, since one may
reasonably postulate a progression in time from the lover to
the traveller to the tramp.

Voice B begins with the image of lovers already referred
to. In the broken tones of almost-suppressed pathos it
describes those despairing and evanescent vows, made in
whispers, that is to say scarcely made, on a stone
unfortunately reminiscent of a millstone, by a couple who
neither touch nor gaze at each other. Like Krapp's memory of
lovers floating on the stream of time, this sentimental
memory is the memory *par excellence*: 'one thing could ever
bring tears till they dried up altogether that thought' (p.
10). Of course tears, like romantic meetings, are in the
protagonist's past. Indeed, the protagonist has passed
through several phases of his life since the interlude on
the stone. To begin with he has ceased to believe in the
reality of the meeting. Standing or, like the character of
the prose poem *Still*, sitting before a window, he has played
the game most Beckett characters play, that of invention.
Surely there never was any love, it was all a story created
for the purpose of reassurance:

by the window in the dark harking to the owl not a thought
in your head till hard to believe harder and harder to

> believe you ever told anyone you loved them or anyone you
> till just one of those things you kept making up to keep
> the void out just another of those old tales to keep the
> void from pouring in on top of you the shroud. (p. 11)

In a sense the shroud had been present all along, as had the
void. It existed in the spaces of separation, in the
silences, in the image of the stone, rather evocative of a
tomb. Now the unreality of human contact is acknowledged.
Assuming the old Beckettian role of the artist, the Joycean
forger, the protagonist freely invents and, inventing,
elaborates. To the time on the stone is added that on the
towpath or, again, on the sand, by the water. Unavoidably,
though, as in a dream which modulates into nightmare, the
sun, once shining over wheatfields, now slowly sets and the
current, gathering flotsam, brings with it a dead rat. The
lovers, who now act out a puppet role, are less and less
convincing, as if they existed on a cinematic screen as an
image increasingly conventional and mechanical. Thus the
pose becomes more strictly geometric – a parallel of figures
on the sand, for example – the presence less corporeal
('just blurs on the fringes of the field' – p. 12), the
place more and more vague.   Finally it is as if we were
witnessing a film projected in slower and slower motion:

> stock still side by side in the sun then sink and vanish
> without your having stirred any more than the two knobs on
> a dumbbell except the lids and every now and then the lips
> to vow and all around too all still all sides wherever it
> might be no stir or sound only faintly the leaves in the
> little wood behind or the ears or the bent or the reeds as
> the case might be of man no sight of man or beast no sight
> or sound (p. 13)

Variations now enter with a kind of detached contempt. The
drowned rat may have been a bird, in the sky may have been a
glider, the woman may have been there or not, it may have
been a time 'before she came after she went or both' (p.
15). Or perhaps after all the protagonist was always alone,
on his stone, on the sand, or wherever. In the end the voice
returns us to the solitary figure by the window and to a
final metamorphosis, the time when, like tears on a previous
occasion, the stories dried up and emptiness took over. The
experience, clearly feared for so long, is, as it turns out,
something of a relief:

> that time in the end when you tried and couldn't ... hour
> after hour hour after hour not a sound when you tried and

tried and couldn't any more no words left to keep it out
so gave it up gave up there by the window in the dark or
moonlight gave up for good and let it in and nothing the
worse a great shroud billowing in all over you on top of
you and little or nothing the worse little or nothing
(p. 16)

This is the moment of conversion for so many Beckett
characters from Murphy onwards. It ought to lead to the
asylum or the open road. In this case, there is a particular
complication, though, a second interlude which completes a
cycle by returning us from silence to speech. The story of
voice A is that of the traveller who comes by ferry (the
Holyhead to Dun Laoghaire, perhaps?) to revisit a scene of
childhood. In the event he symbolically rejoins or rather
re-enacts the past he would like to forget. What this past
involves is a child of ten, eleven or twelve who comes to an
overgrown ruin to hide from — searching parents perhaps, to
sit, like the lovers, on a stone, another image of mortality, to read or, more significant, to talk. Because the boy
protagonist invents reality, as does the lover, and for the
same reason, for *company*: 'talking to himself being together
that way where none ever came' (p. 14). In fact the picture
of personality divided within itself in a process of multi-
plying identities is exactly the same as that of Listener
and voices offered by the play as a whole:

talking to yourself who else out loud imaginary conversations there was childhood for you ten or eleven on a
stone among the giant nettles making it up now one voice
now another till you were hoarse and they all sounded the
same well on into the night ... (p. 11)

This inward disintegration has its counterpart in the ruins
of the setting. Its progress demands an identification of
visitor and child, and this occurs at the climax of voice
A's narrative. What happens is that the visitor to his own
past finds himself unable to get to the ruin. The tram, a
number 11, which recalls the child's age, is gone, only old
rails remain, like a memory. Since there is no train either,
the visitor, like the lover faced with the inrush of the
void, 'gave it up gave up and sat down on the steps ... a
doorstep say someone's doorstep' (p. 13), sitting on stone
as did the lovers and the child. Gradually another metamorphosis is affected, one which involves negation of previous
knowledge — 'little by little not knowing where you were or
when you were or what for' (p. 14) — and then an uncontrollable flood of speech: 'till there on the step in the pale

sun you heard yourself at it again ... drooling away out loud' (p. 15). At this point the themes of verbal invention and identity are one, since, in his gabble, the visitor seems to create the entire story of which he is the supposed protagonist. The child and the ruin perhaps exist only in the visitor's imagination. More than that: the visitor himself now appears as a fiction perpetually recreating itself: 'making it all up on the doorstep as you went along making yourself all up again for the millionth time' (p. 15). And this is of course the situation of the child, prattling helplessly and endlessly like dozens of other Beckett characters, from Lucky to the Unnamable. By the end of the A narrative the visitor returns to the ferry without ever reaching his original goal. The past of mother and childhood which he abominates travels with him as before: the time of the visit was after all identical with that of childhood, and indeed with all other time, all time being 'that time', the time of crisis – that is to say, of living.

The C narrative, which now remains to be considered, can be thought of as representing the final stage of the Beckettian tramp's progress; in any case it has the last word in the play. Its content is the simplest and the most moving of all. The protagonist is a down-and-out who haunts a wintry cityscape, finding his first refuge in a portrait gallery and sitting, inevitably, on a stone seat, the play's fourth and final image of the grave. Here he experiences the first of what he terms rather sarcastically his 'turning-points'. As he gazes at an oil portrait 'black with age and dirt' (p. 10), he becomes aware of a face next to him, presumably his own. After this, the tramp is, as he puts it, 'never the same' (p. 11), and, one might add, in the fullest sense of the expression. The consciousness of self-identity has been shaken, in a fulfilment of the prophecy implicit in the child's game of otherness, but, then, had such a consciousness ever really existed?

> ... never the same but the same as what for God's sake did you ever say I to yourself in your life ... could you ever say I to yourself in your life turning-point that was a great word with you before they dried up altogether always having turning-points and never but the one the first and last that time curled up worm in slime when they lugged you out and wiped you off and straightened you up never another after that never looked back after that
> (pp. 11-12)

In fact there had never been any crisis-point in the protagonist's life save one, the fact of birth (unsolicited, naturally), the fact of life itself. And *that* lacked credibility. We recall that the voices A, B and C, who address themselves to a silent Listener throughout the play, always do so in the second person, never in the first. The inexplicable tragicomedy of life happens, as always in Beckett, not to oneself but to oneself-as-other, to a stranger. Still the phenomenon has some status of reality and some relevance to oneself by virtue of its being painful; and, at this stage in the play, the protagonist still has two critical situations to face.

The first of these eventuates in the Post Office, another place of shelter from the cold and rain. The tramp who, after his moment in the gallery, finds himself inhabiting an alien identity whose words are not his own, and who vainly tries, by the old formula of invention, to reintroduce himself into the third-person narrative of his own life, has now come to a stop. Like the lover's his words have 'dried up', and like the lover and the visitor he has 'given up', or, rather, 'it gave up whoever it was' (p. 13). Now it is Christmas, season of goodwill, as the tramp hesitantly takes a seat in the Post Office and sneaks a look at the rest of mankind, 'at your fellow bastards thanking God for once bad and all as you were you were not as they' (p. 15). The logic of the protagonist, though unstated, is clear. If you find it difficult to believe in your own identity, in your own existence, then you seek out the other's objectifying gaze, you find a witness in whose look you will see proof of your own being. We recall Murphy's valiant attempts with the gloriously unseeing eyes of the lunatic Mr Endon and the long Kafkaesque series of perceivers and perceived in Beckett's work, all fulfilling the requirements of Berkeley's famous dictum, *esse est percipi*. As we might expect, the tramp in the Post Office is unsuccessful: 'you might as well not have been there at all the eyes passing over you and through you like so much thin air' (p. 15). Accordingly, he moves on to the Public Library, where the final revelation awaits him. In fact we reach at this point the climax of all three narratives of the play. As voice A describes the visitor's flight from the place and memories of childhood, and voice B the ex-lover's once-and-for-all surrender to the void, the tramp of C's narrative reaches his last turning-point. Seated with old people at a library table, in a wasteland more absolute than any conceived by Eliot, he hears the ultimate sermon, 'What the Dust Said':

not a sound only the old breath and the leaves turning and then suddenly this dust whole place suddenly full of dust when you opened your eyes from floor to ceiling nothing

only dust and not a sound only what was it it said come
and gone was that it something like that come and gone
come and gone no one come and gone in no time gone in no
time (p. 16)

These are the last words of *That Time* and they look back
to the title of an earlier play, *Come and Go*. Of course they
constitute a restatement of the one truth *That Time* has
pursued throughout, that of disintegration, mortality, loss.
Beckett's play, in so far as it illustrates the failure of
memory, may be regarded as one of many comments on the great
Proustian theme, all of them final; in its implicit denial
of Molly Bloom's conclusive 'Yes', it may be taken as yet
another last judgement on Beckett's other *maestro di color
che sanno*, Joyce. Or we may choose to see it as another
portrait of Beckett's Shem the Penman, an artist and therefore one of Murphy's 'higher schizoids' (p. 125), those
uncaring vessels of divine election whose role it is to be
spoken through for ever and ever. Certainly the image of the
Listener, besieged by the voices of time, evokes all these
associations. But there is more to it than that and it is
precisely this more which is at the heart of Beckett's work.
The situation of the Listener may be one of breakdown, of
ruin, but the conclusion is not simply that of Ecclesiastes.
Beyond the facile *vanitas vanitatum* lies a more tantalising
truth: that the Listener, amid his ruins, *endures*. The message of the dust is, to be sure, *nothing*: 'come and gone no
one come and gone in no time gone in no time'. Yet in the
going there is of necessity a coming, in the no one an
identity, in the no time temporality, in the nothing of the
message a *something*, otherwise there would be no message.
That time, then, which is time itself, any time so long as
it is that of living, that is to say of dying, is, in the
final reckoning, non-time, but a non-time which *is*. Time,
like the identity of the Listener or the tramp, has the
quality of a non-event which does, however, *take place*.
Likewise the engulfing dust of the library has the same
miraculous nature as the sand in *Watt*:

The change. In what did it consist? It is hard to say.
Something slipped ... suddenly somewhere some little thing
slipped, some tiny little thing. Gliss-iss-iss-STOP!
(p. 41)

In this fall of sand, nothing - has occurred. That same
nothing occurs in the unimaginable step forward in the sand
which gives no foothold in *Lessness* and in the inexplicable
heap of *Endgame*: 'Grain upon grain, one by one, and one day,

suddenly, there's a heap, a little heap, the impossible heap' (p. 12). Whether because they come into being or because they cease to be or, more important, because they continue in being in spite of endless diminishment — that is, they exist *as diminishment* — Beckett's units of reality, his presences on the page and on the stage, his events, changes or turning-points, are all of them miracles. And the *fact* of their nothingness endlessly intrigues their creator. Beyond hope and despair Beckett is stirred by the ultimate philosophical curiosity at this tantalising irreducible: that, when all that is conceivable is removed from life as contingent, as inessential, an inconceivable essential remains. It would be no exaggeration to say that all of Beckett's work has, from the beginning, sought to uncover this one mystery, this unnamable. *That Time* takes up the old search with time as its central theme. *Not I* does so with identity as its concern.

The stage arrangement of *Not I* is as simple as that of the other play. It allows the audience to make out, in partial darkness, the figure of the Auditor, who, like the Listener of *That Time*, has no lines, and the outlines of a mouth which functions in much the same way as the voices in *That Time*. As Mouth speaks, Auditor listens and occasionally reacts by a lifting of arms. Mouth's utterance is garbled, quietly panic-stricken and feminine. In fact it is decidedly reminiscent of Winnie of *Happy Days*, particularly when it reflects, somewhat unconvincingly, on God's 'tender mercies' (p. 19). But the bourgeois frivolities and genuine charm of Winnie are gone, replaced by a personality akin to that of Molloy or Malone or, if it comes to that, the protagonist of *That Time*. Mouth tells yet another Beckett story, focusing on what could be termed, without too much reference to Genesis, a fall. Actually the story begins at the beginning, though it feels no compulsion to linger over trifling details:

> out ... into this world ... this world ... tiny little
> thing ... before its time ... in a godfor — ... what? ...
> girl? ... yes ... tiny little girl ... into this ... put
> into this ... before her time ... godforsaken hole called
> ... called ... no matter ... parents unknown ... unheard
> of ... he having vanished ... thin air ... no sooner but-
> toned up his breeches ... she similarly ... eight months
> later ... almost to the tick ... so no love ... spared
> that ... no love such as normally vented on the ...
> speechless infant ... in the home ... no ... nor indeed
> for that matter any of any kind ... no love of any kind
> ... at any subsequent age ... so typical affair ... noth-

ing of any note till coming up to sixty when - ... what?
... seventy? ... good God! ... coming up to seventy ...
(p. 13)

What happens at seventy is a collapse. Wandering over a
field in spring, the female protagonist suddenly finds herself in darkness or near darkness in an indeterminate
position, without the use of her senses or nearly so. The
symptoms are those of the earlier Unnamable, more or less.
There is a fitful ray of light, image of mind, and a buzzing
in the ears like embryonic speech; for the rest, little or
no feeling or activity of any kind except of course that of
the unsilenceable brain. It is perhaps a death of sorts, a
Beckettian death which brings not oblivion but continuation
of life. Like Teresa in rapture or the subject of a cata-
tonic trance, Beckett's protagonist experiences an *ex-
stasis*, a withdrawal beyond the range of everyday sen-
sations and faculties. Thus it seems she is weeping and
therefore perhaps in pain, since her eyes are moist. But the
sufferer is not *herself*, any more than it was in an earlier
experience at the wonderfully named Croker's Acres:

one evening on the way home ... home! ... a little mound
in Croker's Acres ... dusk ... sitting staring at her hand
... there in her lap ... palm upward ... suddenly saw it
wet ... the palm ... tears presumably ... hers presumably
... no one else for miles ... no sound ... just the tears
... sat and watched them dry ... all over in a second ...
(p. 18)

The refined and cultivated tear of the Man of Sentiment,
Sterne's despairing and self-indulgent 'alas, poor Yorick',
has not disappeared but has become incomprehensible, even to
itself, like one of Krapp's tapes played years after the
event. A similar fate has overtaken the expressionist
scream, with which the protagonist briefly and casually
experiments. One thing remains, however, and with a vengeance, or rather it begins gradually to assert itself:
uncontrollable speech. The protagonist, it seems, once
avoided words:

even shopping ... out shopping ... busy shopping centre
... supermart ... just hand in the list ... with the bag
... old black shopping bag ... then stand there waiting
... any length of time ... middle of the throng ...
motionless ... staring into space ... mouth half open as
usual ... till it was back in her hand ... the bag back in
her hand ... then pay and go ... not so much as good-
bye... (p. 16)

At times an obscenely naked need to communicate had taken possession of her, but only briefly:

> sometimes sudden urge ... once or twice a year ... always
> winter some strange reason ... the long evening ... hours
> of darkness ... sudden urge to ... tell ... then rush out
> stop the first she saw ... nearest lavatory ... start
> pouring it out ... steady stream ... mad stuff ... half
> the vowels wrong ... no one could follow ... till she saw
> the stare she was getting ... then die of shame ... crawl
> back in ... (pp. 19-20)

Now the words return, in a rush and with the compulsion of a nervous fixation. At first it is possible not to recognise a voice so rarely heard, but, clearly, it is the protagonist's. The woman attempts to pretend she has nothing to do with it, until she feels her lips moving and not only her lips but her whole face:

> lips ... cheeks ... jaws ... tongue ... never still a
> second ... mouth on fire ... stream of words ... in her
> ear ... practically in her ear ... not catching the half
> ... not the quarter ... no idea what she's saying ...
> imagine! ... no idea what she's saying! ... and can't stop
> ... no stopping it ... she who but a moment before ... but
> a moment! ... could not make a sound ... no sound of any
> kind ... now can't stop ... imagine! ... can't stop the
> stream ... and the whole brain begging ... something
> begging in the brain ... begging the mouth to stop ...
> pause a moment ... if only for a moment ... and no
> response ... as if it hadn't heard ... or couldn't ...
> couldn't pause a second ... (p. 17)

The protagonist's moment of crisis obviously parallels that of the visitor in *That Time*, although the portrayal of compulsive speech in *Not I* is more detailed and indeed more heartrending. What has occurred amounts in each case to a turning-point — in the words of *Watt*, a 'change' — a conversion away from everyday normality with its normal, everyday horrors to — what? Like the prattling of the child and, later, the visiting adult or, again, like the invention of the lover and, in another context, of the tramp in *That Time*, the outburst in *Not I* suggests the interchangeability in Beckett's world of the phenomena of consciousness, madness and art. Mouth opens to utter the first word of the play — 'out'; it opens, like a vagina, to give birth to a 'tiny little thing', a baby girl or, simply, to a word, the *logos* which is the 'I am' of consciousness in general and of art in particular, Coleridge's Primary and Secondary Imagination. In this context the image of Auditor and Mouth, like that of Listener and voices, carries triple connotations. It indicates the functioning of the mind in self-awareness and self-communion – that is, as subject and object to itself – and, again, it evokes the internal situation of the lunatic, divided within himself, and of the artist, inspired by an other-than-himself, the muse. At the same time the protagonist's transition to compulsive speech has the same finality of revelation as has, in *That Time*, the lover's submission to emptiness and the tramp's to the message of the dust. Of course, an explanation of the key event of *Not I* in terms quite other than those given above is forthcoming from the protagonist herself.

She sees her situation as one of punishment, reiterating concepts which may be found in Beckett's work from the excruciating tale of Belacqua's boiling lobster to the theological speculations of Vladimir and Estragon. In fact the thought of divine vengeance is the first thought to occur to her after her collapse – until she realises that, after all, she is not exactly suffering. With sublime irony and with the wonderful imaginative resources of the Beckettian she wonders if, perhaps, she is *meant* to be suffering. It is perfectly possible, given that in her life she frequently found herself in situations of *supposed* pleasure which were not pleasurable at all. Why not the reverse? In that case it might be as well to *act the part* of one suffering, just in case, to confuse the powers in control, by groaning, writhing or screaming, for example. However, the initiative for such complex deceit is lacking and the protagonist remains in her passivity. Still she continues to speculate. For a start, her punishment may well be a punishment not for sin but – a more satisfying concept – for its own sake: in Malone's words, 'so long as it is what is called a living being you can't go wrong, you have the guilty one' (p. 260). Seemingly, it is a torment like that of the Ancient Mariner: the protagonist is required, by an obscure authority, to say something, to tell a story, though *which* is not clear. Like the subject of *The Unnamable*, she is in a Dantean or rather Kafkaesque hell, speaking through Mouth to an Auditor who, in this context, suggests the scribe of other Beckett stories, stationed beside Mouth to receive and possibly to report on the correct story. Obviously the punishment is eternal, just as the correct story is always out of reach.

Viewed this way, *Not I* records a situation in which consciousness exists as its own torment, a situation which begins with the protagonist's compulsion to speak and which

has no end. But this is by no means the only or indeed the
most significant element in the play. *Not I* differs from
That Time in that its dramatic climax is disguised and
comes not at the end but in the body of the play. Five
times in the course of the narrative, Mouth repeats the
formula 'what? ... who? ... no! ... she!' Five times, in
other words, it responds to a prompter who, we may assume,
suggests that it speak of 'she', the protagonist, in the
first person. In each case and most forcefully on the last
occasion, the answer is no: Mouth refuses stubbornly to
speak of 'I'. That refusal is the key to the meaning of the
play. Now Mouth is prompted by the voice of the female protagonist, repeating, often wrongly, the rush of words which
originate in the protagonist. Thus, for example, when it
misinforms us in the matter of the woman's age, it is
interrupted and put right: 'nothing of any note till coming
up to sixty when – ... what? ... seventy? ... good God! ...
coming up to seventy ...' (p. 13). At the same time Mouth
will not identify with the subject of its own story, who
remains insistently not 'I' but 'she'. So the voice which
issues from Mouth is and is not that of the protagonist,
it is a divided voice, speaking on the one hand for the
protagonist and on the other for an unknown. This voice is
required to tell something, perhaps 'how it was ... how she
– ... what? ... had been ... yes ... something that would
tell how it had been ... how she had lived ...' (p. 19). But
another story of a down-and-out is not what is called for:

> what? ... not that? ... nothing to do with that? ... noth-
> ing she could tell? ... all right ... nothing she could
> tell ... try something else ... think of something else
> ... oh long after ... sudden flash ... not that either ...
> all right ... something else again ... so on ... hit on it
> in the end ... think everything keep on long enough ...
> then forgiven ... back in the – ... what? ... not that
> either? ... nothing to do with that either? ... nothing
> she could think? ... all right ... nothing she could tell
> ... nothing she could think ... nothing she – ... what?
> ... who? ... no! ... she! (p. 19)

What is called for is, it seems, unthinkable, unable to be
told. At one level, the voice is asked to name itself, or
rather to identify its true source, beyond the mind of the
helpless protagonist. Because it cannot do this and consequently substitutes a story – that of the protagonist – it
effectively reduces the entire play to a digression, an
evasion of the truth – which has nothing to do with 'she',
the protagonist. At another level the voice is asked to say

'I' rather than 'she', to identify itself as none other than
the woman in question. This it will not do, its true identity being an unknown. On the face of it we are left with a
double frustration, the inability of Mouth to utter either
the unutterable truth or the facile lie, the 'I' which, one
supposes, would satisfy the observing Auditor. But Beckett's
play is not ultimately concerned with failure. While the unknown which is present within the voice or consciousness of
the protagonist as her ultimate reality cannot be named, it
can and is indirectly revealed. Every element of Beckett's
drama - the woman, the voice, Mouth - is inexplicable
taken by itself. Further, woman, voice and Mouth lack
cohesion, their interconnection is mysterious, even negative, like the Occasionalist link which joins or rather
fails to join mind and body in so many Beckett characters,
beginning with Murphy. Yet there is *some* cohesive force,
something of necessity in the contingency of the situation
of the protagonist and her voice; otherwise there would not
be speech, a certain *naming* and, above all, a *refusal* to
name. The very disjunction of the elements in the play indicates the need for a presence beyond them to unify them, not
the dubious 'God' mentioned by the protagonist but an
unknown, able to guarantee the protagonist and her voice a
minimal status, that of a *fact*, tenuous in the extreme yet
inexorably, eternally *there*. That Unnamable is, as in the
trilogy, Beckett's fundamental concern. It is not simply a
matter of depicting the agony of indestructible consciousness, but of evoking, however obscurely, the ground as it
were on the basis of which the action of the play becomes a
possibility, the mystery which sustains consciousness and
which distinguishes itself from it as 'not I'.

To say that Beckett's play dramatises a rejection of selfhood or ego, then, would be to miss the greater part of the
point. Beckett is not primarily interested in the shedding
of a restrictive concept of self, understood as mask or
persona or role-playing, not even in the sophisticated
Pirandellian or Sartrean sense. Identity, for the Pirandello
character, is a matter of *costruirsi*, self-construct; in
Sartre's world it is a matter of *pretending*, *mauvaise foi*,
of *being* the waiter or diplomat one is *not*, in bad faith. In
both cases, identity is a way of being oneself *for others*
and so of being Other to oneself. Such alienation may be
overcome: as, for example, when the Pirandellian actor sees
his own reflection in a mirror and becomes aware of the
(inescapable) charade, or when the Sartrean one discovers
his subjectivity in the moment of freedom - that is to say,
by *doing* something, by ceasing to exist as object. But, in
spite of surface similarities, Beckett's character is no

Enrico Quarto or Kean. *His* removal of the mask was effected
before the lifting of the curtain, it is from the start a
fait accompli, not the end-product of the process of
discovery but its prerequisite. In complete nakedness from
the beginning, Beckett's protagonist removes his skin, then
his flesh and his bones, pausing, but without interest, at
the old, clacking windmill of consciousness only to receive
second wind and to penetrate, like Murphy, layers of mind
and to reach the mind-within-the-mind, mind-no-longer-mind,
myself-no-longer-me. In an invisible room resides the one
to whom I say 'not I' or, more accurately, the one who first
says 'not I' to me. This identity is not to be trivialised
by a name or, what amounts to the same thing, by facile
association with myself. None the less, in so far as I exist
I do so by virtue of a minimal, even negative, connection
with it, that is, I exist by virtue of its saying 'not I' to
me, by virtue of its *denial* of me. We are returned to the
phenomenon of the non-event in *That Time*. The voice which
issues from Mouth has the same quality as the presence of
the Listener in the other play: it is really nothing at all
- painfully *there*, its ultimate identity a 'tiny little
thing', the tiniest thing of all, like a slipping of grains
of sand or a movement of the dust. Wisdom, in this context,
is largely a question of unknowing what one knows. The
Beckett character *en route* to Damascus is thrown to the
ground, exposed to the merciless light which reveals nothing
except more pricks than kicks and is forced to groan, 'not I
but the Other lives in me'. It is not a conversion in the
Cartesian tradition, from the seventeenth century to Sartre
- a turning, in doubt, to the *cogito* - but a movement to a
deus absconditus more remote than the 'spirit' which Teresa
identified as the essence of 'soul', in fact, to a point
philosophically and experientially indistinguishable from
nothing. Of course, there is the further truth, that nothing
is more real than nothing. Beckett retraces this path from
the no-man's-land of his character to an aboriginal ground
of being over and over. Nothing could be more natural or
simpler than such a search. It happens that, as Heidegger
might say, the thing that is most present is also most
difficult to reach. Sartre would probably dismiss the search
as futile. You cannot reach yourself because you are already
there, or, more accurately, you cannot *be* and *know* yourself
at the same time - that is, be both subject and object to
yourself at once. Only God, who doesn't exist, can do that.
But Beckett finds only the impossible worthy of an attempt;
anything less would not be worth the trouble.

NOTES

1. References to Beckett's work given in the text are to the
   following editions, all published in London:

   That Time (1976);
   Mercier and Camier (1974);
   Lessness (1970);
   Molloy, Malone Dies, The Unnamable (1959);
   Murphy (1963);
   The Lost Ones (1972);
   Watt (1963);
   Endgame (1964);
   Not I in *Ends and Odds: Plays and Sketches* (1977).

8 Reflections of Mortality: Max Frisch's *Triptychon: Drei szenische Bilder*

MICHAEL BUTLER

I

For a writer whose international reputation rests largely on his contribution to the theatre, it is a surprising fact that Max Frisch's new work, *Triptychon: Drei szenische Bilder* (1978), is not only his first play for over a decade but only the second he has produced since *Andorra* in 1961. Such apparent reticence *vis-à-vis* the theatre has been frequently explained, however, by Frisch himself. For example, he put forward his previous play, *Biografie* (1967), as an attempt to seek a way out of a dramaturgical impasse first delineated in his 'Schiller-Preisrede' of 1965. There Frisch spoke of his increasing dissatisfaction with his earlier experiments with the parable play, specifically *Biedermann und die Brandstifter* (1958) and *Andorra* − plays which followed 'eine Dramaturgie der Fügung, eine Dramaturgie der Peripetie' (V, 366 − 'a dramaturgy of Fate, a dramaturgy of peripeteia').[1] What concerned Frisch in the middle 1960s − no doubt under the impact of the radical debate on the nature of literature developing at that time in West Germany − was an uneasiness about the predictable nature of the didactic-parable form itself where 'das Gespielte hat einen Hang zum Sinn, den das Gelebte nicht hat' (V, 368 − 'What is played tends to develop a meaning which is not possessed by the lived experience'). He was looking for a theatre which could more truly reflect an experience of life in which chance always seemed to play the greatest role, 'eine Dramaturgie, die eben die Zufälligkeit akzentuiert . . . eine Dramatik der Permutation' (V, 368f. −'a dramaturgy which emphasises fortuitousness . . . a dramaturgy of permutation') - a theatre in other words which would emphasise openness, experiment and the possibility of change.

However, what had already proved an effective aesthetic principle in the novel *Mein Name sie Gantenbein* (*A Wilderness of Mirrors*, 1964), by virtue of the fact that its central character never revealed himself but remained an undefined presence at the centre of a web of shifting inventions, turned out to be untranslatable into the concrete terms of the theatre. The ironically named Kurmann, the protagonist of *Biografie*, could not in the event escape the complex interrelationships of his past, because his essential self was deeply rooted in that past. The medium of the theatre itself, far from stressing the 'play' or arbitrary character of life and thus the possibility of endless variation, merely had an actor confirm Kürmann's fictive identity and reveal him as effectively chained to his biography. Despite Kürmann's reiterated attempts to test alternative patterns of behaviour, he succeeded only in demonstrating the power of linearity, the very sense of 'Fate' masquerading as 'Chance' that Frisch was at pains to deny. *Biografie* in effect turned against its author's intentions.[2]

Some ten years later *Triptychon* - as its title implies - represents a rejection of this experiment with a 'dramaturgy of permutation' in favour of a more radical break with the traditional linear movement of dramatic language. Surprisingly, however, Frisch has refused for the time being to allow his new play to be tested in the theatre. The ostensible reason for this unusual decision was given in an interview published simultaneously with the play:

Die vörlaufige Auffuhrungssperre ist . . . nicht etwas Pathetisches, sondern ich möchte mir Ruhe einräumen. Und ich möchte auch das nicht mehr: daβ ein neues Stuck da ist, es auf den Markt kommt, irgendeine Buhne meint es spielen zu müssen, im Grunde findet sie es gar nicht gut, aber sie wollen eine Uraufführung haben - diesen ganzen Marktrummel wollte ich mir einmal ersparen.[3]

[The temporary ban on production is not an emotional response but a desire on my part to gain a period of rest. One thing I don't want any more is to have a new play come on the market, some theatre or other thinks it ought to stage it, basically it doesn't think much of the play, but they need a world première - I wanted to spare myself this whole marketing business.]

Deprived thus of the traditional first night, the initial
reception of the play in Germany and Switzerland has proved
extraordinarily hesitant if not nonplussed, wavering between
respectful generalisations, muted praise and the occasional
polite reservation.[4] The first serious attempts to get
to grips with the text, as opposed to the simple phenomenon
of its appearance, range from non-committal summary to a
study of comparative elements and undisguised disappoint-
ment.[5] None of these preliminary essays, however, have
gone much beyond a discussion of the play's content or the
apparent influences on it; its unusual structure has tended
to be ignored. And yet it is the structure, the shaping of
Frisch's ideas, rather than any startling originality of
thought, that could prove to be the most arresting aspect of
Triptychon once it appears in the theatre. An effective
analysis, therefore, must take into account not only the
play's content but also its dramaturgical form.

II

Any student of Max Frisch's work will readily perceive
the continuity of theme in *Triptychon*. Indeed, the play's
essential concern with transience and death can be found
already well-established in the author's earliest narratives, *Jürg Reinhart* (1934), *Antwort aus der Stille* (1937)
and *Die Schwierigen* (1943/1957). The recurring elegiac lines
from the latter, 'Alles wiederholt sich, nichts kehrt uns
wieder, Sommer vergehen, Jahre sind nichts' (I, 559, 593,
599 – 'Everything repeats itself, nothing returns to us,
summers pass, years are as nothing'), could well stand as an
adumbration of the thematic material of *Triptychon*. More
recent work, too – for example, the *Tagebuch 1966-1971* and
Montauk (1975) – has intensified Frisch's prolonged meditation on mortality via discussion of the function of memory, the problem of aging and contemporary attitudes towards
death. But, more importantly, Frisch's lastest play can be
seen to fit into his persistent examination of the peculiar
propensity of *language* to obscure and distort reality
rather than express it. However, whereas in earlier novels
and plays Frisch demonstrated how language was the *source*
of fatal *Bildnisse* (images), in *Triptychon* he goes one stage
further and shows language itself in the very process of
petrification.[6]

Thus the play consists of three separate but related
explorations of the inadequacies of language: the first *Bild*
(picture) depicts the linguistic embarrassment of a hetero-

genous group of mourners; the second the dead in a process
of gradually falling into silence as they wander in Hades;
the third the desperate but futile attempt of a man to
'recall' his dead mistress and make up for opportunities
lost in life.

Although conceived and written last,[7] the opening scene
succeeds in establishing the tone of the whole. For here we
see — at a common enough existential moment — the dispirit-
ing clichés of people who use language, like Walter Faber
in *Homo Faber*, as a means of obfuscating reality: 'Er hat
einen schönen Tod gehabt . . . und siebzig ist ein schönes
Alter', 'Sterben müssen wir alle', 'Ich stehe auf dem Boden
der Tatsachen', 'Irgendwie hat der Mensch auch eine Seele'
(pp. 9ff. — 'He had a fine death ... and seventy is a fine
old age', 'We've all got to die', 'I face the facts', 'One
way or another Man has got a soul as well'), and so on —
lifeless phrases from living people whose emptiness is
dramatically highlighted on stage by the unseen presence
of the deceased Matthis Proll sitting in his rocking-chair.
The 'social' nature of these clichés is underlined on the
one hand by the incongruity of the Pastor with his intact
Christian faith,[8] and on the other by the 'angry young
man' Roger who brushes aside what he considers to be mere
superstition in order to express his awareness of the
reality behind appearances:

Ich weiß nur, daß es ein menschliches Bewußtsein ohne bio-
logische Grundlage nicht gibt. Schon eine Gehirnerschüt-
terung macht mich bewußtlos. Wie soll mein Bewußtsein sich
erhalten nach dem materiellen Zerfall meines Hirns? — zum
Beispiel wenn ich mir eine Kugel in den Kopf schieße ...
Ich will nur sagen: als biologisches Faktum ist der Tod
etwas Triviales, eine Bestätigung der Gesetze, der alle
Natur unterworfen ist. Der Tod als Mystifikation, das ist
das andere. Ich sage ja nicht, daß sie inhaltlos sei. Aber
eine Mystifikation. Auch wenn die Vorstellung eines ewigen
Lebens der Person unhaltbar ist, die Mystitikation besteht
darin, daß der Tod letztlich die Wahrheit über unser Leben
ist: Wir leben endgültig. . . . die einzelnen Ereignisse
unseres Lebens, jedes an seinem Platz in der Zeit,
verändern sich nicht. Das ist ihre Ewigkeit. (p. 15)

[All I know is that there cannot be any human consciousness without a biological basis. It only takes a simple
concussion to render me unconscious. How is my consciousness supposed to survive the material disintegration of my
brain? — For example, if I put a bullet through my head
... What I really mean is: death as a biological fact is a

trivial matter, a confirmation of laws to which all Nature is subject. The other way of looking at it is to see death as mystification. I don't claim that this concept has no content. But it *is* a mystification. Even if the idea of eternal life for the individual is untenable, the mystification lies in saying that death is the *ultimate* truth about our lives: We *live* with finality. . . . the individual events of our lives, each with its allotted place in time, do not change. That is their eternity.]

A careful ear, however, will pick out the oddly unconvincing cadences of this superficially fluent and rational mode of thinking. Francine, to whom the words are addressed and who is similarly detached from the conventionality of the other mourners, certainly does so:

Francine: Haben Sie schon einmal einen Menschen verloren, den Sie geliebt haben wie keinen anderen?
Roger: Warum fragen Sie mich das?
Francine: Sie denken so vernünftig.[9]

[*Francine*: Have you ever lost someone whom you loved more than any other person?
Roger: Why do you ask me that?
Francine: You think so rationally.]

The full significance of Roger's 'certainties' is, in fact, only made clear once the 'triptych' has been filled out in the third *Bild*, where the ineffectuality of his initial, brash confidence – once he has been confronted by experience – is finally revealed.

Weaving through this web of social dishonesty and spiritual blindness is the central figure of the funeral feast: the widow, Sophie Proll. It is her preoccupation with her complaints against her late husband that enables *her* to see him – to conjure him up, as it were – sitting in his rocking-chair. By this device of concrete hallucination Frisch introduces a theme which runs practically through the whole of his *oeuvre*: the paralysing power of *Wiederholung* (repetition). For the death of her husband makes no essential difference to Sophie's long marital relationship: absurdly, she continues to reiterate her arid self-justifications against a man now fallen into ultimate silence. The old skirmishes of their marriage continue unabated in her head and point to a paradoxical symbiosis: the spiritual numbness of the living feeds on the eternal indifference of the dead – a vicious circle of pointlessness. The gradual fading away of Matthis Proll points up the melancholy fact that his physical presence was never really necessary in the ,first place for Sophie to indulge her moribund monologues.

The central *Bild* of *Triptychon*, as befits the form it imitates, is the fullest and thus the dominant one. Here, in his own version of Hades, Frisch develops to its logical conclusion his old fear of image-making, that process of stultification in which human beings — wittingly or unwittingly — make persistent efforts to control or repress their own and others' true natures. In Frisch's underworld there is no possibility of change, no redemptive suffering, no opportunity of revision, any more than there is in Sartre's *Huis clos*, which the scene superficially resembles. Unlike Sartre's vision, however, there is no desire here to convince others of fervidly held but essentially spurious truths. A bare stage indicates the time as the 'cruellest month', April — a repetitive and mocking spring. In such sterile and monotonous surroundings the seventy-year-old Proll meets again his father, who had died young. But their relationship, despite the incongruous age difference, remains stuck in that groove of insensitivity and mutual incomprehension it had gouged out in life. Elsewhere, a convict protests his change of heart and complains of injustice to no one in particular; a lover continually rehearses a solipsistic quarrel; a pilot goes over and over the last moments before his airliner crashes; the Pastor from the first *Bild* appears still unshaken in his belief in the Resurrection; and so on. Unlike Sartre's Garcin, Estelle and Inès, Frisch's characters hardly communicate with each other at all. Their hell is *not* other people. Hell does not exist — for there is no feeling and therefore no punishment. Old relationships are merely repeated, fossilised forever at the final stage they reached in life. This 'eternal', emotionless Easter — even the ironically interpolated *Te Deum* is a gramophone recording — acts as a faded backcloth for constellations of characters who themselves are in the process of fading. For all they have left is their individual stories — now deprived of any audience — and, worse, only an intermittent desire to articulate them. In the timelessness of eternity there can be no development, no surprises and ultimately therefore no need for self-expression as a means of self-discovery. The self has *been* expressed: the last words of the play are, 'Das also bleibt' (p. 115 — 'That, then, can't be changed').

Amidst the large number of characters (representatives of widely different 'deaths' but all linked in this particular corner of Hades by chance events in their previous lives) only two seem to possess any degree of consciousness of their predicament: Matthis Proll and the young girl

Katrin - and this may simply be due to the fact that *they* are 'recently' dead and have not yet fallen into the grey rhythm of their seniors. It is Katrin, a young suicide, who is made to utter the familiar Frisch text, 'Es geschieht nichts, was nicht schon geschehen ist. . . . Es kommt nichts mehr dazu' (p. 31 - 'Nothing happens that has not already happened. . . . Nothing more will be added'), and who declares without pathos, 'Daβ wir uns nur noch wiederholen' (p. 40 - 'We are only repeating ourselves'), and, 'Wir sagen uns, was wir schon einmal gesagt haben' (p. 72 - 'We're telling each other things we have already told each other before'). All the other characters wander through this arid landscape as fragments of an unrealised world. What becomes painfully clear is that even this level of consciousness will not remain. For both Proll and Katrin, by their very prescience, realise more acutely than the others the utter pointlessness of continuing to speak. The constant repetition of 'stories', Frisch indicates, will quickly pall once they are consigned to 'eternity' and thus robbed of any possibility of variation.[10]

An intriguing character wandering through the general barrenness is the Clochard. Too promptly he has been taken to be the mouthpiece of Frisch himself.[11] But this is clearly not the function of the Clochard. Although he does utter sentiments that might be said to appeal to Frisch - for example, 'La mort est successive' or 'Es ist schade um den Menschen' ('O poor humanity!') - it is significant that these are themselves quotations (in this case, from Diderot and Strindberg), just as the designation 'Clochard' (tramp) seems too obvious a cliché reference to Samuel Beckett. In fact, the Clochard's major contribution to the text consists predominantly of quotations, including crassly predictable ones from *Hamlet*. It thus comes as no surprise to learn that the Clochard was an *actor* who ended his career as a drunk. In other words, his sentiments are as secondhand as the lives of other characters around him appear to have been. Furthermore, until the very end of the central scene the Clochard is constantly presented as someone set aside, ignored, deprived of his *raison d'être* - an audience. This state of affairs inevitably relativises even the words he utters apparently as his own - in particular, when he declares,

Ich strecke meine Mütze nicht mehr hin - die Toten betteln nicht. Sie fluchen nicht einmal. Sie pinkeln nicht, die Toten, sie saufen nicht und fressen nicht, sie prügeln nicht, die Toten, sie ficken nicht - sie wandeln in der Ewigkeit des Vergangenen und lecken an ihren dummen

Geschichten, bis sie aufgeleckt sind. (p. 43)

[I no longer hold out my cap – the dead don't beg. They
don't even curse. They don't pee, the dead don't get
drunk, they don't stuff themselves with food, they don't
brawl, the dead don't fuck – they wander in the eternity
of what's past and lick away at their stupid stories until
they're all lapped up.]

Such sentiments may indeed be taken as a fit comment on his
companions in the underworld, but they are even more applic-
able to his own life, in which he apparently played role
after role until he lost all contact with what was genuine
in himself. Thus his remark, 'Ich erzähle, wie ich gestorben
bin. Es dauerte dreißig Jahre. Man ist nicht plötzlich tot'
– (p. 49 – 'I'm telling the story of how I died. It took
thirty years. Death is not a sudden event'), though a variation of the general theme, is readily perceived as a
borrowing from Rilke's *Malte Laurids Brigge*. And here, it
would seem, lies the true significance of the Clochard
figure. He is essentially a parody of the artist, the poet-
seer, *der unbehauste Mensch* – the voice in the wilderness
which claims to have detected the daily subterfuges of
ordinary living, as for example in his comment on family
life, with its strong Beckettian undertones:

Jetzt wirft das Kind, jetzt fängt der Papa, jetzt wirft
der Papa, jetzt fängt das Kind – nein, es fängt nicht,
aber der Papa holt den Ball und wirft noch einmal, jetzt
fängt das Kind. Und der Papa klatscht. Jetzt wirft wieder
das Kind. Aber zu tief, und der Papa muß sich bücken.
Genau wie es gewesen ist! – und jetzt fängt das Kind,
jetzt wirft es, jetzt fängt wieder der Papa. (p. 81)

[Now the child throws, now daddy catches, now daddy
throws, now the child catches – no it doesn't catch, but
daddy fetches the ball and throws again, now the child
catches. And daddy applauds. Now the child throws again.
But too low and daddy has to bend. Just as it was! – And
now the child catches, now it throws, now daddy catches
again.]

But the Clochard remains in this context, of course, a
surrogate artist (an actor), a man who mouths other men's
words. Above all, he is a lonely, ignored alcoholic who cannot remember his own lines and a man who hides self-pity behind a mask of knowing cynicism.[12] He is at the same time
both an embodiment of a specific German tradition of *Kultur-*

pessimismus and Frisch's comment on it. If, traditionally, the artist is the living memory of his race, the man who can communicate and combine the disparate and often frightening elements of reality into an aesthetic and constructive whole, it is precisely this function which is mockingly cancelled at the end of the central scene: 'Mein Gedachtnis ist aufgebraucht, die Rolle meines Lebens spielen jetzt andere, und langsam verleiden die Toten sich selbst' (p. 83 – 'My memory is exhausted. Others are now playing the role of my life, and slowly the dead grow tired of themselves and each other').[13]

The final 'wing' of Frisch's triptych takes its significance, like the first, from the play's central image of Hades. The halting and ebbing flow of conversation in the Underground is here replaced by the loquacity of Roger, now presented as a latter-day Orpheus who tries to rescue Francine (the woman who became his mistress after the chance meeting at Proll's funeral) by words alone from the realm of the dead. But the same lack of contact is made clear. Roger's constant 'So hast du gesagt' ('That's what you said') clicks like a linguistic metronome, mocking the lack of rhythm in this one-sided 'conversation' and the erstwhile relationship it vainly tries to conjure up. His reiterated plea, 'Sag etwas' ('Say something'), merely underlines the fact that Francine's words are themselves repetitions that come and go, fading in and out of Roger's memory. Here particularly Frisch shows his originality over the banal debates which pass for 'conversations of the dead' in Sartre's *Les Jeux sont faits*, a play with which the first reviews constantly compared *Triptychon*. For what we have in this final scene is a mimesis of Roger's mental structures. Thus we can observe in uncomfortable proximity the man's excuses, his *mauvaise foi*, his egocentric struggle to assert *his* view of reality, the false pathos bolstered like the Clochard's cynicism with arch references to Hamlet, the Portuguese Nun and the Song of Songs. Roger's efforts, in fact, constitute desperate attempts to seek confirmation of thin experience from the rich storehouse of literature.

It becomes rapidly plain in this bleak scene that it is only the fitful power of *memory* which is keeping Roger from being sucked, as it were, into the central *Bild*. But, as he is forced to recognise, memory runs on limited batteries; for only a creative relationship with a *Du* can keep them charged and thereby enable memory to acquire, store and process knowledge and feeling to promote further growth. The third *Bild* imitates exactly this process of energy running down: Francine's 'answers' pile up at the end like so many disjointed, mechanical utterances, bereft of all spontaneity and life. In Frisch's play, memory is presented as the instrument of a dull, repetitive routine rather than as the supremely creative process it should be, and certainly was, say, for Kierkegaard or Proust.

The appearance of the Clochard as a silent harbinger of death brings Roger to a final perception of his dilemma: Francine cannot be recalled from the underworld; his look backwards at their relationship merely underscores its original lack of vitality, merely conjures up the rigidity of worn-out reflexes and responses. The Clochard points inexorably back to the central *Bild* (where Francine in fact belongs), and Roger's subsequent suicide in its very *kitschig* elements serves only to emphasise the unreality of a life lived in a dishonest way. The Roger of the first *Bild* - forthright and seemingly so clear-headed and self-controlled - ends not with a theatrical bang but with a drawn-out and painful whimper.

III

The foregoing analysis of *Triptychon* has shown that the play cannot claim any particular originality of theme. There is nothing in this new work that Frisch has not said many times over the last forty years in his novels, plays and diaries. But such an analysis, with its necessarily linear argument, cannot do full justice to a structure that gives *Triptychon* more than a passing fascination. For the dramaturgical problems which in part make Frisch hesitate to release his new play for production lie precisely in its iconic form. What Frisch has tried to do is present the three *Bilder* as one interrelated and simultaneous image of reality - even if a highly abstracted one. The two subordinated 'wings' are not meant to be read or seen successively but gain their full meaning only in relation to the dominant central scene. They are linked to it thematically and concretely by the 'hinges' of Proll (who appears in *Bilder* 1 and 2) and the Clochard (who appears in *Bilder* 2 and 3) and to each other by the pairing of Roger and Francine with that hint their relationship gives of primeval discord rooted in *Erkenntnis* (knowledge). (Both are clearly depicted as intellectuals in the opening scene.) The harmony of the triptych is further enhanced by the balancing woman-and-dead-man/man-and-dead-woman configuration of the outer two scenes. The whole composition, however, is held together in terms of a parodic reflection of the integration and equilibrium of the traditional triptych form. For the latter has its origins in the secure world of Christian cultic tradition: the triptych was above all an altar-piece conceived as a backcloth to a meaningful and life-giving celebration.[14] Frisch's wry version fits neatly into the gradual secularisation of this tradition, which led first to the triptych's liberation from the requirements of the liturgy and ultimately to a complete loss of the religious dimension itself. Like the painful Expressionist triptychs of Max Beckmann or the equally bleak vision of Otto Dix, Frisch's linguistic creation is a record both of the cruel finality of man's images and of his spiritual deadness in a world he has ruthlessly defined in his own terms.[15]

It is important to see, however, that *Triptychon* functions not just as a reflection of themes long familiar in Frisch's work, but also as a comment on literary production itself. Hence one of the persistent guises of 'repetition' in the play is the device of overt or covert quotation of literary tradition - a phenomenon which could lead to charges of plagiarism and thus to a misunderstanding of Frisch's purpose. For, despite the apparently pessimistic reflection of literary activity, which is the concomitant feature of the negative portrayal of lives characterised by missed opportunities and failed personal relationships, this triptych can be seen on the contrary as a visually concrete warning. For the pale, indeed fading, reflections of the people in the *Bilder* themselves enables the reader/spectator to see something of his own self reflected back at him. The formal brilliance of this play, it might be said, raises the banality of its theme to the level of art. Rejecting the wit and polish of traditional theatrical essays set in Hades, Frisch aims at the demystification of death and shows that what he calls 'das Tödliche' in all its subtle and unexpected manifestations is more to be feared than death itself. For, whereas death is a necessary end and can have a positive function as a definer of life,[16] 'das Tödliche' ('Lethal negativity') is at work insidiously at every stage of life, poised to corrupt any relationship at any time - and always with the co-operation of the principals.[17]

Thus *Triptychon* can be 'read' not as the statement of a weary pessimist, but as the warning of a very much alive moralist.[18] In a sense, Frisch has returned, paradoxically, to a didactic tradition which in the early 1960s he had declared as a dead end: the theatre as 'eine moralische Anstalt' (a moral institution). The didacticism, of course, is suitably muted, but *Triptychon*, for all its dramaturgical innovation, is nevertheless the work of a sceptical moralist in the mould of Michel de Montaigne, whom Frisch implicitly praises in *Montauk* - a moralist who, whilst perceiving the general weakness in himself, still possesses the energy (as Frisch once put it) of 'painting the demons on the wall' ('Der Autor und das Theater'; V, 350). Frisch's constant weapons are parody, irony and paradox. And their impact on us is all the greater for the fact that, characteristically, he has first turned them on himself.

NOTES

1. This essay was first published in *German Life and Letters*, XXXI, 1 (October 1979), 66-74. References are to *Max Frisch: Gesammelte Werke in zeitlicher Folge*, 6 vols (Frankfurt a. M., 1976). Roman numerals refer to volume, arabic to page. Page references to *Triptychon* are to the 1978 Suhrkamp edition.
2. Cf. Frisch's entry in his *Tagebuch 1966-1971*, dated 8 Feb. 1968: 'Stück aufgeführt, BIOGRAFIE EIN SPIEL, mit vierfachem Sieg der Bühne (Zürich, München, Frankfurt, Düsseldorf) über den Autor; er besteitet die Fatalität, die Bühne bestätigt sie – spielend' (VI, 103 – 'Play produced, BIOGRAFIE EIN SPIEL, with a quadruple victory of the theatre (Zurich, Munich, Frankfurt, Düsseldorf) over the author; he denies Fate, the theatre confirms it – in performance').
3. 'Abschied von her Biografie' (interview with Peter Rüedi), *Die Weltwoche*, 19 Apr. 1978. A slightly modified version of the play was in fact broadcast on 15 April 1979 by the West German Deutschlandfunk (in conjunction with the Sender Freies Berlin, Süddeutsche Rundfunk and Westdeutsche Rundfunk) and repeated on 4 April 1980 on Swiss radio. Since this paper was delivered, however, *Triptychon* has been given its world première after all – but in a French translation by Henry Bergerot! Directed by Michel Soulter and designed by Jean Lecoultre, the play opened on 9 October 1979 in the Centre Dramatique de Lausanne. Frisch's guarded comment before the opening night throws a slightly different light on his earlier hesitations: 'Ich wollte durch die Umsetzung in eine andere Sprache Distanz zu meinem Stück gewinnen, und ich wollte es nicht auf einer grossen Bühne verheizen, sondern es behutsam ausprobieren lassen' ('By having the play translated into another language I wanted to gain distance from it, and I did not want to expose the play recklessly in a major theatre but have it tried out cautiously') – quoted in an unsigned review, 'Von der

Unfähigkeit, zu lieben und zu leben', *Der Bund*, 11 Oct. 1979. After a second try-out in Warsaw, directed in Polish by Erwin Axer, Frisch — presumably satisfied with the positive reception — released the original text to the Frankfurt Schauspielhaus for staging in January 1981. A complex row between the Suhrkamp Verlag, on the one hand, and the theatrical management and actors, on the other, led first to the postponement and finally to legal proceedings for broken contract. (Details of this unsavoury episode can be found in *Frankfurter Rundschau*, 19 and 20 Dec. 1980 and in *Der Spiegel*, 29 Dec. 1980.) *Triptychon* was eventually given its German première on 1 Feb. 1981 in the Akademietheater, Vienna (director: Erwin Axer). The immediate critical reception, ranging from undiluted praise to severe drubbing, merely added to the confusion and mystification surrounding the play's bizarre odyssey from page to stage.

4. The inadequacies of the 'Feuilleton' reception have been examined by Walter Schmitz: 'Zu Max Frisch: *Triptychon, Drie szenische Bilder*' in Gerhard P. Knapp (ed.), *Max Frisch: Aspekte des Bühnenwerks* (Bern, Frankfurt a. M. and Las Vegas, 1979) pp. 401-24.

5. Respectively, Jürgen H. Petersen, *Max Frisch*, Sammlung Metzler Band 173 (Stuttgart, 1978); Gerhard P. Knapp, '"Daβ wir uns nur noch wiederholen." Jean-Paul Sartre und Max Frisch: Notizen zur literarischen Tradition', and Alexander von Bormann, 'Theater als Existenz-Erfahrung? Die Wende von Max Frisch zum christlichen Laienspiel', both in Knapp, *Max Frisch*, pp. 437-49 and pp. 425-36.

6. Frisch's cultural roots clearly stretch back beyond post-1945 Existentialism to the *Kulturpessimismus* of the turn of the century as evinced in such key documents as Hofmannsthal's *Ein Brief* (the 'Chandos Letter', 1902) and Rilke's *Die Aufzeichnungen des Malte Laurids Brigge* (1910). For a discussion of the literary-historical connections, see Schmitz, in Knapp, *Max Frisch*, pp. 406ff.

7. See the interview with Peter Rüedi cited in n. 3.

8. That Frisch does not intend any attack on Christianity in his play, however, is clear from his remark to Rüedi, 'Es ist eine sicher nichtchristliche Todesvorstellung, aber keine polemisch antichristliche' ('My concept of death is certainly a non-Christian one, but not polemically anti-Christian').

9. It is the fate of a number of important Frisch characters to arrive at the painful discovery that knowledge is not exclusively a matter of the intellect but also one of feeling. Walter Faber springs to mind and also

Rolf, the Staatsanwalt in *Stiller*, who at a critical moment of emotional stress is forced to confess: 'Dabei wuβt ich nicht, was tun. Meine Vernünftigkeit kam mir selber sehr schal vor' (III, 761f.; 'I didn't know what to do. I felt myself that my commonsense approach was very shallow').

10. It was this very possibility of variation that kept the anonymous narrator of *Mein Name sie Gantenbein* going. In contrast, none of the characters in *Triptychon* has his 'story' fleshed out; they remain ciphers, their biographies thin and uninteresting. Frisch remarks in the interview with Rüedi that this was the *result*, not the intention, of his work on the text: 'Das [the central scene] sollte das Stück überhaupt werden, dieses Dialogwerk. Es wurde dann immer knapper und knapper, weil sich ja gezeigt hat, daβ die Toten sehr maulfaul sind, die reden nicht mehr sehr viel' ('That was meant to be the whole play, this collection of dialogues. But the scene grew briefer and briefer because it turned out that the dead are verbally lazy, they don't have much left to say to each other'). This is where Frisch can be differentiated from Samuel Beckett, who Petersen, for example, seems to think has decisively influenced him (*Max Frisch*, p. 181f). For many of Beckett's characters exhibit extraordinary verbal energy precisely *against* the overwhelming evidence of the absurdity of their situation.

11. For example, by Peter Iden, 'Gespräche am Totenfluβ', *Frankfurter Rundschau*, 6 May 1978; and Hans Bertram Bock, 'Der Rest ist Bitternis', *Nürmberger Nachrichten*, 8–9 July 1978.

12. Cf. Walter Schmitz's perceptive remark: 'Der Clochard, ehemaliger Schauspieler, beschreibt seine Rolle als Zyniker in seiner Rollensprache. Der *Gesprächszerfall* ist total' ('The Clochard, a former actor, describes his role as cynic in the language of his role. The disintegration of linguistic communication is complete') – in Knapp, *Max Frisch*, p. 416

13. Memory as the uncertain key to knowledge and above all to the maintenance of personal identity is the theme of Frisch's latest work, *Der Mensch erscheint im Holozän: Eine Erzählung* (Frankfurt a. M., 1979).

14. See Klaus Lankheit, *Das Triptychon als Pathosformel* (Heidelberg, 1959).

15. Interestingly, Lankheit discusses the decline of the religious triptych in terms strongly reminiscent of Frisch: 'Die christliche Gestaltkunst [ist] von der Krisis der Abbildlichkeit betroffen, die mit der Wendung

zur Unanschaulichkeit in aller Erkenntniszweigen einget-
reten ist. Die Krisis des Altarbildes ist zunächst die
Krisis des anthropomorphen Gottesbildes. . . . Denn die
Krisis des christlichen Kultbildes ist weiterhin eine
Krisis der Bilderfahrung überhaupt' (p. 85 — 'Christian
art has been deeply affected by the crisis of represen-
tationality which came about with the trend towards
impenetrableness in every branch of knowledge. The
crisis of the altar-piece is primarily the crisis of the
anthropomorphic image of God. . . . For the crisis of
the image in Christian worship is moreover a crisis in
the way we experience images altogether').

16. Cf. Frisch's remark in his *Tagebuch 1946-1949*: 'Erst aus
dem Nichtsein, das wir ahnen, begreifen wir für Augen-
blicke, daβ wir leben' (II, 500 — 'Only through the
faint perception of non-being do we grasp for moments
that we are alive').

17. The impetus to write *Triptychon* came apparently from
just such an episode in Frisch's own life. In an interview with John Barak, Frisch touched on this seminal
incident: 'I had a friend with whom I once was close. We
had a squabble and for seven and a half years had no
contact. The squabble was minor in comparison with our
former accord, and yet if either one of us had died during this interval the event of death would have immor-
talised the pettiness of the squabble' — 'Max Frisch
Interviewed', *New York Times Book Review*, 19 Mar. 1978.
Later in the same interview Frisch tacitly admitted that
the friend in question was Friedrich Dürrenmatt.

18. Cf. Frisch's comment on his play to Rüedi: 'Meine
Hoffnung wäre gewesen (ob das zum Ausdruck kommt, weiβ
ich heute noch nicht), daβ das nicht etwa eine Absage an
das Leben ist, sondern im Gegenteil: was stattfindet,
findet in dieser Zeit statt, also vor dem Jenseits oder
der Ewigkeit. Das ist eine Bejahung der Existenz als
einzigem Zeitraum, in dem etwas sich verwandeln, in dem
man umdenken kann' ('I would hope — whether I have
expressed it I don't know even today — that the play is
not any kind of rejection of life but its opposite: what
takes place, takes place here and now, that is, before
the next world or eternity. It's an affirmation of
existence as the only temporal sphere in which things
can be changed and in which one can re-think one's
position').

9 Auden and Brecht

JOHN WILLETT

I

In 1957, when I was writing my book *The Theatre of Bertolt Brecht*, I wrote to W. H. Auden to know if he was at all influenced by Brecht's work. I had heard about their collaboration on a version of *The Duchess of Malfi* in the United States, and I had been impressed by a translation by Auden and James Stern of Act V of *The Caucasian Chalk Circle* that had appeared in the *Kenyon Review* in the spring of 1946, about a year and a half before Brecht left America. I wasn't quite sure who Stern was, though I seemed to recall that in the late 1930s a story by him had appeared in John Lehmann's *New Writing*, which had also printed a poem and a short scene by Brecht. But I had seen various parallels between Auden and Brecht — for instance, in the former's balladesque poem 'Victor', which recalled Brecht's 'Apfelboeck' — and wanted, as an admirer of both poets, to find out more.

Auden, then staying on Ischia, told me that he had met Brecht a number of times, particularly when working on the *Malfi* adaptation, which he called 'an appalling flop'.[1] He had lost the script of the *Caucasian Chalk Circle* translation, and wrote that 'The early Brecht, like *Hauptpostille*, *Mahagonny Stadt* and the *Drei Groschen Oper*, have certainly influenced me.' *Sic*, *sic* and *sic*: what he was referring to was *Die Hauspostille*, Brecht's first book of poems; *Aufstieg und Fall der Stadt Mahagonny*, his opera with Weill; and the *Dreigroschenoper*, better known to us as *The Threepenny Opera*.

Eighteen months later I wrote to him again, because I had been told via Eric Bentley and Brecht's son Stefan that Auden had once made a translation of *The Threepenny Opera*

162

too. I had also been talking to John Cullen of Methuen about the publication of some kind of English Brecht edition, and wanted to know if Auden had ever translated any of the poems and whether he could tackle any further plays. He answered, again from Ischia, 'No, I never did a translation of the *Dreigroschenoper*, though I should have liked to very much.'[2] He had done none of the poems apart from the *Caucasian Chalk Circle* songs, but said that he had 'toyed and still toy with the thought of some day translating *Baal* [by which I think he meant the introductory chorale or hymn from that play] and *Das ertrunkenes Mädschen* [i.e. 'Die Ballade vom ertrunkenen Mädchen', another song from *Baal*]'. As for plays, he had just completed his version of *The Seven Deadly Sins* with Chester Kallman for performance that November, but 'I don't really want to spend much time translating Brecht or anyone else.' At best he and Kallman might be interested in doing *Aufstieg und Fall der Stadt Mahagonny*, because it was 'all sung', and the problem is making an English version rather than a translation in the strict sense'. This they were in fact to do some two years later, though their version remained long unperformed and was only published in the United States in 1976. It and *The Seven Deadly Sins* now make volume II part iii of the Eyre Methuen *Collected Plays*.

Then in 1971 Auden published his commonplace book under the title *A Certain World*. Here he includes a section called 'Unfavourites and Favourites', with a list of what he terms 'my pets': a select team of fourteen of those 'elder modern poets . . . from whom I have learned most'.[3] At their head is 'Berthold Brecht (the lyric poet)'. *Sic*.

That is where I started to become curious again, and began seriously trying to find out what the relationship between the two writers really was. What I have managed to put together is still full of gaps and unsolved puzzles, but here it is in its present incomplete state.

II

Auden was at Oxford from 1925 to 1928, going down that summer. Breon Mitchell, who wrote a paper in *Oxford German Studies*[4] on the subject, quotes him as saying that 'he knew no German and no German literature' at that time. More recently Gabriel Carritt, who was one of Auden's closest Oxford friends, told me that Auden had lent him books on Toller and Brecht, and was already talking about the latter before leaving for Germany in August 1928. This would have been surprising, as Brecht at that time was still relatively unknown. If Auden knew of Toller – which is likelier, since there had by then been a number of translations of his plays and of his *Swallow Book* of prison poems – it could perhaps have been from a student performance: there is no record of any Toller production at the Oxford Playhouse in his time.

But in the autumn of 1928, when Auden arrived in Berlin for a year's stay, *The Threepenny Opera* opened in Berlin, and he did see that – apparently very soon after arriving. I think he must also have got hold of the *Hauspostille* (which had been published the previous year, though the poems in it all dated from before 1923), and it is possible that he came to know *Mahagonny* from records. He himself did subsequently write some more or less frivolous poems in German (which have not been published). As for his friend and collaborator Christopher Isherwood, who followed Auden to Berlin about six months later, he neither met Brecht at that time nor came into contact with his work, though he had some rather nebulous dealings with Willi Münzenberg's organisation International Workers'Aid (or IAH, or Mezhrabpom, a body directly responsible to the Comintern), where Brecht's name would have been – sometimes approvingly, sometimes censoriously – a household word. Gerald Hamilton, the slippery original of Isherwood's Mr Norris, did, rather amazingly, speak on Münzenberg's platforms; he may have been somebody's spy.

Hitler came to power, Isherwood left Berlin, Brecht went into exile. At the end of 1933 the Brechts moved into the Danish cottage where they were to spend the next five and a half years. From October to December 1934 Brecht was in London, staying with the composer Hanns Eisler in lodgings in Calthorpe Street off the Gray's Inn Road, just behind New Printing House Square, working on film projects and Communist songs. Auden, who had begun writing plays – notably the very Expressionist *The Dance of Death* the previous year – was then schoolmastering. Whether Brecht made any English contacts outside the film business is not clear; if he did, they have left no mark. In 1935, however, he got to know John Lehmann in Moscow, and perhaps that is why the next year, when he again came to London to work on a film – a terrible-sounding version of *Pagliacci* with the tenor Richard Tauber – he did meet a number of people connected with Auden in one way or another.

Thus, William Coldstream, at whose house in Upper Park Road, Hampstead, Auden stayed when working for the GPO Film Unit, vaguely recalls seeing Brecht at the unit's offices in Soho Square; Basil Wright likewise half-remembers having lunch with Brecht, Cavalcanti, Lotte Reiniger of silhouette-

film fame, and her husband, Carl Koch, at a Soho restaurant.
Eric Walter White, Benjamin Britten's biographer, visited
Brecht in Abbey Road, where he was staying with the Van
Gyseghems of Unity Theatre, and recalls discussing the
Pagliacci film. A. J. Ayer, then on the point of becoming my
philosophy tutor, once told me that he too had met Brecht in
London, but now remembers nothing about the occasion. And it
must have been around the same time that Brecht, apparently
more than once, visited Rupert Doone and Robert Medley of
the (London) Group Theatre, which had presented *The Dance of
Death* and the Auden-Isherwood *The Dog Beneath the Skin* - the
latter in February of that year. I talked to Medley, who was
vague about dates but recalled Brecht's inviting them both
to Denmark if there was a second world war.

Undoubtedly Brecht must have made some kind of contact
with Auden in 1936, if only on the telephone, because when
he got back to Denmark that August he wrote saying,

> dear comrade auden,
>   before i left london i made a small arrangement with an
> american literary agent by which he would pay you an
> advance of £25 for an english version [*Nachdichtung*] of
> one of my plays. it's not a large advance, but it's some-
> thing. one of them, die rundkoepfe und die spitzkoepfe
> [i.e. *The Round Heads and the Pointed Heads*], is probably
> going to be produced in copenhagen this autumn. if you
> came to see me you could see one or two of the rehearsals.
> i hope you haven't forgotten your promise to come? i would
> be very glad if you did.
>   yours cordially,
>   bertolt brecht[5]

It is my guess that Auden had considered visiting Copenhagen
on the way either to or from the *Letters from Iceland* trip;
however, he never did so, and Brecht's letter must have
reached England some weeks after he and Louis MacNeice had
set off. (MacNeice himself, incidentally, never met Brecht
and, according to his wife Hedli, did not like what he knew
of Brecht's work.) The term 'comrade' in the letter - the
only time in their slender correspondence that Brecht so
addressed him - suggests Auden's political position a few
months before he decided to volunteer for the International
Brigade: if he wasn't actually in the Communist Party at
that moment, he must have been very close.

Another thing that Brecht must have done at some time
during his second London visit was to arrange for the
English publication of his *Dreigroschenroman* - the *Threepenny Novel*, first issued in 1937 by Robert Hale as *A Penny*

for the Poor. Isherwood translated the verses for this, most of them being taken from the songs in the play. But he still had no direct contact with Brecht, his participation having been arranged by the main translator, Desmond I. Vesey, then a newly appointed director of Robert Hale's publishing firm but previously in Berlin, where Brecht's right-hand woman, Elisabeth Hauptmann, had known him. Vesey, who is now dead, was the son of an Indian Army general and was rumoured to be working for the British Secret Service in Germany just before the Reichstag Fire. When I met him in the 1960s he struck me as a plausible candidate for such a role; he was certainly in MI5 in the Second World War.

That more or less concludes the story of the Brecht–Auden relationship as it began in England in the 1930s. It was appreciative enough on Brecht's side for him to include Auden and Isherwood, as well as Rupert Doone the dancer-director, in the proposed Diderot Society, or society for *Theaterwissenschaft*, which he inconclusively tried to set up the next year: this would have been a group of about a dozen like-minded persons in different countries, among them Eisenstein, Piscator, Jean Renoir and Archibald Macleish. He may also have read the Auden–Isherwood plays (in fact Medley now[6] recalls actually seeing *The Dance of Death*, though he is not otherwise thought to have been in London in February 1934, when the Group Theatre performed it), since he referred to them approvingly in his 'Notes on the Folk Play' of 1940, written in Finland while waiting to leave for the United States.[7] What he didn't care for, he said, was their use of symbolism — something that comes across most strongly, of course, in *The Ascent of F6*. The Group Theatre probably had the script of this work by the time of Brecht's 1936 visit, prior to its publication on 24 September and its première on 26 February 1937 (both these dates being after Brecht had returned to Denmark).

III

The Second World War broke out, Auden and Isherwood settled in the United States, and in 1941 the Brechts followed. Like Auden, Brecht had been asked to teach at the New School in New York, but instead he settled in Santa Monica, an attractive seaside suburb of Los Angeles where he finally met Isherwood through their joint friend Berthold Viertel, the Austrian film and theatre director and excellent poet, who was the prototype of the unforgettable Bergmann in Isherwood's novel *Prater Violet*. 'This I wrote this morning', says Bergmann in a scene that is clearly taken from life, 'after reading your book [i.e. Isherwood's second novel, *The Memorial*]. . . . My first poem in English. To an English poet.' 'I took it and read', says Isherwood, who goes on to quote:

> When I am a boy, my mother tells to me
> It is lucky to wake up when the morning is bright
> And first of all hear a lark sing.
> Now I am no longer a boy, and I wake. The morning is
>   dark.
> I hear a bird singing with unknown name
> In a strange country language, but it is luck, I think.
>
> Who is he, this singer, who does not fear the gray city?
> Will they drown him soon, the poor Shelley?
> Will Byron's hangmen teach him how one limps?
> I hope they will not, because he makes me happy.

After being introduced by Viertel on 19 August 1943, Brecht asked Isherwood to dinner on 20 September, and according to both men's accounts it seems that they got on well, though Brecht by then was aware of the new religious preoccupations of the two English writers, describing Isherwood in his journal as 'ein kleiner mönchersatz' - a little imitation monk in his Buddhist garb. Admittedly Isherwood got up and left that particular party when Brecht said that Aldous Huxley was 'gekauft', had sold out. But Brecht later gave him *The Good Person of Szechwan* to read in the hope that he might translate it. Isherwood politely refused (unfortunately he cannot remember whether it was the new, shortened version of the play or the standard 1940 version) but offered to lend Brecht one or two hundred dollars to tide him over till he could get a production set up. This struck Brecht as 'a lot', so he noted in his journal, 'as I know he's got nothing'.[8]

The *Szechwan* play was among various projects which Brecht had been discussing with the actress Elisabeth Bergner, whom he knew from Munich and Berlin, and who was then hoping that her prewar London successes would help her obtain recognition as a star in the American theatre and cinema, something she never in fact achieved. In New York a few months earlier, however, they had settled on an adaptation of *The Duchess of Malfi* which Brecht was to make for her, simplifying and redrafting the story himself (in a mixture of English and German) but leaving any new writing to the American poet H. R. Hays. Hays, who came from one of the earliest New York families, had worked with Hanns Eisler on a satire called *The Medicine Show* for the Federal Theatre in 1939, and had also scripted a rejected Davy Crockett musical for Kurt Weill. Possibly through these connections he became interested in translating some of Brecht's work (for instance, he did the first English version of *Mother Courage*, which James Laughlin published in *New Directions* in 1941) and had helped supply affidavits so that the Brechts might be admitted to the United States. An underrated writer, he was one of the only two English-language poets since Kipling whom Brecht himself translated, the other being not Auden but the Santa Monica writer Albert Brush.

Hays completed two or three scripts on the basis of Brecht's polyglot draft scenes, then in the winter of 1943 he was surprised to learn from Bergner's producer husband Paul Czinner that Auden too was to be brought in. This followed a letter from Brecht to Auden at Swarthmore College asking him to take part and saying, 'As you can imagine I would get great satisfaction from being able to work with you'.[9] Bringing in Auden must in my view have been Brecht's own decision rather than Czinner's, and he may well have talked to Isherwood about it, though Isherwood himself cannot remember. In any case, Hays promptly left in a rage, and ever afterwards refused to let the adaptation be performed or published with both his and Auden's names on it.

Auden and Brecht saw each other in New York early in 1944, but in fact their subsequent versions still contained a lot of Hays's work. Auden's hand is apparent in some of the later scripts, most clearly in the Echo scene, the Epilogue (which is half Auden, half Webster, and very beautiful) and also – in my opinion – in the shortened rendering of Brecht's soldiers' song 'Als wir kamen vor Milano' (a phrase whose word-order is, anyway, English rather than German):

> I wrote my love a letter
> When we entered fair Milan:
> Oh the war will soon be over
> For the cook has lost his coppers
> And the captain's lost his head
> And we've shot away our lead.
>
> But when we left the city
> Then a second war began
> Though the first was scarcely over
> And I'll drink a thousand beakers
> With a whore upon my knee
> Till my love again I see.[10]

This occurs in Act II, scene i of the last script copy-

righted under Brecht's and Hays's names only, and thirty
years later Hays insisted to me that it must be his work.
But it sounds to my ear much more like Auden, and both
Isherwood and Stephen Spender (whom I also consulted) agree.

While the *Duchess* was under way, and within a few weeks of
his first approach to Auden, Brecht had got involved with
another Germany émigrée actress who wanted a Broadway play
from him. This time it was Luise Rainer, who had made a
great hit in the film of Pearl Buck's Chinese novel *The Good
Earth* and now had Brecht commissioned by a would-be New York
impresario called Jules Leventhal to write her *The Caucasian
Chalk Circle*. At first Brecht seems to have wanted Isherwood
to do the English text, but Isherwood pleaded commitments,
and so on completing the first version of the script, in
June 1944, Brecht proposed that Auden be commissioned
instead. Auden, however, only received the script some two
months later, after a preliminary translation had been made
(for $250) by James and Tania Stern, close friends of his
who had been sharing a shack with him on Fire Island. James,
I later discovered, was an Irish-born writer descended from
a Frankfurt banking family; his father was an officer in the
13th Hussars and his brother became champion jockey of
Ireland. Tania, a gymnastics-teacher, was German, being the
sister of the former Soviet art administrator Alfred
Kurella, sometime secretary to Henri Barbusse and later
chief cultural pundit of the East German Socialist Unity
Party.

Auden's first reaction, even before seeing their rough
version, was that the play would probably 'have to be completely remodelled'.[11] Then a few days later he suggested
that he and the Sterns might collaborate, but only if and
when the producers 'got serious'.[12] How serious they might
have got is hard to make out, since Luise Rainer abandoned
the whole project once she came back from entertaining the
armed forces and saw the script. But it was still on in
December, when Brecht had read the rough translation and
was looking forward to the finished *Nachdichtung* which Auden
had just contracted to make. 'This matters enormously to
me', Brecht wrote (in German) to Stern. 'I mind more about
having an English version by him than about getting a
Broadway production.'[13] In the end, however, Auden only
translated the verses — which Brecht was at this stage
expecting Eisler to set — and made adjustments to the
Sterns' dialogue. Two finished scripts were then typed by
Stern, who later destroyed one of them. The other was sent
in November 1945 to John Crowe Ransom, who in due course
printed the last act in the *Kenyon Review*.

By that time the war was over, but *The Duchess of Malfi*,

like Mother Courage and her cart, dragged wearily on. Work on both plays had been interrupted shortly after the German surrender by Auden's departure for some four months as a member of the Morale Division of the US Strategic Bombing Survey, to report on the effects of the war on the civilian population. Stern, who was part of the same team, has given a vivid account of their findings in a now unobtainable book called *The Hidden Damage*; meantime his wife Tania stayed in Vermont, where she had the company not only of the Czinners but also of Viertel, the Zuchmayers and the Budzislawskis – Hermann Budzislawski being a Communist journalist who worked for Dorothy Thompson. Brecht too was there in July.

On his return that autumn Auden was summoned to Chicago by the Czinners to do what he called some rehashing of the *Malfi* script: 'scholars', he told a friend, 'will be *appalled*'.[14] As things eventually turned out, they were not, because, rather than let Brecht direct it, Bergner brought over George Rylands, who decided to go back to Webster's original text. All Brecht's and Hays's work was thrown out of the window; Brecht had his name removed from the whole undertaking, leaving only Auden to figure as author of a song or two (these, along with Webster's lovely dirge, being set by Britten, who, however, was out of sympathy with the whole production, so that according to Eric White none of his music has survived). The play opened in Providence in September 1946, was seen in Boston by an appalled Brecht, moved to the Ethel Barrymore Theatre in New York and folded after a month. Two years later Auden had still not been fully paid. 'God forbid that anyone should get hold of that *Duchess of Malfi*', he wrote to me in 1958. 'I cannot recall the incident without a shudder.'[15]

To round off the story of Brecht and Auden in America: it was in 1945 that Reynal and Hitchcock, who were Hays's publishers, decided to bring out an edition of Brecht's poems in Hays's versions. Hays told me that Brecht had wished Auden to take part in this too, but the publishers had 'stood by' him and not allowed it. The following year this developed into a more ambitious scheme for an American Brecht edition, again with Reynal and Hitchcock, for which Eric Bentley was to select and edit some plays. Bentley told Stern that he wanted to include *The Caucasian Circle of Chalk*, as it was then called, and after the publication of the *Kenyon Review*'s extract he got the script from Ransom. However, only the fifty poems translated by Hays ever appeared (under the title *Selected Poems*); Reynal and Hitchcock were swallowed up in another firm, and the rest of the edition never materialised.

Brecht appears to have understood from Bentley that Auden

would have no objection if he and Maya Apelman made a new translation of the play – though, according to Stern, Auden subsequently denied this. Anyhow, the three earlier translators lost track of their one surviving script, and very soon they had lost interest in it too. It has never been traced. Thus, when the play was finally staged in May 1948 in a mid-Western college production by Henry Goodman, it was in Eric and Maya Bentley's translation. This was copyrighted in 1947 and published along with their translation of *The Good Woman of Sezuan* under the title *Parables for the Theatre*.

IV

I myself only came into the story in 1956, by which time Auden was spending much of his time in Europe and Brecht, of course seemed ensconced in his theatre in East Berlin. I went there to see him that summer – it was not long before his death – and was told by his young daughter Barbara that the one suitable translator for his work was someone she called Arden; it took me a moment to realise who it was she meant. Later I was to find this view borne out by her brother and her mother, though none of the family seemed very clear as to what Auden translations there might already be. So I wrote to him, and in due course set about finding a copy of the Auden-Stern *Caucasian Chalk Circle* script. Bentley put me on the track of a microfilm which Brecht's Danish mistress Ruth Berlau had made and had deposited in the New York Public Library, and after some false alarms Robert Macgregor of *New Directions* eventually located it and had it copied for Methuen, to whom I had proposed it for their first Brecht play volume.

As the translation was still in rather a rough state and did not entirely tally with the final German text, Auden and the Sterns undertook to revise it. In October 1959 Auden wrote to Stern from the Austrian village of Kirchstetten, where he had now settled:

Methuens sent me pages from the Chalky Caucasus, which I have revised as best I could. It's terrifying when a fifteen-year old corpse which one has completely forgotten suddenly comes out of its grave. The only places where I have been deaf to your question-marks are the Azdak lyrics and Mrs Plushbottom limerick. When the words are to be sung, the translator has either to do a version which will correspond exactly to the music (I have never seen the

music for this play. I suppose it exists)[16] or assume
that new music will be written for the English version: in
either case the suitability of words to setting is much
more important than being literal, I believe: my practice
is to read the original first for its meaning (my German
is much better now) and then put the original out of my
head and re-create.[17]

At the end he added a PPS: 'There is one line, I have left
to you since I am very uncertain what it means. *Schrecklich
ist die Verführung zur Güte.*' This sentence – 'terrible is
the temptation to goodness' – is, interestingly enough, the
key line of the play.

The revised translation is now in volume seven of the Eyre
Methuen edition of the *Collected Plays*, along with the final
Hays version of the *Duchess of Malfi* script, which includes
the song which I think is by Auden. The Auden-Kallman *Seven
Deadly Sins* and *Mahagonny* have likewise appeared as part of
volume two. Hannah Arendt wrote of these in the *New Yorker*
that she knew of 'no other adequate rendering of Brecht into
English'. They are very good, but I don't agree. Auden's
translations of the *Mother Courage* songs, which he did for
William Gaskill's National Theatre production of May 1965,
are in his *City Without Walls*; Spender thinks them among his
best work, but they don't fit Paul Dessau's settings, and
they diverge too much from the originals for my taste, in
both meaning and gist. Nor did they really tell in the
production, where they were very badly sung to wishy-washy
settings by Darius Milhaud. Not long after that, Spender
told me that Auden would like to translate the whole play,
so I wrote again to him in August 1971 to ask if he was
still prepared to do this. He answered from Kirchstetten on
6 September:

On thinking it over, I have decided I cannot do *Mother
Courage*. The truth is that I think Brecht was a great
lyric poet, but a second-rate dramatist. His natural
poetic sensibility was pessimistic, even Christian, and he
tired to harness this to an optimistic philosophy, e.g. he
apparently wants us to take *M.C.* as a picture of what
life is like under capitalism, but I can only interpret
the play as 'That is what, since Adam fell, life is like –
period.'

At that time I was beginning to get together the English
language edition of Brecht's poems, which eventually saw
the light after various cumulative idiocies, being finally
published in London in 1976 and in New York in 1980. I had

already asked Auden in 1969 if he could translate some of
the poems, and he answered that at present he had no time
and it would not be fair to say that he might do some at a
later date. Little did he know how long it would all take.
So, two years later, I asked him again and discovered, a bit
to my surprise, that he had never seen the collected German
Gedichte, which had appeared between 1960 and 1967, full of
previously unpublished stuff and revolutionising many
people's ideas about Brecht's work. Once he could lay his
hands on these, he said, he would 'see if I think I can do
anything, but I can't promise anything'.[18]

I got the publisher to send him the posh leather-bound
edition, and also organised an unrelated but agreeably co-
incidental *bonne bouche* in the shape of a small and very
good lunch-party to celebrate the fiftieth anniversary of
the St Edmund's School Literary Society — this being the
preparatory school on the borders of Surrey and Hampshire
where Auden minor and C. Bradshaw Isherwood both went and
I later followed - the society's founders having been himself, Harold Llewellyn-Smith and the headmaster's daughter,
my dear godmother Winnie Morgan-Brown. Encouraged by his
geniality on this occasion, I afterwards wrote to Auden
sending him an unpublished poem which I had found in Berlin,
called 'Begegnung mit dem Dichter Auden'. It goes,

lunchend mich wie sichs gehört
in a brauhaus (unzerstört)
sass er gleichend einer wolke
über dem bebierten volke

und erwies die referenz
auch der nackten existenz
ihrer theorie zumindest
wie du sie in frankreich findest

This can be found on p. 418 of the *Poems* fairly freely
translated as

Encounter with the Poet Auden
Lunching me, a kindly act,
In an alehouse (still intact)
He sat looming like a cloud
Over the beer-sodden crowd

And kept harping with persistence
On the bare fact of existence
I.e., a theory built around it
Recently in France propounded.

I thought that this might amuse him, and asked if he could tell me anything about the occasion referred to. He answered, after thanking me for getting up the lunch,

> I'm afraid I must cry off the Brecht translations because I cannot do ånything for some time, and, evidently, time presses. So sorry.
>
> I was amused [or it could be 'amazed'] by the verses you sent me. I recognise neither the locality nor the opinions I am supposed to have expressed. The last time I saw BB was, I think, in East Berlin in 1952.[19]

I have never managed to find out any more about their meeting, and it is possible that Auden disliked the allusion to the French brand of Existentialism, which (says Edward Mendelson) he despised. So I couldn't help wondering if paragraph 2 of the letter might not have helped inspire paragraph 1. Had I put my foot in it? Anyway, Auden never translated any of the Brecht poems he so admired — or if he did he kept it to himself. And this was my last contact with him. Alas.

V

Now, what were Auden's real feelings about Brecht? Why, after admiring his writings and collaborating apparently painlessly with him, did he switch to an attitude of apparent distaste for Brecht after the Second World War? In 1975 I got a letter from Charles Monteith of Faber and Faber saying, among other things,

> Auden said to me — not once but many times since it was one of his favourite conversation-stoppers — that of the literary men he had known only three struck him as positively evil: Robert Frost, Yeats and Brecht! When I asked him to expand a little he said, about Brecht, 'He was simply a crook. Never gave up either his Austrian nationality or his Swiss bank account.'[20]

I don't myself think that these are the kind of actions which make a man a crook, let alone positively evil, and I am sure that Auden felt this way about Brecht long before anyone became interested in such details of Brecht's civic and financial status. So I asked another of his close friends what he thought the real reason was. His answer was that Auden had simply been afraid: to have aligned himself

with Brecht in the McCarthy era, following Brecht's own
hearing by the Un-American Activities Committee, could have
done him serious harm. I asked Edward Mendelson; he had no
idea. I asked Isherwood. He said, 'No comment.'

Mendelson's private speculation was that Brecht and Auden
were at bottom very much alike. Both started as romantic
anarchists, then converted to an orthodoxy around the age of
thirty. Auden, he suggested, 'may have felt that *he* converted to the true orthodoxy while B converted to a false
one, and that while he, Auden believed in his, B (Auden may
have felt) did not believe in *his*'[21] — to which I would
add that the opposite feeling, or any twinge of it, could
have been even more alienating. Similarly, Hannah Arendt,
who had an immense regard for Auden but an untenably
ambiguous attitude to Brecht, wrote of Auden as reflecting
'the obvious influence of Brecht, with whom I think he had
more in common than he was ever ready to admit'. Whether or
not they explain Auden's apparent postwar distaste — which
Brecht and his family, so far as I know, never shared — I
think these remarks are largely true, and that as writers
the two men had many common characteristics, while always
being extremely opposed in their private lives and, after
Auden's visit to Spain in 1937, increasingly so in their
political and philosophical convictions.

They liked hymns, the Bible, the poems of Kipling, old
and new popular ballads, scientific thought and technical
gadgets. They were naturally musical; they could laugh. They
had wonderful imaginations, which they could harness to
simply colloquial language and quite rigid and traditional
verse forms. They wrote clearly. They had a subversive,
plebeian angle on things. They didn't try to bullshit you.
I look at Auden and John Garrett's anthology *The Poet's
Tongue*, which to me is the best anthology ever made, and I
find anonymous ballads such as 'Lord Randal', Webster's
dirge from the *Duchess*, 'Casey Jones', one or two Hymns
Ancient and Modern (including 'Hail Thee, Festival Day',
which at St Edmund's we used to sing before the annual
Ascension Day picnic), not to mention pop songs, W. S.
Gilbert, and Jean Ingelow's marvellous long poem about the
tidal wave on the Lincolnshire coast. I read Brecht's
remarks about 'Das Seemannslos', the nineteenth-century song
he quotes in two or three of his plays, and turn to the
corresponding English ballad by Arthur C. Lamb, with its
opening quatrain,

Stormy the night and the waves roll high
Bravely the ship doth ride
Hark! while the light-house bell's solemn cry

Rings over the sullen tide

And I *know* that if Auden had known it he would have put it in.
I read Brecht's song of the cranes in *Mahagonny*. I read Auden's '0 lurcher-loving collier, black as night', written for the film *Coalface* in 1935. I'm glad to have lived when these things were written, and I just cannot take such writers' personal hatreds very seriously. In heaven, in the historical dialectic or, more surely, in the verdict of posterity, these two unique poets will be reconciled.

NOTES

1. Letter from Auden to me, 2 Mar. 1957.
2. Letter from Auden to me, 18 Aug. 1958.
3. *A Certain World* (London, 1971) p. 371.
4. No. 1 (1966) pp. 163-72.
5. Brecht to Auden, Aug. 1936 (Brecht Archive no. 1396/36).
6. Robert Medley, 'The Group Theatre 1932-1939: Rupert Doone and Wystan Auden', in *London Magazine*, new ser., XX, no. 10 (Jan. 1981).
7. See *Brecht on Theatre* (London and New York, 1959) pp. 153ff.
8. See Brecht's *Arbeitsjournal*, entry for 20 Sep. 1943.
9. Brecht to Auden, undated (Brecht Archive no. 210/13).
10. Act II scene i of the *Duchess of Malfi*, in *Brecht: Collected Plays*, vol. 7 (Random House and Eyre Methuen editions).
11. Auden to the Sterns, postmarked 7 Aug. 1944.
12. Auden to the Sterns, 11 Aug. 1944.
13. Brecht to James Stern, postmarked 13 Dec. 1944.
14. Auden to T. Spencer, 17 Nov. 1945.
15. Letter from Auden to me, 18 Aug. 1958.
16. Hanns Eisler later said that he felt unable to supply the kind of setting for a Homeric epic that Brecht wanted. So Paul Dessau wrote the music when the Berliner Ensemble staged the play in 1954.
17. Auden to James Stern, 13 Oct. 1959.
18. Letter from Auden to me, 1973.
19. Letter from Auden to me, 2 Nov. 1971.
20. Letter from Charles Monteith to me, 29 Aug. 1975.
21. Air-letter from Ed Mendelson to me, 11 Mar. 1977.

Index